THE DEAN OF NEW THINGS

Praise for the work of John Mogulescu and his team

"[John Mogulescu] would have been surprised, at age eighteen, to learn he would be heralded as one of America's most important visionaries in the field of public higher education, his work cited by none less than the president of the United States."

—**Cathy N. Davidson,** ***The New Education***

"John Mogulescu, who heads higher education's version of a skunkworks at CUNY, has generated a flow of innovations." . . . "[CUNY Start and ASAP] led me into the world of student success."

—**David Kirp,** ***The College Dropout Scandal***

". . . . driving force behind many of the signature CUNY programs that are proven to help with student retention, persistence and graduation. . . . Much of your thought leadership around mapping the future of higher education based on best practices and innovative programming was the foundation for the creation of our latest CUNY educational jewel in the borough of Manhattan, Guttman Community College. . . . Your work has truly impacted and transformed the lives of thousands of people throughout your career and at each level of heightened responsibility you have delivered a better CUNY for all. The City of New York is truly indebted to you."

—**Gale Brewer, former Manhattan Borough President**

Praise for *The Dean of New Things*

"After spending nearly 50 years in academic and administrative positions at the largest urban public university in the US, John Mogulescu has chronicled his experience bringing change to the hardscrabble environment of The City University of New York. More than a memoir, this book tackles some of the impediments and challenges facing Higher Ed today: Scarcity of resources, unwillingness or fear by some faculty to embrace new modalities in the delivery of pedagogy, interference by people and institutions outside of the academy imposing their will, and the general fact that fresh thinking is hard to implement. Throughout a staggering number of newly innovated programs initiated by John Mogulescu and his team, there are hard lessons learned. Strong leaders surround themselves with smart people who are encouraged to be creative and are given authority to act. They are bold, listen carefully to dissent and not fearful of altering course. But they are fighters when they have to be. John Mogulescu is all that. This is an important book that should be a guide for future leaders in Higher Education."

—Matthew Goldstein, Chancellor Emeritus,
The City University of New York

"John Mogulescu's expert and personal account of nearly fifty years of making change at the nation's largest urban public universities should matter to all institutions of higher education, especially as they look to the future. Written with the passion of a gifted leader, the book generously shares an extraordinary wealth of experience and understanding of the challenges faced by universities and the communities that sustain them, both within and outside. The book's unflinching assessment of resistance to change as the author encountered it over the course of his career is tempered by his stellar record of success. *The Dean of New Things*, Mogulescu's story, makes for an important book."

—Louise Mirrer, Ph.D., President and CEO,
New-York Historical Society

"*The Dean of New Things* by John Mogulescu is a rare animal in the literary-scholarly forest: a policy memoir. It is simultaneously an inviting, reflective story of one person's career, with all its ups and downs, and a revealing analysis of how to innovate strongly and capably within a large, change-resistant, public organization. The author invites you into his life – sharing his anxieties, his hopes, his origins, and his destinations. His is truly a New York, or perhaps better a Brooklyn life: the child of Jewish immigrant origin parents with radical leanings, graduate of Midwood High School, and a steadily rising career through the many facets of the City University of New York. It also offers many insights into why the City University, despite all its constraints, performs small miracles. John Mogulescu accomplished simply amazing things not as a charismatic person, but as a practical idealist whom his mentors supported because he could seize opportunities and reach worthy goals and whose co-workers he inspired to join his teams and empowered to do their best. Throughout he showed great integrity in admitting to and learning from institutional flaws and shortcomings, making no excuses about the need to remedy them, and tackling them to enhance opportunities for even the most challenged students.

—John Mollenkopf, Distinguished Professor of Political Science and Sociology, Graduate Center, CUNY, and Director, Center for Urban Research

"*The Dean of New Things* is essential reading for everyone interested in the condition of public higher education. CUNY is America's largest urban public university (think 243,000 degree students), and for many years, John Mogulescu was its senior lieutenant, pressing—often successfully—for creative reforms and highly innovative solutions that have changed the lives of countless thousands. In this engrossing book, the reader is taken on a journey of striving, frustration, stamina, and political courage that is at once moving and perceptive, offering seminal insights into the realities of higher education and the myriad challenges confronting those who put the interests of students first."

—Dr. David Steiner, Executive Director, Johns Hopkins Institute for Education Policy, Former Commissioner of Education, NYS.

"Whether you are currently involved in higher education, or just a person who's interested in the relevance of colleges and universities today, you will find this story of one man's success in applying passion, perseverance and creativity to the challenge of keeping a public university—The City University of New York—true to its mission, both a fascinating read and a source of inspiration. Within a large bureaucracy such as CUNY, the task of moving programs, policies and hundreds of professionals forward into a new way of thinking often is daunting. It becomes easy to just keep the status quo. Students enroll, some make it through, budgets are approved, the union stays happy, everyone gets paid and the years roll along. But for John Mogulescu, this attitude was never enough. He sees what could be. With the skills of an excellent administrator, he puts together a team that believes in success for all students, excellence in all teaching, and that a university needs to be a resource for its community. Such thinking finds this "agile band of brother and sister professionals" teaching the NYC Police Department, winning Emmys, creating online degree programs, improving graduation rates, and even developing the first new community college in the City in decades. And, as if that were not enough, raising over a billion dollars in grants to fund the work. When you read *The Dean of New Things,* you will find both joy and hope in the power of one man to make a difference and the promise of higher education for this city and its people."

**—Regina Peruggi, President Emerita,
Kingsborough Community College, CUNY**

"For over 40 years John Mogulescu has been one of the most innovative higher education leaders in the nation, creating one program after another that provides opportunities to immigrants, adult learners and students of color that even the best public colleges have not always been able to motivate and retain. As someone who has worked with three of the programs John has created, CUNY Prep, Guttman Community College and College Now, I have seen firsthand how John's risk taking, student centered approach can change lives. This book, part memoir, part institutional history, provides an invaluable guide to how higher education can adapt to challenging circumstances and become a force for democratic change in a polarized nation."

**—Dr. Mark Naison, Professor of African American Studies
and History; Founder and Director, Bronx African American
History Project, Fordham University**

"John Mogulescu is a supremely dedicated public servant who devoted his professional career to expanding the reach and impact of the City University of New York. Over the course of five decades, beginning as a student intern and ending as the Senior University Dean for Academic Affairs, he created or managed a host of education and training programs, mostly for nontraditional students, that transformed thousands of lives. This remarkable book, part memoir, part treatise on policy making and program management in the public sector, tells the story of his many accomplishments in a way that is both engaging and instructive."

—Richard M. Freeland, President Emeritus and Distinguished Professor, Northeastern University

"A captivating narrative and a profoundly personal history of America's largest urban university. It is a must read for anyone seeking to understand the transformative power of higher education as the engine of social mobility."

—Peter Sloane, CEO, Heckscher Foundation

THE DEAN OF NEW THINGS

Bringing Change to CUNY and New York City

JOHN MOGULESCU

Hardback ISBN 979-8-9893748-0-9
Paperback ISBN 979-8-9893748-1-6

CONTENTS

PART 2: SO MUCH MORE AHEAD

Expanding Our Vision, Making Connections, and Creating Partnerships

To Bonne, my partner for this book and so much more

and

To my colleagues, who made everything possible

CUNY

The City University of New York is the nation's largest urban public university, a transformative engine of social mobility that is a critical component of the lifeblood of New York City. Founded in 1847 as the nation's first free public institution of higher education, CUNY today has seven community colleges, 11 senior colleges and seven graduate or professional institutions spread across New York City's five boroughs, serving over 226,000 undergraduate and graduate students and awarding 55,000 degrees each year. CUNY's mix of quality and affordability propels almost six times as many low-income students into the middle class and beyond as all the Ivy League colleges combined. More than 80 percent of the University's graduates stay in New York, contributing to all aspects of the city's economic, civic and cultural life and diversifying the city's workforce in every sector. CUNY's graduates and faculty have received many prestigious honors, including thirteen Nobel Prizes and 26 MacArthur "Genius" Grants. The University's historic mission continues to this day: provide a first-rate public education to all students, regardless of means or background.

—***CUNY Media Relations, 2023***

PREFACE

IN THE FALL OF 1972, AS A SECOND-YEAR GRADUATE STUDENT IN social work in the community organizing concentration at New York University, I began a three day a week field work assignment at New York City Community College, then one of six community colleges in the City University of New York system. In January 2022, after close to fifty years at CUNY, I retired.

A few months before my retirement, the university Office of Communications released a podcast Interview about my CUNY career. Rick Firstman, the producer of CUNY podcasts, who conducted the interview, called it: "Imagine That: How John Mogulescu became the Dean of New Things." I loved the title and also Rick's introductory remarks: "John Mogulescu is affectionately regarded as the founding father of many of CUNY's most innovative and consequential programs of this century. He's been an unstoppable force and a guiding spirit bent on breaking down educational and career barriers for New Yorkers of all backgrounds. This spring, after a prodigious career spanning nearly 50 years, he announced his retirement. To many, CUNY won't be the same without him."

This book tells the story of "How John Mogulescu Became the Dean of New Things." But although the book is organized around my career and the work of my team at CUNY, it is also—and importantly—about CUNY, New York City, and institutional change. It focuses on a group of unusual educators who believed that CUNY was not as good as it needed to be, that dramatic change was essential, and that generating new ideas was crucial to sparking that change. And it attempts to expand on the role and responsibility of an urban public university in a city challenged by widespread social policy issues related to poverty, inequality, and race.

The book came about gradually. Shortly before my retirement, I had lunch with Bill Kelly, a former colleague and friend. Bill had been the president of the CUNY Graduate School and the CUNY's interim chancellor before becoming the New York Public Library's Andrew W. Mellon Director of the Research Libraries in 2015. Besides connecting with an old friend, I hoped to get his reaction to the idea of my writing a book about my career and sharing what I had learned. Bill responded with encouragement, saying that despite the many books about higher education, my story was unique. My team and I had brought the kind of lasting change to CUNY that few thought possible in higher education, and to a degree changed New York City as well.

Others had encouraged me to write about my years at CUNY. Seven years earlier, in 2014, Distinguished Professor of History at John Jay College and the CUNY Graduate Center, Gerald Markowitz, volunteered to work with me on an oral history project about my time at CUNY. Like Bill Kelly, Jerry believed it was important to record my story. For two years Jerry and I sat down bi-weekly to record interviews that were later transcribed. His only requirement was to always tell the truth as I believed it to be. Throughout the project, Jerry urged me to turn the oral history into a book. In addition to Jerry and Bill, many colleagues and friends have also pushed me in this direction, and such a project had been in the back of my mind.

In the early 1980s, CUNY established the Division of Adult and Continuing Education (ACE) as a component of the CUNY Office of Academic Affairs. I joined ACE in 1986, became its dean in 1990, and continued to lead it for thirty years. Over those years, I was promoted and the unit evolved and transformed, becoming the Office of the Senior University Dean for Academic Affairs (SUD), with a far more expansive agenda. We grew from a staff of ten to nearly 350 people, virtually all supported by outside grant and contract money. None of our staff were full-time CUNY faculty, advanced degrees were not essential, and all members of our senior staff were expected to raise public and private dollars. That last factor was crucial to our success. SUD became the largest grant getting entity at CUNY, raising over $1.3 billion dollars during the first 19 years of the 21st century. On an annual basis, SUD secured almost a quarter of all of the grants and contract monies generated by the rest of the university, including all 25 colleges and professional schools.

Our accomplishments, fueled by a fierce commitment to students, were broad and lasting. We created two new CUNY institutions, Guttman Community College and the CUNY School of Professional Studies (SPS); built and administered ASAP, perhaps the most successful community college success program in the United States; reimagined remediation and ESL instruction through CUNY Start and the CUNY Language Immersion program; built one of the largest dual enrollment program in the country and created twenty new early college high schools; worked with the New York Police Department (NYPD) to change the Police Academy curriculum; established an institute that dramatically improved working conditions for early childhood educators; won television Emmys; and developed any number of successful workforce development and continuing education programs.

Our unit became a major training arm of New York City and New York State, working with virtually every agency, as issues of social policy intersected with higher education. Our programs grew through five different mayoral administrations and were recognized by local and national foundations, many of which supported our work generously.

A series of chancellors and vice chancellors of academic affairs came to designate us informally as the innovative shop of CUNY. A host of efforts to develop new university programs were assigned to us. As Chancellor Matthew Goldstein said repeatedly during his 14-year tenure (1999–2013), we were his "go to" unit. He recognized the talent of our staff whom he often praised as the most gifted staff in the university. He also understood that not only did we generate fresh ideas, but those ideas were translated into successful programs. We were good implementors who paid enormous attention to timelines and detail.

Beginning in 2003 until I retired, in addition to my senior university dean position in the CUNY Central Office, I also held the position of founding dean of the CUNY School of Professional Studies, an innovative school designed for adults. SPS created 27 baccalaureate and master's degree programs and pioneered online degrees at CUNY, while offering an array of non-credit programs to over 30,000 New Yorkers annually.

We fought many battles during this time, at both our Central Office SUD unit and at SPS, winning most but losing some important ones. Often our programs were not popular with faculty governance leaders, the faculty union, some college presidents, and some Central Office administrators. With the support of chancellors, we were able to duck under or refute the criticism and move on with the projects. Budgets and politics are always intertwined with policy in public higher education and public service generally. That was certainly the case in the turbulent years that form the backdrop for this story. Clear vision, dogged persistence, judicious flexibility, and carefully nurtured relationships often helped sustain the work even when budgets dwindled or policy was opposed.

The Dean of New Things illustrates some of the many kinds of projects developed by our team at the Central Office and also at CUNY SPS. It concludes with a reflection and an epilogue. In the reflection section, I examine the question of whether through our work we really were able to transform CUNY. It reviews the central themes, strategies, approaches and obstacles involved in providing educational and economic opportunity to the most educationally and economically disadvantaged New Yorkers.

The epilogue, What's Next for Higher Education, considers why higher education in the United States is under threat, both from within the academy and even more worrisome from the larger community. In the face of an uncertain future and the growing view that earning a degree is not essential and may actually be an obstacle to addressing issues of inequality, I offer suggestions as to how higher ed should respond, not by constricting its historic mission but by expanding it creatively and decisively.

PART 1

Becoming an Educator

My career came about through a series of lucky accidents and with the guidance of great mentors. Although no one, and certainly not I, would have predicted that I would have a career in education, in retrospect, two of my earliest influences—sports and politics—paved the way. My parents nurtured a deep conviction that everyone deserves a fair chance and taught me that it was important to stand up for your convictions. Sports taught me not only the benefits of a team but how to be a member—and a leader—of a well-functioning team. These and some personal quirks—impatience, persistence, and even anxiety—help explain how the boy who wouldn't go to kindergarten became "The Dean of New Things."

As I found my way into education, first as a teacher and then at a community college and CUNY's system office, mentors who were both smart and committed to justice guided me. I began to understand the potential of continuing education to serve the community, as well as learn the skills to organize effective programs and to navigate increasingly complex and challenging environments.

CHAPTER 1

A New Teacher

Unprepared and Insecure

ADELPHI STREET IN THE FORT GREENE SECTION OF BROOKLYN rang with the angry shouts of teachers picketing in front of Public School 20. It was September 11, 1968, and the United Federation of Teachers, under the leadership of President Albert Shanker, had gone out on strike. More than 50,000 teachers (approximately 93% of the teaching force) had joined the strike, entirely shutting down the vast majority of the public schools in the city and leaving over one million children without access to education. The causes of the strike and the complex underlying issues are still subject to debate. The immediate cause, however, grew out of a Ford Foundation-funded experiment in Brooklyn: community control of a largely Black school district in Ocean-Hill-Brownsville. The local school board had involuntarily transferred a group of mainly white and Jewish teachers and administrators out of the district. The teachers' union, the United Federation of Teachers (UFT), clashed with the community school board over the transfer, which they termed antisemitic, and the UFT called a system-wide strike.

Amid the noise of the picketers, I walked down Adelphi Street filled with anxiety, my body almost shaking. I was headed to Public School 20, to begin my first job out of college as a sixth-grade teacher. It was hard enough to think about teaching a sixth-grade class with virtually no preparation for the job, but in addition to that challenge, I was about to cross a picket-line.

As I neared the school, I could see that the loud, angry shouts were not coming only from the picketing teachers in front of the entrance. Parents and other neighborhood residents had gathered there as well, equally loudly, but in support of me and the other teachers entering the building to keep the school open for their children.

I couldn't help but be struck by the fact that the vast majority of the teachers—both those picketing outside the school and those crossing the picket line—were white, while the neighborhood parents and the students entering the building were almost entirely Black. At that moment, though, I was mainly concentrating on envisioning myself as a teacher. Only later could I give more attention to the implications of that racial divide and its future impact on New York City as well as the fact that I would be teaching a class of largely Black students. Eventually, I came to understand that in addition to crossing the picket line and starting a new job, some of my initial anxiety was likely related to being in an environment that was unfamiliar to me. I didn't know how I as a white teacher would be perceived by my largely Black students and the adult members of the community. I was worried about it.

Most of my thinking the previous few days had been focused on whether I would cross the picket line—something I had been taught by my parents since childhood never to do. Now I walked silently into the building, went to the main office to pick up my room keys, and then directly to my classroom on the second floor to prepare to meet my students. Having crossed the line, my focus shifted to how I was going to teach the nearly 30 students on my register. I had taken a few education courses in college but had not spent one minute student teaching or even observing an elementary school classroom. My total preparation since graduating from college in May consisted of a few short conversations with my brother's close friend who taught sixth grade elsewhere in the New York City system.

I had not planned to become a teacher. As a psychology major at Brown University, I expected to attend graduate school in social work right out of college. As I approached my senior year, however, the war in Vietnam continued and with it the requirement that all young men register for the military draft. The thought of graduate school was overshadowed by the need to avoid being drafted into the military and sent to fight in the Vietnam war, a war I strongly opposed. Teaching in an inner-city public school, at a time when schools were desperate for teachers, provided a deferment from serving in the military. I chose that avenue. The education courses I had taken, together with a number of child psych courses, qualified me for a teaching certification exam. I passed and was assigned to P.S. 20.

Because of the strike activity outside of the school, my students didn't line up out in the schoolyard as usual. Instead, they came directly to the classroom, entering one by one. It was obvious that many in my class had stayed home because of the strike. Only about a dozen of my 30 students appeared that first week. This turned out to be one of the few good things about the strike; the smaller class size made a huge difference in my ability to manage the students that first week. As the strike continued, almost all the children came back, while the picket line gradually dwindled and then disappeared.

The students were verbal, energetic, smart, and very observant. P.S. 20 tracked students according to academic performance (largely test scores); of six classes in the sixth grade, mine ranked second in educational preparation. Most of my students read at grade level, with some reading a bit above and others below. Math scores were a little below that, but far higher than most of the other students in the grade at our school. Virtually all of my students were Black and from low-income backgrounds.

I began the year with a combination of enthusiasm and fear. While I hadn't planned on becoming a teacher, I was excited to have my first real job and actually get a paycheck. There was, of course, that one problem: I didn't have a clue about how to teach. That thought was scary. I was assigned an experienced teacher as a mentor, but that was confined to casual discussions outside class. When the classroom doors closed, I was on my own. I also was overwhelmed by having to teach all subjects. I was pretty good at teaching math, less good at teaching social studies, and truly horrible at science. As for reading, I initially felt fortunate that the school district was experimenting with the Sullivan Reading program, a prescribed series of self-paced reading units that utilized the teacher mostly as a guide/facilitator. The students seemed content with the program, but I quickly saw that it had major limitations and didn't provide my students with the opportunity to read real books. To supplement Sullivan, each month we ordered children's books from Scholastic Press. The students selected from a long list those books they wanted to read. When the books arrived, there was excitement in the class as the students grabbed the books they asked for, opened them and started reading. It was always a wonderful moment.

While these students were relatively good readers, they also were demanding. As a new, inexperienced teacher, I found classroom management to be a persistent challenge. There were a few students I couldn't control. Too often those students led to wasted time for everyone. I found myself yelling a lot and saying things to students that were clearly inappropriate. It doesn't do much good to holler at a twelve-year-old, "If you don't start paying attention, you'll never learn anything." In fact, hollering never works; it only makes things worse. Overall, my teaching was a mixed bag. Some of the lessons I planned really worked and others did not. When a lesson didn't work, the end result was often a loss of control, with kids shouting and laughing and ignoring me. It was frustrating, and I at times felt helpless.

There wasn't a day during my first year of teaching when I didn't leave school exhausted. My best friend from childhood and one of my college roommates were also teaching elementary school in the system, one in Brownsville and the other in Bedford-Stuyvesant. Having similar experiences, when we talked on the phone or got together on weekends, we shared stories, laughed about daily incidents, and tried to support each other with encouragement and suggestions. I was lucky in that my school was fully open and continued to have huge support from parents and community members. In contrast, their schools were barely functioning, with only a very few teachers in attendance and the rest out on strike. Parents at those two schools were not as well organized in support of the nonstriking teachers.

When the school strike ended on November 17, the striking teachers returned. At P.S. 20 that was about two-thirds of the teaching staff.

They were furious at their colleagues who had not gone out on strike, but their strongest hostility was reserved for the new, young teachers like me, most of us teaching to avoid the draft. We were recently out of college, publicly opposed to the war, largely leftwing in our politics, and clearly on the side of the Black community that was trying to take control of the public schools in their own neighborhoods. Few of us were going to be career teachers.

My focus for the rest of that first year was on the children in my class and figuring out how to teach. I had good days and bad, often determined by whether I lost control of the class and whether it seemed that my students were learning. At times I felt exhilarated by a good lesson or by something a student said, but the exhausted feeling took a toll. During the year I had a horrible case of the measles, followed by pneumonia and the flu.

By Friday afternoon of each week, it was pretty clear that the kids also were tired and needed a break. My solution was at 1:30 p.m. to hand out art paper and turn on the "Best of the Temptations" album. The kids were free to draw, read, gather in small groups to socialize, or just listen to the music. As soon as the music went on, everyone relaxed, and the rest of the day went smoothly. I still have that old Temptations album and play it a few times a year as I remember its effect on my students—and on me.

Yet there were some wonderful moments. The high point was the play on the Civil Rights Movement that the students and I wrote together. The students fully embraced the project. We spent many hours rehearsing, getting ready to perform it for the entire fifth and sixth grades. The play incorporated freedom songs from the movement, such as "If You Miss Me at the Back of the Bus" and "Oh, Freedom." Fortunately, a teacher who played guitar joined us at rehearsals.

The play's sole performance was fabulous. The students performed with enthusiasm and passion, belting out the songs with incredible energy. The highlight was Joy Palmer, who delivered Martin Luther King's "I Have a Dream" speech to a totally engaged audience. The play ended with the class singing "We Shall Overcome," joined by an auditorium packed with students, parents, and guests. They gave the class a standing ovation.

Of all of the students in that first year of teaching, the most memorable for me was Joy Palmer. Joy was assertive, smart, witty, and very angry. You could feel her presence in class every day. While most days she was a pleasure to teach, she might also explode at any time. It was no surprise I selected her to deliver the "I Have a Dream" speech; she was a compelling public speaker with a loud, dynamic voice.

As that first year of teaching progressed, I got a little better at controlling the class. I improved my teaching techniques. I came to know the students very well and worked hard to try to be fair to all of them. I had some favorites, but in truth I liked all of them, even those who presented challenges every day. One of those students was Richard, a really nice kid, but volatile. When something bothered him or he just was in a bad mood, he could be impossible.

I hated the idea of keeping students after school as a punishment. (Of course, I wanted the day to end so I could go home, too.) But when kids were really disruptive, I would make them stay in class after school was dismissed. In 1968, that kind of punishment was still permitted.

One day I kept Richard and two other students after school. In order to keep them from running out of the room, I parked my chair directly in front of the door, blocking the exit. After a few minutes of shifting restlessly in his chair, Richard walked decisively over to the window, opened it, leaned outside, and shouted, "Mr. Mogulescu, I am going home one way or the other." I guess I could have called Richard's bluff, but I knew him well enough to realize that it was quite possible he would jump out of that second floor window. I gave up. "Go home, Richard," I said. We would fight this battle another time.

I was fortunate to work at a school that had good leadership and functioned smoothly. Richard Alexander, the first-year school principal, was a decent, capable person who worked hard and knew how to relate to children and their parents. His assistant principals were also competent and supportive of the teachers. I quickly realized how much good leadership mattered. Compared to the stories I heard from my friends teaching elsewhere in the system, P.S. 20 was a good place to be.

We ended the school year with an upbeat graduation ceremony. I wished the students well on the last day of school. Most of them would be going to a junior high school down the block. I felt confident that most of them would do okay. Although I was elated that the school year was over and I would have a break of two months, I was also emotional and a little teary with the realization that the students I had come to know so well would be leaving my life.

In early June I had given the students a writing assignment that asked them to answer the question "What is a friend?" Below is the short statement that Richard wrote. It is revealing in so many ways.

"A friend is like Mr. Mogulescu. He's the best friend, and teacher I ever had. He is not like the other teachers I had. He is a fair man. Sometimes he is wrong, and a lot of times I am wrong. I should not be bad to him, but I cannot help it. I think I shouldn't have went with Mr. Mogulescu cause I am bad today. A friend is when you be good and not bad, like I am sometime. I try hard to be good, but it doesn't help. I just be bad. But I do my work. A friend is someone that is kind, grateful, and a lot of other good things. Mr. Mogulescu is one of them. He is kind. I will try and be good for the rest of the day and Friday. I am sorry that I have been bad to you friend. You the best. The end"

The summer seemed to move quickly. By mid-August I began to think about my second year of teaching. I hoped that, given a year of experience, I would have an easier time. That was not to be. The second year was far more difficult. At the same time, it helped frame much of my later thinking about race, inequality, education, and social justice.

For my second year of teaching, I was assigned the lowest-performing class. It was clear from the outset that one year of teaching was not enough preparation or experience to manage this group of students. As was not unusual in a lowest-tracked class, many of the students were 13 or 14 years of age, having been held back at least once in the early grades. Of the 26 or 27 kids in the class, seven or eight could not read at all, and none could read above the third-grade level. To keep these students occupied for the entire day was next to impossible for me. At least part of every day I lost control of the class. At times there were fights, often started by some verbal slight between students. While the students didn't read well, their verbal skills were well honed. Teasing came easy. Insults, often beginning in jest about a family member or their welfare status, ended with harsh statements. Words like "fag" and "Jew" were in frequent use. To break up fights, I would grab the more aggressive student, and drag him/her out of the classroom and down to the principal's office.

Despite the persistent problem of classroom management, I liked virtually all of the students. I was particularly engaged with the group of boys who were most unruly. During lunch, after school and even on the weekends, I would play basketball with them, take them to local sporting events and community activities, and introduce them to my friends. I always got permission from their parents to take them out, although I don't recall asking my principal whether this was a good idea or even legal.

As the boys got more comfortable with me outside of the classroom, they would often show up at my apartment on the weekend, ringing the buzzer downstairs. "Hi, Mr. Mogulescu," Gary or Baron would say. "Is it okay for us to come upstairs?" At the time, I was in a serious relationship with one of the other teachers in the school and we would have them come up for a while, asking whether their parents knew where they were and letting them know that they couldn't do this again. That warning would work for a week or so, but never fully resulted in ending their visits.

Throughout the year, I would turn to Ms. May for advice on how to manage and teach this group of students. Ms. May, a middle-aged, soft-spoken Black woman, married to a local pastor, had taught this same group of students the previous year. While she admitted that the class was the hardest she ever had, she almost never lost control, didn't raise her voice, and got students to respect each other. While Ms. May offered thoughtful advice, it didn't magically translate into making me a more effective teacher.

I had good days, lessons that worked, and lots of laughs with the students. But overall, it was a troubled year. My guess is that the students didn't learn a whole lot. I was proud of working with the kids on a little student newspaper. We called it the Mini Matter Press, and for a while the students were really engaged with putting it together. And I did have some success in teaching basic arithmetic. I did a lot of self-reflection during the year, wondering whether it was my fault that the kids often acted out, or was it that too many of the kids had emotional problems. I concluded that it was some of both.

I tried to follow the kids after they left P.S. 20, particularly those boys I became closest to. A number of them went to jail, and only a few left the neighborhood. About ten years after I left teaching, I learned that Baron was murdered while incarcerated. I did keep up with Gary for a long time. When I had begun my CUNY career at New York City Community College and was directing an adult literacy program, I thought that it might be good for Gary to enroll. He did, but over the next year or two, he made no real progress in improving his reading ability. It was clear that he had some kind of disability that we were unable to address.

Perhaps the craziest incident of the year revolved around Ellis. He was one of the better prepared students in the class and was incredibly verbal and funny. He was one of the tougher kids as well. Ellis recognized when he was beginning to lose it and would usually give me a heads up that he was about to erupt. When that happened, he would disappear into the teacher's closet, which was just big enough to hold a student. I let Ellis do that, for it calmed him down. He usually didn't stay long and would reenter the classroom on his own. One day Ellis was in the closet when Mr. Alexander, the principal, entered the room. He had noticed that the class was noisy as he walked by and looked in to check. During the few minutes Mr. Alexander was in the room, no one said a word about Ellis. The principal left, Ellis came out, the class cheered, and we went on with our business.

That second year of teaching left me feeling demoralized, overcome with a sense that I had failed the kids. I understood that successfully teaching a group of students so poorly prepared would not be easy for even the most experienced teacher. I also recognized there was something wrong with the system where so many students entered the sixth grade so far behind. Still, I felt I owed the students more. While I wanted to run away from another year of teaching, the war was still on. Leaving teaching could result in being drafted.

In my third and last year of teaching, I was assigned the top-level class in the sixth grade, called the "intellectually gifted" class. Almost all of the students were far above grade level in math and reading. While almost all of the students were Black, they more often came from families that were much better off economically. Many of their parents were college educated and employed in professional jobs. In Fort Greene, even before gentrification dramatically changed the neighborhood demographics, there was a middle-class Black population.

That year was my easiest teaching year by far. I now had two years of experience. More importantly, the students were so much better prepared and far easier to control. Now I had to make sure I was challenging these students, particularly those at the highest level, but most of the discipline issues disappeared. I enjoyed teaching those students but somehow didn't get the same level of satisfaction as working with the students from the previous two years.

On December 1, 1969, halfway through my second year of teaching, the first national draft lottery was held. It determined the likelihood that you would be called up and probably have to serve in Vietnam. I drew number 291. By early 1971, it was clear that a number that high meant I would not be drafted. In March, having been accepted again by NYU for its master's in social work program, I let Mr. Alexander know I would be resigning at the end of the school year.

I left teaching with a mixture of relief, frustration at my lack of success, and anger. It was clear that the many students who were years behind in the sixth grade would likely never catch up. They deserved better. I had become a better teacher, but certainly not yet a good one. I admired the successful career teachers. They seemed to combine a passion for teaching, sound content knowledge, and the skills needed to manage a classroom. They also liked children and believed deeply in their potential.

At the same time, there was a small number of teachers who really disliked the kids and couldn't relate to them at all. Some were abusive to the children, calling them demeaning names and questioning their intelligence. Often, those teachers provoked confrontation. I recall one teacher, a large man who far outweighed the students, picking a fist fight with a student. Why they continued to teach was a mystery. Given that many of them had been teaching for many years and had job protection through the union, there was not much that administrators could do to take corrective action.

I also left believing that despite understanding from an early age from my parents that you should never cross a picket line, breaking the strike had been the right thing to do. I strongly believe that Al Shanker called the strike over issues of power and control and not, as the union claimed, about 19 teachers being transferred. Some of the veteran striking teachers in P.S. 20 never forgave those of us who opened the school. I guess that was to be expected. During those three years of teaching, I developed a more complicated view of the value of teacher unions. I acknowledged that teachers, like other workers, needed the advocacy and protection afforded by the union. I understood, too, that because teachers often have to present ideas and concepts at times considered controversial, they might require additional protections. At the same time, I continued to be critical of union actions that protected incompetence or upheld procedural concerns over what seemed the greater good. Principals' meetings were routinely held from 2:00 to 2:45 p.m. and generally ended on time. Regardless of the importance of the discussion, however, at 2:42 p.m. a group of teachers would pointedly pack up their bags, so that they could reach the door at 2:45 on the dot. There was no chance they would stay even one minute overtime for any reason. I found their behavior infuriating. My view was further complicated as my career continued at CUNY and I gained positions of responsibility and worked to change the university.

Through observing the lives of my students, I left teaching understanding as never before that the world was not fair. Most of the students at P.S. 20, despite their individual talents and traits, were severely disadvantaged in comparison to children growing up in better economic circumstances. While this should have been obvious to me beforehand, teaching for three years in Fort Greene brought it to the forefront of my thinking. It also helped determine my own future and some of the career choices I would make. Those were formative years for me.

My last three months at P.S. 20 were dramatically affected by an article entitled “A P.S. 20 Teacher Speaks Out” that I wrote in March 1971 for a newsletter put out by the school’s parents. The article captured some of my anger and frustration at the union, the lack of accountability for teachers, and the fact that three-quarters of the children in the school read below grade level. The UFT Chapter Chair responded to my article with a letter entitled “A brief reply to some uncritical nonsense.” It was a strident, sarcastic, and very personal attack on me. The school’s assistant principal, who had been a supportive colleague, also responded with a more professional but no less critical letter. Soon after, one of the leaders of the Parents Association replied to the assistant principal defending me and the content of my letter.

Looking back at this episode and rereading my article many years later, I could see that much of what I wrote was unfair to the many hard-working teachers at the school. I had ignored the need for a union to protect teachers. I had presented an exaggerated, dismal picture of the conditions at the school. What also became clear to me later in my career was that teachers received only minimal professional development support, were not paid enough, and too often had class sizes far too big. I guess I could say I was 25 years old, lacked maturity, and certainly did not fully understand the many factors, both inside and outside the school, that contributed to students underachieving. That being said, what I believed then and throughout my career at CUNY and still today is that the system led to student failure for so many low income, children of color. The system needed significant change. That change would come only with bold action and a refusal to accept the status quo.

Over the next 50 years, I thought a lot about my public school teaching experience. Without doubt, it was the most demanding job I ever had. Nothing else came close. In the classroom, there was never a moment to relax. If you were not fully prepared for each day, the six or so hours spent at school could feel like a week. Despite three years of exhaustion, many wonderful moments are sketched in my memory. Those moments were directly related to the relationships I established with the kids. They made me laugh. They made me cry.

In 2007, nearly 40 years later, I was the dean of the CUNY School of Professional Studies, presiding over a graduation ceremony for an Advanced Certificate in Disability Studies program. At the conclusion of the ceremony, we presented certificates to the graduates. Across the stage at the CUNY Graduate Center walked a middle-aged woman. Her name was called: "Joy Palmer." I looked at her and she at me. We broke into huge smiles. It was the Joy Palmer who wowed the crowd with Martin Luther King's "I have a Dream Speech" in our class play on the Civil Rights Movement all those years ago, back in sixth grade. We hugged as I gave her the certificate. After the ceremony, we found each other and talked about the class and our lives since 1968. Without going into detail, she told me she had a very difficult life. Whatever the issues were, she had overcome them and was now a direct care worker in the field of developmental disabilities. The CUNY School of Professional Studies program was a career advancement opportunity. Joy and I have kept in touch since that time. After getting her certificate, she became a supervisor at her agency. She then enrolled in the master's degree program at SPS, earning that degree while continuing to work. With that, she became an adjunct professor at CUNY, teaching in the Disability Studies Program.

During one conversation, I asked Joy about her memories of me as a teacher. I was pretty good, she allowed. But mostly she remembered that I liked the kids. That was heartwarming, for while I felt it to be true, to hear it from one of my former students was important to me.

The night of the graduation ceremony where Joy and I reconnected, I went home and pulled out a scrapbook I had kept during my first year of teaching. It contained a poem that Joy had written. It was about race, and it was angry. I sent her a copy. The poem speaks to feelings that Joy shared with many others in my class:

Struggles
We are music makers
But not money makers
We are prayers
We are not traders of food or grain
We are black

But not so proud
We live in slums
And white live in suns
We are disadvantaged
While whites are advantaged
What am I guess what a
SLAVE!!
Joy

The day after I sent Joy the poem, she wrote me the following email:

> Just wanted to take this opportunity to touch base with you to let you know that I received your note and was overwhelmed with emotion after reading its contents. It only validates the fact that I knew then, as I do now, that I am very talented and that it is my destiny to be successful. I plan on showing it off in class and at work tomorrow. Sure means a lot to me that you kept the poem and that you remember so much about me. I still can't get over seeing you after almost 40 years and you still look the same. Again, thank you, take care of yourself, and I hope to see you again soon. Be blessed and well.
>
> Respectfully, Joy Durinda Palmer

CHAPTER 2

Brooklyn Roots

Family, Sports, and Politics

IT WAS MY FIRST WEEK OF KINDERGARTEN. I CRIED EVERY DAY when my mother tried to leave the classroom after dropping me off. By the end of the week, my parents decided that I was not ready for kindergarten. They withdrew me from school. I spent the rest of the year at home. For first grade, rather than sending me to the local public school, my parents enrolled me in an independent private school offering small classes and lots of individual attention. That worked out well, although it was hard to explain to my friends on the block why I wasn't at the public school with them, and why instead of walking with them I came home by a private bus. It was embarrassing. For second grade I returned to public school, P.S. 199, and found myself well behind the other students. The private school was nurturing, but it hadn't taught me a whole lot. This was not a great start to my formal education experience and hardly auspicious for someone who would spend a career in higher education. But it spoke to my insecurity and the endless worrying that followed me for much of my life.

I was born in Brooklyn in 1946 and, except for my college years, have spent my entire life there. We lived in the Flatbush section, first in a small, attached house on East 17th Street and later in a much larger home on the corner of East 22nd Street and Avenue M. My father, Joe, was born in Camden, South Carolina. His father, a Jewish merchant from Romania, had settled in Camden, opening a dry goods store to support his family. When my father was a teenager, the family moved to

Brooklyn. At New Utrecht High School, he met Milly Greenwald, who had grown up in Bensonhurst. They later married and had two children, my older brother Bill, born in 1943, and me.

My early life revolved around the vibrant street life of Brooklyn. We were almost never in the house, spending most of our time playing games outside. Even at an early age, we were able to play without parental supervision. When it got dark, parents would shout from the doorstep for us to return to the house in time for dinner. The games I played—punchball, stickball, stoop ball, box ball, and slap ball—have all disappeared. Back then on those Brooklyn streets, I came to realize that I was really good at games with balls, and that playing them brought me immense joy. Much of my early life was centered around sports and that included my early reading interests, which were almost always related to sports heroes like Brooklyn Dodger stars Jackie Robinson or Duke Snider as they battled the hated New York Yankees or to fictional characters from the Chip Hilton book series authored by famed basketball coach Claire Bee.

My father was a successful businessman. He and two of his brothers opened an interior design firm in the early 1950s. Called Designs for Business, it became one of the leading design firms in the city. DFB's talented designers and architects created the interiors of many office buildings in Manhattan and beyond. DFB enabled my parents to live an upper-middle class life and to buy and renovate the beautiful corner house on 22nd street when I was nine years old.

That house became the clubhouse for my friends and my brother's, with a basketball hoop in the driveway, and pool and ping-pong tables in the basement. On our quiet street, only an occasional car interrupted our games. Neighborhood kids flocked to the house daily. My mother seemed to really enjoy having a house full of boys. She fed them, talked to them, nursed them when they hurt themselves playing ball, and made them feel her home was theirs, too. She even got to know the local police. Our next-door neighbor, plagued by the constant noise of our daily basketball games, often ran out of his house to take our basketball away when the ball rolled onto his property. Two or three times a week he called the police to complain about the noise. The police always came to investigate, but before very long were drinking coffee, eating cookies, and talking about the world with Mrs. Mogulescu.

While my early life revolved around sports, the life inside our house focused on politics. Early in the Depression my mother's father, a banker, committed suicide by hanging himself in the basement. My mother, a teenager at the time, blamed capitalism for his troubles. She became an ardent supporter of the Soviet Union and an almost full-time activist. It was embarrassing to be walking home from school and see my mother handing out leaflets on Avenue M, trying to enlist her neighbors in electing some left-wing candidate, or criticizing the proliferation of nuclear weapons, or asking people to write letters in support of the Rosenbergs. She was particularly active in opposing Senator Joe McCarthy and the many other state and local politicians who accused so many people, including many of her friends, of being communists. The accusations cost some of them their jobs and careers.

Despite his success in business, my father held similar views, but he was more of a political theoretician, spending hours reading and analyzing the latest political news and opposing the Cold War policies of the United States. As activists, my parents also embraced issues related to the civil rights struggles and the racist history of the United States.

From an early age, my brother and I were observers of the daily political conversations in our house. These were highlighted by a regular discussion group led by Jack Foner that met at our house throughout our childhood. Professor Foner, a historian with a doctorate from Columbia, had been fired from his teaching position at City College for suspected membership in the Communist Party. Then he had been blacklisted from securing another job. To make a living, Professor Foner gave lectures in private homes, including ours. Many of my parents' left-wing friends attended. My brother and I often sat on the stairs to listen, trying to understand why everyone was so unhappy with the United States and so supportive of the Soviet Union.

In 1969, Professor Foner at last received an academic appointment at Colby College in Maine, where he established one of the first Black studies programs in the United States. Jack Foner was the father of Eric

Foner, who as a Columbia professor became one of the nation's leading experts on the Civil War and Reconstruction.

By the early 1960s, with the civil rights movement gaining momentum and the beginning of protests against American intervention in Vietnam War, I had come to appreciate my parents' views and their activism. Rarely did I attend a demonstration against the war, either in New York City or Washington, when I didn't bump into my parents or arrange to meet them at a demonstration site. Their political influence on Bill and me was profound, and while we didn't always agree, particularly as it concerned the Soviet Union, we grew to share many of their values and political instincts.

Along with politics, the other constant in our house was sports. Sports became my outlet, enabling me to overcome much of my shyness and insecurity. I was a gifted athlete who excelled at any activity with a ball. Because I loved the Brooklyn Dodgers, my first love was baseball. In Little League, I actually pitched consecutive no-hitters. Although my father loved baseball and enjoyed having catches with me in the street and going to my Little League games, his favorite sport was tennis. When he introduced me to the game, it turned out that I was better at tennis than baseball. By age 13 I began to play tournaments. By my senior year in high school, I was one of the best players in the city, and our high school team won the city championship.

Because there were no indoor tennis courts in the city then, in the winter I played a lot of basketball. I was excited to make the Midwood High School basketball team. Midwood competed against some of the best teams in the city in what was called the "Suicide League." It included teams with national reputations like Boys High, Erasmus, Wingate, and Thomas Jefferson. I was most proud when we beat a Thomas Jefferson team. Their star was Jim McMillian, later a first team All-American at Columbia, who had a long, successful career in the NBA with the Los Angeles Lakers.

The members of the Midwood team were largely Jewish and Irish. Competing against other high schools and playing ball in the parks of Brooklyn introduced me to competing against Black players, who had begun to dominate the game throughout the cities of America and certainly in Brooklyn. Travelling to some of the poorer neighborhoods of the city to play games, I began to understand my own feelings about race, including my fear of entering neighborhoods that didn't feel safe to me. I also encountered racist attitudes expressed by a few of my teammates. Although horrified by some of their comments, I am ashamed to say I never confronted any teammates about what they were saying, not wanting to start a controversy and upset the team chemistry.

Entering my senior year in high school, I began to think about college. Although a decent student, probably having a class rank of around 120 in a class of 1,200 students, I had spent far more time concentrating on sports than on my studies. Unsure of my ability to handle the work, I also had avoided taking any honors or AP courses. I was not much of a reader, and my English SAT score was not impressive. Because I was an athlete, however, I was recruited by several colleges. I applied to Clark University because my brother was there, and it was a Division III college where I likely could play both tennis and basketball. I also applied to Brown University and the University of Pennsylvania, Ivy League schools that never would have considered admitting me were it not for sports.

I was accepted by Brown and Clark. Only later did I fully grasp that Brown accepted me solely because I was a recruited athlete. Looking back, it seems unfair for me to be admitted to an Ivy League school while classmates with far better academic records were not. My mother came home one day and said that the mother of another Midwood student had stopped her on the street and screamed at her that it was unjust that her son did not get into Brown despite his class ranking of 16. She had a point. Throughout my years at CUNY, I had many a conversation with my colleagues about the advantages that recruited athletes have in the college admission process, even at the most elite colleges. Whenever there were discussions about affirmative action, I would point out that the largest affirmative action effort at Ivy League and other elite colleges is for recruited white athletes, given the large number of sports teams that these schools support. Teams like soccer, lacrosse, gymnastics, hockey, crew, skiing, swimming, and many others have a scarcity of students of color, and all of them recruit aggressively.

In September of 1964 I entered Brown, arriving with a cast on my leg as a result of a broken ankle received playing basketball two days before I left Brooklyn. That was just the beginning of what turned out to be a disastrous first semester. When I walked into my freshman dorm room, looking forward to meeting my roommate, a huge surfboard rested on one of the beds, along with what I learned later to be a skateboard. I knew that my roommate's name was Greg Donaldson and that he too was a recruited basketball player, but was he really a surfer? Greg came from Levittown, on Long Island. In addition to playing basketball, he had indeed been a Jones Beach lifeguard and a surfer. Most of all, he was a character and a gifted storyteller. Every evening after dinner he would entertain a group of freshman athletes in our room with stories about Levittown, his hometown "boys," surfing, basketball, and any number of other trivial topics. At some point, I would kick everyone out of the room, either to get in some studying or simply to go to sleep.

The athletes self-segregated. Many of us felt that we were at Brown only because of sports and concluded that this meant we were not as intelligent as the other students. We were most comfortable around other athletes. That was certainly true for me. I doubted that I was smart enough to be at Brown, and the first semester convinced me that was the case.

All Brown freshmen took four courses, including English Composition. My first assignment for that class was an in-class essay on the topic "What is the Intellectual Life?" When the paper was returned, it was a sea of red ink. For a reason I cannot now fathom, I had written that the intellectual life was a phony life filled with snooty people who wore smoking jackets and thought they were smarter than everyone else. The grad assistant who marked the paper didn't appreciate my thoughts and made me rewrite it three times. I ultimately got a D in the course.

For the first exam in my European History class, I mistakenly wrote on the wrong British civil war and got an F. That error was minor, however, in comparison to the stupid decision I made in preparing for the final. For the reading period, we were assigned *The Heavenly City of the Eighteenth-Century Philosophers* by Carl Becker. Because there would be a choice of questions on the final, I decided not to read the book and instead to concentrate on other course content. I entered the exam room to learn that there were two 90-minute questions, both on the Becker book. I let out a loud scream realizing that I had to write on a book I had never read. The result was an F on the final and a gift of a D minus for the course. I got another D in French and a C in Calculus, winding up with a 1.25 grade point average and a letter informing me that I was on probation.

It wasn't that I didn't study. I actually did. I just had no idea how to be a college student. I finished the basketball season, starting some games on the freshman team. But realized that I wasn't good enough to get playing time on the varsity. I decided not to play freshman tennis in the spring to concentrate on my studies. A 2.5 average that semester got me removed from probation.

I never fully recovered from the debacle of the first semester, though, and felt uncomfortable academically during much of my four years at Brown. I studied hard, and by my sophomore year had become a B minus/ C plus student. I decided to major in psychology. Psychology interested me, but there was also a practical reason. I got my first B grade in a psych class, and a B average in the major was required to graduate. Having chosen a major, I planned to become a clinical social worker and volunteered to work with disadvantaged high school students in Providence as kind of a big brother. I joined the varsity tennis team, compiling a good record playing 2nd and 3rd singles for three years and becoming co-captain of the team my senior year. I also made some wonderful lifelong friends at Brown, most of them basketball players.

During my latter years at Brown, the Vietnam war began to loom larger and larger. As American involvement deepened, growing numbers of young men were drafted and sent to serve in a conflict halfway across the world that many Americans opposed. While not a student activist, I was an early critic of the Vietnam war and attended many protests on campus as well as many major demonstrations in New York and Washington, D.C., including the 1967 March on the Pentagon.

By graduation, I had regained some of my confidence. But I left college uncertain of the future, scared to death that I would be drafted and sent to Vietnam. Certainly, I had no idea that I would ever have a career in higher education. I returned to Brooklyn to become a public school teacher, which most importantly earned me a deferment from the draft. My life as an adult was about to begin.

CHAPTER 3

Fannie Changes My Life

My Introduction to CUNY, Community College, and Prison Education

AFTER THREE YEARS AS A SIXTH GRADE TEACHER, I ENTERED THE graduate program in social work at New York University in September 1971. Although I had planned to become a clinical social worker, I changed my focus during the first year in the program. Rather than working with individuals, I was more interested in working in communities to bring about social change. Having selected the community organization and planning track, I was ready to begin my second-year field placement. Field placement is a major component of social work education. In addition to formal courses, I would spend three full days a week working in an agency under a field supervisor. In the fall of 1972, I walked into a small, third-floor office at New York City Community College of CUNY to meet my field supervisor, Fannie Eisenstein. This assignment made little sense to me. I had no idea why a second-year major in community organization would be assigned to a community college. Actually, I had close to no idea of what community college was. I was greeted by a short woman who had wavy gray hair. She looked really old to me. In seconds, I had written her off and determined that my placement at this college must have been some kind of mistake.

An hour later, as I walked out of the office, my life had changed. As soon as Fannie Eisenstein began talking, I realized that I was in the presence of an extraordinary woman—intensely passionate and committed to creating new opportunities for the most disadvantaged New Yorkers. She was brimming with ideas, verbally gifted, energetic, and both fierce and brilliant. Fannie had spent most of her working life as a social worker/community organizer. In her fifties she applied to become associate dean of the Division of Continuing Education at New York City Community College. Given her lack of experience in higher education, it was to the credit of Vic Lauter, the division dean, to hire her.

Some years later, a colleague in the division told me about reading a memoir by Arthur Laurents, the screen writer and Tony award winning playwright, director, and producer, perhaps best known for his work on "West Side Story" and "La Cage aux Folles." Laurents recounted trying to figure out the character that Barbra Streisand would play in the movie "The Way We Were." He had been asked to write the script for the film, co-starring Robert Redford. He described talking to Streisand in her apartment and thinking about the character:

> But as she tummeled, she kept reminding me of someone else, a girl I had once known. Who, where, when, I couldn't place her. I couldn't see her. Like Barbra, unlike Barbra; younger, another time, an earlier time, against another Background. Cornell! Frizzy hair and sensible shoes, a brown skirt and blouse, a red scarf, handing out leaflets in 1937 on the Arts campus. Stop Franco! Stop the war in Spain! Her name—the coincidence was surely an omen—was Fanny Price. While this journey was taking place in my head, I was talking away a mile a minute with Barbra, but looking at her, I knew Fanny Price was going to be transformed into the heroine of the movie I was going to write for her. The lack of a story was momentary; with Fanny's outrage and convictions, the story would tell itself.[1]

Laurents's Fanny Price at Cornell was now my Fannie Price Eisenstein at New York Community College. They had been at Cornell at the same time. The courage and conviction that Laurents recalled still animated Fannie as I listened to her talk during our first meeting. Almost immediately, I understood how fortunate I was to be assigned to be supervised by her.

At the end of our conversation, Fannie introduced me to Judy

McGaughey, a senior member of the Continuing Education staff, who actually had faculty status although her responsibilities were administrative. Judy, who developed and supervised a number of the Continuing Ed programs at the college, would become my daily supervisor. She was an excellent supervisor, whose judgment I came to trust.

My field placement assignment for the year was to organize and administer an education program at the Brooklyn House of Detention, a city jail facility located in downtown Brooklyn within walking distance of the college. Although a life-long resident of Brooklyn, I'd been unaware that there even was a 12-story jail in downtown Brooklyn. As I listened to Judy and Fannie describe the need for a program, I felt excitement. And fear. It had been almost a year since the riot at the upstate prison in Attica had filled the national news. I had followed the event closely. Protesting conditions at the prison, inmates had taken 42 corrections officers and staff hostage. The inmates presented a list of 30 demands. After several days of negotiations, although considerable progress had been made, Governor Nelson Rockefeller sent state troopers and police in to retake the prison. Ten corrections officers were killed, along with 33 inmates. At first the governor claimed the prisoners had murdered the corrections officers; however, it was established that all or almost all were actually victims of bullets fired by the law enforcement officers. I had been outraged at Governor Rockefeller for approving the strategy to take back the prison and restore order and then lying about how the corrections officers being held hostage were killed. Throughout the disturbance, which dominated the news, I became emotionally attached to the inmate leaders of the rebellion, who spoke so passionately and articulately about the conditions at Attica that led to the rebellion.

Having started my first job out of college as a teacher in the midst of the New York City teacher strike, I now would be following that up inside a jail a year after the most significant prison uprising in the history of the United States. Trying to put aside my anxiety, I concentrated on what an amazing opportunity this was to create a program that mattered. But I had no idea what I was supposed to do, nor what it was like to be inside a jail.

Judy and I approached the Brooklyn House of Detention (BHD) for our first planning meeting. As I walked down Smith Street from the college, crossing Fulton Street, past the Brooklyn Criminal Court and Abraham and Straus department store, I looked up at the large building looming on the corner of Atlantic Avenue. From a distance the building looked cold and dreary, its windows covered with bars. The forbidding front entrance let you know that this was not a building open to the public.

We entered the facility, showed our identification, and were escorted through a series of gates to a bank of elevators that took us to our meeting with Deputy Warden Guzman. The "Dep" as I learned to call him, was a no-nonsense, experienced corrections professional. He let us know that the facility had no education programs, and he welcomed the involvement of the college in creating one.

In 1972, the BHD housed more than 2,000 men, almost all awaiting trial or other court appearances. Some men were there because they had violated parole or probation and awaited hearings. Generally, though, the detainees were being held before being tried because they couldn't meet bail or in some cases had no bail. Those with the most minor charges had the lowest bail. They stayed the shortest amount of time, either because they met bail or had their cases settled. Those with the most serious charges generally had the highest bail. Most cases were ultimately settled with plea bargain arrangements, although a small percentage of the men did have jury trials. Interestingly, 50 years later, the issue of cash bail has become a heated political issue throughout the United States.

Each housing floor of the facility held more than 200 men—two men to each tiny cell equipped with a sink and toilet and bunk beds. The floors had two levels, divided into four parts. Cells were located down four corridors on each level, with approximately 15 cells per corridor. All of the housing floors had four small dayrooms, with a television in each and some space for other activities. Meals were served on the floor. The building had a small law library for detainee use, a chapel, and an enclosed rooftop recreational area with two basketball hoops. Our classes would be held in a second-floor general purpose room.

To enter a housing floor, you got off the elevator into a small vestibule area, walked a few steps to an iron gate, and tried to get the attention of the corrections officers to let you in. You quickly learned to shout "On the gate" as you approached the floor entrance. As you entered the floor, it was hard not to smell the remnants of breakfast or lunch. The level of noise was unrelenting. On each floor, two corrections officers were responsible for maintaining order and attending to the needs of the 200 inmates. The corrections officers were unarmed, to avoid the risk of detainees overpowering them and getting a gun. The officers relied on common sense, intelligence, and experience to see that the floor was under control and serious incidents kept to a minimum.

Dep Guzman talked to us bit about the educational background of the students. It made sense to start by organizing a high school equivalency test preparation/literacy program. I would be the entire staff for the program, serving as both administrator and sole teacher. As I was in the facility only a few days a week, Judy and I decided to try to recruit detainees who already had a high school diploma, some college, or a college degree to help teach the men who signed up for the program.

I had no difficulty recruiting tutors for the program. With no real activities at the jail, boredom was common. And many of the men genuinely welcomed the opportunity to tutor and help other detainees. I provided a brief orientation to the tutors, introducing them to the teaching material we would be using. For literacy instruction, we used some of the same reading kits that I had used when I was teaching sixth grade. I also was able to purchase some high school equivalency preparation books and materials for detainees who had better basic skills and would be preparing to take the equivalency exam.

By early fall, our small program was meeting three evenings a week, with around 15–20 students and a comparable number of tutors, all participating voluntarily. Three corrections officers (COs) were assigned to bring the students from their floors and stay in the makeshift classroom to ensure that order was maintained. These COs loved the program, which took place after their regular daytime shift and therefore paid overtime. All three officers were nearing retirement, and these extra hours added a significant amount of money to their pensions.

The program ran smoothly. The relationship between the detainee tutors and their students was respectful. The detainees who participated as students were serious about their studies. Like the vast majority of the detainees in the entire facility, almost all of the students were Black or Hispanic. What made the program most challenging was that it was impossible to know who would be attending class on a given day. Students accused of more minor crimes often were able to meet bail and simply disappeared. We soon learned that students facing more serious felony charges would attend for longer periods of time, and for that reason we preferred having them in class.

As I got to know these students, they would talk to me about their lives, usually without going into detail about why they wound up in jail. At times, they asked me to pass along messages to family members or contact friends. Many professed that they were not guilty of their charges and were in fact political prisoners. Getting to know these men over months in a school setting, recognizing their intelligence and their desire to learn or tutor, reinforced for me that something was wrong with a society that resulted in so many Black and Hispanic young men being incarcerated. On the other hand, I also romanticized the men, putting aside the reality that some of them had committed violent, horrible crimes. I wanted to believe that they were indeed political prisoners, victims of poverty and a racist society that provided them with little opportunity. A number of the men asked me to write character references for them or even attend sentencing or other court hearings to provide references in person. More than a few times I attended court only to learn that the person I had known in the classroom as a caring and giving person had been convicted of a brutal crime. None of this added up to me.

Beyond spending time in the jail during that graduate school year, I also was considered a member of the Division of Continuing Education staff at the college. Under Fannie's leadership, the division was an exceptional place where I was surrounded by smart, committed people who wanted to build programs and create opportunities for the most economically and educationally disadvantaged adults in the city. They viewed noncredit workforce and pre-college programs, as well as programs targeted to specific populations in the community—prisoners and ex-offenders, older adults, people with disabilities, to name a few—as logical extensions of the mission of a community college. Fannie placed no restrictions on our desire to develop programs, other than we had to figure out how to pay for them. And that last point, figuring out how to pay for them, led most of us in the division to seek out grants from private or public sources in order to translate good ideas into funded programs. Grants also enabled us to provide educational opportunities to students for free.

It is hard to overestimate how much I admired Fannie and how much I learned from her. Although her commitment was boundless and her vision broad, she recognized that passion and ideas were not enough; ideas had to become successful programs. Fannie understood the importance of paying attention to detail as well as having vision. Securing funding for a program was only the beginning. The program had to be well run. Fannie was a stickler for good business practice. She started all meetings on time and had no patience for anyone being late or cutting corners. Phone calls were to be returned the day you received them, and program deadlines would be met. She stressed the importance of building relationships and treating everyone respectfully. She never worried about academic credentials in her hiring, but rather looked to hire people who foremost had ideas, intelligence, and passion. Fannie herself was a gifted writer who expected the staff not only to be able to conceptualize, but also to express new thoughts in coherent language. She was humble, never taking credit for the successful programs we developed or new funding we received. That was the work of her staff.

Fannie was also the single best public speaker I ever worked with. When Fannie was asked to speak at a program graduation or event, she was always well prepared. Her written remarks were eloquent, often drawing on her prodigious reading. What made her unique, however, was how she related to her audience, particularly if the occasion was for students. She would enter a room and always find something that she would incorporate into her comments. It could be a picture on the wall, a conversation she had with a student before the event started, or something that she had read in the morning newspaper. To listen to Fannie speak was to listen to a great orator.

A speech Fannie gave in 1995 displays her eloquence and passion. Then 80 years old and still working full time at Goddard Riverside Community Center, she was invited to give the keynote address at the New York State Continuing Education Association Regional Conference. The title of the conference was "Opportunity in Adversity." Fannie framed her remarks around the recent election when the Republicans had regained control of the U.S. Congress and introduced the legislation called Contract for America. She expressed the need to develop a different strategy in the way we worked with our constituencies:

> Your conference brochure recognized the new climate. It signals the need for strategies to influence legislation and lobby for change. It projects an examination of new models of education which cross the borders of rigid separation between continuing education and credit programs and knit their vital, inter-relating nutrients together. These themes of advocacy in the public sphere and interconnection in education can direct us to the struggles for survival all around us.
>
> It is not true that there is no money for education, health, and welfare. In the richest country in the world there is money. The question is one of choice.
>
> A fight-back has begun and is growing . . . Our challenge and opportunity is here . . . in drawing into common struggle all of us who have no private escape hatch, only our shared condition, and a vision of the possibilities we give each other in a caring polity.[2]

While Fannie held her staff to high expectations, she also nurtured them. In public, she praised staff members generously, even those whose performance was just average. In private or in small division meetings, however, she could be sharp and critical. She also was direct. You knew exactly how she felt. You knew when she believed that you were falling short of her expectations, and why. Because we all held Fannie in such high esteem, we did everything possible to impress her. Over the years, as many of the Continuing Ed staff went on to leadership positions elsewhere at CUNY or beyond, we would get together as friends and former colleagues. Much of our conversation was about Fannie, who had been not only our mentor, but also our hero. As I assumed higher level positions in my career with greater authority and power, I incorporated into my own thinking many of the strategies that Fannie had taught me.

The second year of the jail program, beginning in 1973, brought dramatic changes. I had graduated from social work school and, thanks to grant funding I'd secured from the State Education Department, I now assumed the paid position of director of the program. I was a full-time member of the Division of Continuing Education at New York City Community College.

One day, Dep Guzman abruptly informed us that the second-floor dayroom could no longer be used for the program. That decision was largely a result of the huge overtime expense for the three COs assigned to the program. It turned out to be game changing—for the better. One entire floor in the facility became a dedicated school floor, and all detainees accepted into our program would be transferred to that floor. All four dayrooms on the floor, instead of just one, would be used as classrooms during the afternoon hours. Recruitment became much easier because I was granted access to the entire building, which enabled me to go to all of the housing floors to recruit students.

With a school floor and a real budget, we totally redesigned the program. Instead of relying on detainee tutors for instruction, the program could hire a teaching staff. We offered separate classes in reading, writing, math, and what we called Life Skills.

My first challenge—and opportunity—was to hire teachers and a program counselor. Hiring excellent teachers turned out to be the single most important thing I did for the success of the program. Recruiting teachers proved not that difficult. The pay was good, starting at $20 per hour, which at the time was very high for a continuing ed teacher in a non-credit program. Also, a year after Attica, teaching in a jail seemed exciting and consistent with the values of many young people who had grown up in the politically charged 1960s. Nevertheless, teaching in the jail was not for everyone. I learned a lot about hiring people over the next two years. I made a few hiring mistakes. But I learned. Over time,

I got better at picking excellent staff. That skill helped me throughout my career.

Over the next two years, I spent part of almost every weekday at the jail, mostly on the school floor. I would arrive early in the morning, walking down the cell block tiers to announce the time that classes would begin, encouraging students to attend class, and occasionally waking up sleeping detainees. I learned to be sensitive about pushing the men to attend class; on any given day detainees might receive negative court rulings, possible jury convictions, or bad news from home. Most of the men didn't need much prodding to attend class, though. They were active and enthusiastic students, eager to be challenged by our instructional staff. The school floor had less tension and fewer incidents of violence and confrontation than the other floors in the building. Perhaps the relative calm was because the men were occupied for a portion of the day with class and homework assignments. But in my mind an even more important factor was the corrections officers assigned to the school floor.

James Frye was the regular daytime CO assigned to the school floor. Other officers rotated on the floor, but Frye was the lead officer and the one I got to know best. Like Ms. May at P.S. 20, who controlled even the most difficult class without raising her voice, Frye was in charge. He gave the detainees respect and could be flexible at times in interpreting unreasonable rules, but also set necessary limits. He used humor in talking to the men, but always treated them with dignity. As a Black officer living in New York City, he was familiar with the neighborhoods where the detainees lived and actually knew some of the men and their family members on the outside. On every floor of the jail, there were "panic buttons" to call for immediate assistance if an officer was threatened or a dangerous incident broke out on the floor. Those buttons rang regularly throughout the facility, and "riot squads" rushed to a floor to address a disturbance. It was scary to view the COs dressed in protective equipment, carrying batons and other riot gear, and getting ready to intervene. I don't recall ever seeing Frye have to press the button. As in my public school experience, where seasoned and competent teachers rarely lost control of their classrooms and treated the students with respect, in the jail some COs virtually never had incidents on their floors, while others had many. For those who lost control the most, the job was terrible—both dangerous and exhausting.

During that second year, our education staff at the jail got to know the COs on the floor and elsewhere in the building well. Noting our long hair, informal dress and left-leaning politics, most officers viewed us skeptically as "do-gooders" who glamorized men accused of violent and heinous crimes. To some degree, the COs were right. We saw the best side of the men on the school floor. Because of our political leanings, we tended to believe that the jail was filled with men incarcerated because of the color of their skin or having grown up in poverty.

Talk about sports provided the way to a major breakthrough we made with the officers. Many officers were huge basketball fans, loving the championship Knicks team of 1969, as did we. They also played the game themselves and fancied themselves as "players." In one of our conversations, I mentioned that a few of our staff also played basketball and would be interested in playing against a team of COs. They laughed at my suggestion, trash talking us, but they finally agreed to play. We arranged a game on a Saturday at a Y on Staten Island. What they didn't know was that Greg Donaldson, who taught in the program, and I had been recruited basketball players at Brown, where Greg was one of the team's high scorers. He was a respectable Division I player. Another staff member, Ray Holloway, had been a good college ball player. I had been a decent high school player at Midwood High School. To fill out our team, I invited one of my other college roommates, Rick Landau, to join our team. Rick was the co-captain and starting guard on Brown's team, and like Greg, could really play.

Not surprisingly, we won easily. In fact, we kicked the COs' asses. They were much friendlier and more accepting of us as we returned to the jail the following week. We continued to play with the COs, occasionally inviting them to the college after work for pick-up games. I became friends with Frye and some of the other officers.

Throughout the three years I spent in the jail, I never felt totally comfortable. To start, I was a young, inexperienced white educator in a community of largely Black and Brown adults, in an environment totally outside my own life experience. From the moment I entered the building, I never forgot that I was in a jail, surrounded by men accused of all kinds of crimes. Also, the building had no open space. Whether on a housing floor or elsewhere in the building, everything was tight. There was no privacy for either detainees or staff. While I felt comfortable on the school floor, I needed to circulate throughout the building recruiting students, and I had to push myself to do that. It helped that the program had something valuable to offer the students. Many earned their high school equivalency diploma there. Others improved their basic skills. For those who were high school graduates or had some college experience, the program offered an opportunity to be challenged with college level work assigned by terrific teachers.

At the end of the year, we held a graduation ceremony to celebrate the achievements of the students. That was a joyous occasion—made even more special because family members had permission to attend and sit with their loved ones. At the end of the ceremony, we distributed certificates to the students, recognizing those who earned their GED or who completed all of the courses in the program. As the students walked to the podium to receive their certificates, the audience greeted them with thunderous applause and shouted congratulations.

We selected one graduate to give remarks. At the last graduation I attended as the director of the program on April 3, 1975, I listened intently as our student speaker talked about what the program had meant to him. The poignant speech affirmed the difference our program had made in the lives of the students:

> Many of us entered this program with understandable apprehension. After all, wouldn't this program be symbolic of the very same institutions that once so casually discarded our future, just as one discards yesterday's newspaper. Or would this be still another rip-off of our integrity: merely a temporary vehicle to further the aspirations of some government official. Well, regardless of the motives involved the old adage of "the end justifying the means" is quite apropos in this situation.

> To our pleasant surprise, we discovered that the teaching staff was determined to teach us in a manner both acceptable and relevant to us. In an atmosphere not conducive to learning combined with a wall of institutional resistance, we maintained an academic society. In fact, this was the essence of what an academic society should be: a reciprocal learning process between teacher and student. Special thanks are in order for the persevering efforts of our instructors, who at present, will remain anonymous in name only due to the time allotted for these graduation exercises. But the seeds they implanted in our brains will continue to grow and flourish, and those seeds bear their name and individual qualities.
>
> The federal grant which made this program possible will expire this year. If it is not absorbed by the state or municipal government it will cease to exist. To those members in attendance today who are the quote "respectable standard bearers of society," particularly the prestigious gentlemen seated behind me on this stage, we urge you to reverse this tide of public apathy. However, if your presence here today is a façade, ponder this: the proverbial human melting pot boiling over with frustration, anger, and hatred at this cruel joke played at our expense, in a word—Rehabilitation. It is your responsibility to transform this over-used, under-practiced and empty word into something tangible for the students of this program.
>
> The journey of a thousand miles begins with but a single step. Honored guests we have taken that monumental first step, but to proceed on this arduous journey requires our sustained efforts along with your pledged commitment to educate the apathetic masses of society, so that we may live to see the day when this vicious revolving-door pathology becomes extinct. [3]

After working for three years at the jail, in 1975 I was able to secure new funding for the college to run a basic education and GED program serving ex-offenders. At the same time, the program funding at the jail was renewed by the State Education Department. Fannie asked one of my colleagues, Mae Dick, to become the director of the jail program. I would direct the ex-offender program, but also supervise the jail program. Like me, Mae had started working at the college as a social work student. We had shared a desk my first few years at the college and become dear colleagues and friends. Both smart and tough, Mae was someone who would intervene on the street or the subway if she saw anyone being treated badly. She would do well working in the jail.

Just as I learned from my three years teaching at P.S. 20, there also were more lessons from the jail experience. Regardless of the mode of instruction, whether you used tutors or experienced teachers, improving reading skills for the lowest level readers is hard to do, and with few exceptions, progress is slow. In the jail program, as in my sixth grade class, it was hard to understand why so many students could be so verbally fluent and yet read below the most basic level. Over the years, as adult literacy programs expanded throughout CUNY and the university developed a community of literacy educators, those of us working in these programs recognized that the answer to that question is enormously complicated. Whether the students' struggle with literacy was due to lack of success in the early grades, undiagnosed learning disabilities, lack of opportunity, poor schools, poverty, early trauma, or other factors, there was no one simple solution or approach. Over time, we became more sophisticated in how we taught the adults enrolled in our basic education and literacy programs and introduced new teaching methods. We continued to find, however, that although most students who came with some ability to read would make real progress, very few who started at the beginning-level class would ever qualify for a GED prep class, let alone earn a GED. This factor would have implications for how we organized future programs and what we could promise our students.

On the other hand, in the jail program, there were many examples of highly intelligent, well-read individuals who lacked a high school diploma because they had left school early. Those students, who read near or above grade level, could earn their GED quickly if enrolled in a well-run program. They could go on to college. Success in college was another question, and one I continued to grapple with.

In those three years working in the Brooklyn House of Detention,

I also learned some things about who populated jails and prisons. The detainees at the BHD, the vast majority of whom had not been convicted of charges, were principally Black and Hispanic men. Virtually all came from specific borough neighborhoods and grew up either in poverty or surrounded by poverty. It was also clear that the court system depended on the plea-bargaining process. That process worked slowly, but it kept the courts functioning, at least to a degree. Still, in every borough of New York City, large numbers of detainees and inmates languished in jails for months or longer awaiting a determination of their guilt or innocence.

Along with the New York City Community College program at the Brooklyn House of Detention, other CUNY community colleges—LaGuardia Community College, Bronx Community College, and Borough of Manhattan Community College—through their continuing ed divisions, began education programs at their neighboring correctional facilities. The program directors and supervisors formed what we called a Correctional Education Consortium, working together to secure additional funding for program expansion and to advocate for the rights of prisoners to receive educational services, even as they awaited disposition of their cases. The consortium also worked to expand our reach to Arthur Kill correctional facility on Staten Island and to a few of the upstate prison facilities. What had begun as a small effort in Brooklyn had now expanded to reach thousands of detainees and inmates each year.

CHAPTER 4

Continuing Education

Creating Educational Opportunities for Underserved New Yorkers

AS I BEGAN MY FOURTH YEAR AT NEW YORK CITY COMMUNITY College in 1976, despite all I had learned at the Brooklyn House of Detention, I was relieved to no longer be going into the jail other than to attend program celebrations or meetings with top corrections officials. While I was comfortable on the school floor, the BHD was a building filled with tension, disruption, and unhappy people, both the jail staff and the men held there.

While working in the jail, as a staff member of the Division of Continuing Education, I attended monthly division meetings and heard about the other programs the division operated. Now, in my new role as director of the adult literacy program, I would be based at the college and immersed in the work of the division. I also began to learn more about New York City Community College and CUNY. Located at the Brooklyn end of the Brooklyn Bridge, New York City Community College was the oldest of CUNY's then six community colleges. Founded after World War II, the college was created to train veterans and those who had been engaged in war-related work to qualify for jobs in the post-war economy. Like all CUNY community colleges, NYCCC offered associate degree programs in liberal arts and in career-focused areas designed to be completed in two years. The college's programs in areas such as machine tool, construction, and graphic arts, among many others, created natural opportunities for Continuing Ed to use the facilities and the expertise of the college faculty to create non-credit entry and upgrade programs in these fields.

With the grant funding in place from the New York State Education Department for a new basic education/GED program, Fannie Eisenstein, Judy McGaughey, and I began to plan for a quick opening. At first the program was going to be only for ex-offenders, but we quickly realized that the pool of possible participants would be too small to fill the seats. This led to us open the program to any adults who did not have a high school diploma, including those at the basic education or pre-GED levels.

In planning the program, we made a major mistake. We thought it would be a good idea to bring the program directly to the community by locating it in one of the several public housing projects near the college. The division already had a relationship with residents of the nearby Farragut Houses in Fort Greene. After consulting community leaders, we agreed to start a program there. It would be an evening program, convenient for residents returning home after work.

Our assumptions were logical but wrong. Despite a robust recruiting and marketing process that saturated Farragut and other nearby housing projects with materials publicizing the program, we had few applications. After several futile weeks spent trying to fill classes, we realized that this site was not going to work. We had overestimated the interest Farragut residents would have in attending an evening adult education program. Also, residents of other Brooklyn neighborhoods who would have benefitted from the program were reluctant to travel to Fort Greene to attend class.

Given that the program was funded for only one year and that in order to be re-funded we had to demonstrate quick success, we faced a major problem. We decided to move the program to space at the college. Fortunately, the college had already rented an elementary school building owned by the Catholic Diocese of Brooklyn across the street from the main campus. The century-old building was certainly not pretty, but it had adequate classroom and office space. Fannie somehow got the college to let Continuing Ed take over the space, and we moved in.

We called the program the Adult Learning Center, and we reached out to not-for-profit and government agencies all over Brooklyn to recruit students. We also added daytime classes. Before very long classrooms were filled with students. We actually had a waiting list. We had hired an exceptional teaching staff. The students liked coming to the college, which they considered an adult environment. Even though it lacked air conditioning or elevators and the heat was at best unreliable, having our own building enabled us to begin thinking about new program possibilities. That launch and re-launch provided a lesson that I carried with me throughout my career. If a program is not working despite being given a fair amount of time to succeed, it is essential to re-examine your assumptions and make significant changes. That may seem obvious, but all too often change is delayed or resisted, and the program winds up blaming student apathy or unwillingness to work hard for its own lack of success. If data shows that students are not coming, if they stop coming, or they are not achieving what was expected, the first place to look is at the program itself. Staff members also need to talk to students in order to understand their experience of the program. With that information—and an open mind—the staff can make informed change. If you're not helping the people you want to help, maybe it's your fault, not theirs.

In the spring of 1976, New York City was deep into a fiscal crisis. The federal government and President Gerald Ford refused to bail out the city. *The New York Daily News* memorialized the situation in a famous headline on October 29, 1975: "Ford to City: Drop Dead." University leaders worked with state legislators to secure permission of the State Education Department to move New York City Community College from city to state funding, which stabilized its budget. That move changed its status from a community college to a senior college, enabling it to offer bachelor's as well as associate degree programs. The college was renamed New York City Technical College, or City Tech.

The period from 1976–1985 under Fannie Eisenstein's leadership was one of exceptional growth for City Tech's Division of Continuing Education. The staff aggressively sought new funding from both public and private sources, and each time we received a grant or qualified for some new state funding, we hired talented staff members. A wide array of new programs was developed, and many existing programs were able to secure additional funding. We were constantly writing proposals.

Grant-funded programs, regardless of the source—government

agencies, private foundations, unions, corporations—are almost never unrestricted gifts. Funders require proposals. These vary in length and specific requirements, but generally a proposal must state the program goals and intended outcomes, provide a plan for achieving the outcomes, tell the funder how the program will be evaluated to determine whether outcomes are met, and include a budget that states in detail how the funds will be spent. At the end of the funding period and often annually as well, grantees must submit reports to the funder.

However complex the submission process might be, I quickly recognized the value of grant-funded programs. Ultimately and importantly, they paid the salary of all but a very few people working in the division. During almost all of my CUNY career, my salary came from grants.

At CUNY, grant funds are managed through a central fiscal agency, the Research Foundation, called for short the RF. Those employed through grant funding work on the projects at the campuses but technically are RF employees. Grants gave us the flexibility to hire staff quickly and be less restricted by rigid hiring criteria. We also could set our own salary scale, although it was expected that generally the staff would be paid at rates comparable to those hired on the college's tax levy budget. Because staff funded through grants were employed by the CUNY Research Foundation and were non-union employees (today, at some CUNY campuses, RF employees are unionized), it was also possible to reward good performance with merit-based salary increases. The downside of this for the employee was the lack of job security and union protections. We made every effort to maintain employment for our grant-funded staff even if a grant ended. As we grew as a division, we seldom lost talented staff, transferring them to work in other programs in comparable positions. When it came to leadership positions in the division, Fannie did not differentiate between RF and "tax levy" staff. Many of the senior level positions were eventually held by grant-funded individuals.

Most of all, grants enabled us to translate good ideas into innovative programs and to offer educational opportunity for free to adults unable to pay even low tuition costs for non-credit programs. Although low-income students enrolled in degree programs at the college received federal and state aid that covered tuition and associated costs, almost no aid was available to non-degree students.

The scope of the programs that we developed during Fannie's tenure was extraordinary. The Adult Learning Center continued to grow, as did our work in correctional institutions. A major new federal grant called the Reading Academy enabled us to increase the number of basic education and GED prep classes we offered, including classes for students at the lowest level of literacy. We added an ESL component for the large number of recent immigrant New Yorkers looking to improve their English language skills. In the career and workforce area, we developed a variety of technical training programs, including welding, automotive repair, machine tool, and electronics. All of these programs were hundreds of hours in length and very rigorous. They led to well-paying jobs and careers. We were fortunate that, in addition to its Brooklyn main campus, the college occupied a large Midtown Manhattan building that housed some of its technical degree programs. Continuing Education worked out arrangements with the college departments offering degree programs to share the space and equipment necessary to run our technical programs.

In addition, we developed the Apartment House Institute to train building superintendents on all aspects of building maintenance and repair; a training program for deaf and hearing impaired adults; the Institute of Study for Older Adults, which ran classes in senior citizen centers and nursing homes all over New York City, largely requested by the residents themselves; and the Non-Traditional Training Center for Women, that offered training in the construction trades for women who had been excluded from these trades. The division's range of programs represented an unusual view of continuing education, one radically different from the more conventional image of continuing ed as offering leisure time activities. Our vision was that the college should endeavor to meet whatever educational needs adults in the community experienced.

Fannie understood that simply developing new programs was not enough. Programs needed to be administered with care. No detail was considered too small, and all of our work focused on eventual student success. Program directors observed classes, evaluated teaching, and surveyed students. Most programs had at least a part-time counselor, who could help students with personal issues and follow up with students who were struggling. Printed matter about the program and instructional materials were reviewed and proofread. Public events received careful attention for several reasons. Graduation or recognition ceremonies were special for the students. Conferences or all-day meetings were opportunities to make the program and the division known more widely to college officials, as well as possible collaborators or funders. We never wanted to hold an event that was badly organized or poorly attended, so in the days leading up to an event we followed up with invitees, checked programs, and double-checked AV equipment.

Although most programs attracted students and met their intended outcomes, not every program worked. I recall developing a program to train students to become food preparation workers for a company doing business with the airline industry. The company promised to place program graduates in well-paying jobs. When the jobs didn't materialize or turned out to be very low paying, we shut down the program.

By the early 1980s, I had become one of the leaders in the division. Judy McGaughey, who had been my supervisor, left to become a dean at LaGuardia Community College. I became the director of planning and development for the division, reporting directly to Fannie and overseeing many of the programs. I had become Fannie's deputy. What had been a relatively small staff when I started in the division in 1972, had grown to more than 150 administrators, instructors, counselors, and support staff.

Throughout my career, my approach to new challenges incorporated much of the thinking I had first encountered during these years at City Tech—about program development, administration, and supervision, as well as about creating a staff that was cohesive, project-focused, and collaborative. As I was to learn again and again, perhaps most important to program success was the staff that was hired. And here Continuing Ed stood out. In part because of our growing reputation for serving disadvantaged populations effectively and because the division was known as a good place to work, we were able to attract gifted professionals/educators who brought commitment, as well as expertise to their jobs. They cared about their colleagues and were interested in building a real community. We enjoyed each other's company and spent time outside of work socializing. The staff worked hard, seldom complained, and loved sharing new ideas and more effective ways to serve students. Many of the staff who were part of the building of the division went on to positions of leadership throughout CUNY and beyond as their careers evolved.

One of those gifted directors was Bonne August, hired by Judy to direct the federally funded Reading Academy. Bonne was working on her Ph.D. in English when she was hired. After several years, she left the division to join the English Department of Kingsborough Community College, one of CUNY's community colleges. She later chaired that department before returning to City Tech as provost from 2005–2020. After working together in the division for a while, Bonne and I started a relationship, fell in love, and were married in 1978.

In 1984, Fannie announced that, in accordance with CUNY's mandatory retirement policy, she would be retiring in 1985, the year of her 70th birthday. She had no desire to retire but could not get around the rule. Thus started a process that led to the most significant disappointment of my career to that point, but also led to an incredible opportunity.

Although it appeared that I was Fannie's logical successor, I was unaware that City Tech's president and the provost at the time were set on taking the Division of Continuing Education in a different direction. Bringing in Fannie Eisenstein's protégé as the new dean would be the same direction, they believed. It didn't help that Fannie wrote a strong letter to the president in support of my candidacy. She also wrote to the provost: "I understand and support affirmative action procedures and open searches. In this instance, however, I believe that the best interests of the College would be served by appointing Mogulescu as Dean of Continuing Education and conducting an open search for his replacement." Not surprisingly, the college ignored Fannie's advice and started a search for a new dean. I later learned that Fannie's letters and her campaign for me only hardened the views of the provost and president that a dean from outside the division was necessary to support their goals of a different direction.

I thought I gave a good interview to the search committee and waited to be invited for a final interview with the president and provost. I was optimistic that, with all that we had accomplished and with Fannie's support, I would get the job. After a lengthy waiting period that seemed like years, but was only months, I was finally scheduled to meet with the president and provost. When I was informed beforehand that this would not be a formal interview, I suspected that the purpose of the meeting was to tell me that they had selected someone else. I had trouble accepting that. When I got to the office the day of my meeting with the provost and president, every member of the Continuing Ed staff was wearing a button with my name on it. They wanted me to get the job, too. I left for the interview warmed by their support.

The meeting with the provost and president was short and to the point. They thanked me for my service, indicated that that they had appointed a woman from NYU as the new dean, and said they hoped that I would stay at the college. They explained that they wanted the division to move away from serving disadvantaged populations and running what they called social service-type programs. Instead, they wanted to develop relationships with the business community and generate more revenue for the college. At the time, I thought their goal was unrealistic. Neither the Continuing Education division nor the college itself was positioned to move in that direction. But I also saw that better serving the business community was a worthy long-term goal and did not necessarily mean moving away from programs for disadvantaged populations. The two goals were not mutually exclusive. I would have welcomed the opportunity to do both, but I would not get that chance.

I walked back to the office sad and disappointed, wondering what the future might now hold for me. A large number of Continuing Ed staff were waiting for me to get back to hear the news. There were tears and words of support, and some anger expressed as well. Telling Bonne and my two young children that I didn't get the job was hard. They were wonderfully supportive.

A postscript to the meeting with the president and provost occurred a few weeks later when the provost invited me to lunch. He told me that one of the reasons I didn't get the job was that I had shown emotional weakness when I spoke at Fannie's retirement celebration. This, he said, demonstrated that I lacked the toughness for the job. I was flabbergasted. And angry. I maintained my composure. But now I wish I had called him out for being such a jerk. I had indeed choked up a few times while giving my remarks at Fannie's retirement party, but why would my affection and admiration for Fannie, my hero and mentor, be seen as a weakness?

In the time between learning that I didn't get the job and the start date of the new dean, my feelings of rejection and anger only increased. But I convinced myself that perhaps I could remain in the division in my present position. While I enjoy being an agent of change, I don't like change in my own life. I didn't want to leave. Perhaps the new dean would be terrific. Within a few days of her arrival, however, I knew that staying would not be possible. She clearly was intent on taking the division in a new direction. That's what she had been hired to do. But she seemed uninterested and even resentful of all that we had accomplished under Fannie's leadership. I felt like she was not listening to me or the other members of the staff and did not have a feel for such a large, sprawling organization. I had to leave.

Fortunately, almost immediately I was offered a new job as associate director of the Literacy Assistance Center (LAC), a small nonprofit agency. Established in 1983, the LAC provided technical assistance to existing literacy and high school equivalency programs in New York City, along with professional development opportunities for practitioners in the field. I had worked closely with Jacque Cook, the executive director of the LAC, in prior literacy work, and she reached out to me when I didn't get the dean's job. She thought that I would be a good addition to her fast-growing agency.

Within two years year after I left the college, most of the leadership of the Division of Continuing Education either had been fired or resigned. Approximately three years after being hired, the dean herself was removed from her position.

I was 38 years old. As I thought about my 13 years at City Tech, I realized how much I had grown and how fortunate I was to work with so many outstanding colleagues. At least five of those colleagues went on to head continuing education units at CUNY colleges or elsewhere. Others became college vice presidents or leaders of large agencies. Several continued to work with me after I went to CUNY's Central Office. So many people who made a difference in so many lives grew up professionally together in City Tech's Division of Continuing Education. We learned many of our professional skills together in the division. When Bonne later became the provost at City Tech, we appreciated the ironic twist. I like to think that if she had been provost back then, I might still not have gotten the job, but she would have grasped the potential of continuing ed. Of my many wonderful colleagues, I will single out two whose impact on my career and life were unique. Bonne, who became my wife and life partner, and was an exceptional educator and higher ed leader, is at the top of that list. Bonne also has been an amazing mother to our two daughters, Amy and Laura, and is now an equally wonderful grandmother to our five grandchildren.

The second was John Garvey. John arrived at City Tech in 1978 with a bachelor's degree from Manhattan College and a history as a New York City cab driver, union activist, and political radical. John had a burning desire and passion to do his work well and provide educational opportunity for those not well served by our city. He started as a tutor in our jail program, but before long became its director. It was obvious to all of us at Tech that John was a gifted educator, a wonderful communicator, and a creative, imaginative thinker. John continued to work with me at the CUNY Central Office through 2010 and was often the person I turned to for new ideas that expanded the scope of our programs. Whenever he came into my office saying, "Would you ever think about. . . . I knew I should listen.

CHAPTER 5

80th Street

The Role and Power of the Central Office

I WAS GRATEFUL TO JACQUE COOK FOR CREATING A POSITION THAT enabled me to leave City Tech, but I spent only nine months at the Literacy Assistance Center. I enjoyed my work at the LAC and appreciated learning about the many facets of operating a small nonprofit agency. I did not expect that I would soon be presented with an opportunity to return to CUNY.

It started with a call from Jim Hall, the vice president of continuing education at York College, inviting me to lunch. Jim was one of CUNY's continuing ed leaders. I respected him. He was smart, funny, and irreverent. Until recently, Jim's deputy had been Regina Peruggi, also someone I admired. Jim, Gina, and I had worked closely together to advocate for continuing education at CUNY and develop strategies to convince the city and state to fund our programs. Gina had left York College a little over a year earlier to assume a position at the CUNY Central Office. She was deputy to Augusta, "Gussie," Kappner, the university associate dean for adult and continuing education.

Over lunch, Jim told me that Gussie was about to be appointed president of Borough of Manhattan Community College. Gina would replace Gussie as the new university associate dean. Would I be interested in talking to Gina about becoming her deputy? Indeed I was. When I met with Gina, she outlined the nature of the position, the structure of the office, and her vision for the future. She also explained the dynamics of the Central Office, stressing the political nature of the place. My title would be the Director of Adult Learning for CUNY. The office generated some grant money, most of which supported the CUNY adult literacy program. If I accepted the offer, I would once again be an employee of the Research Foundation as I had been at City Tech, and my salary would be paid by those grant funds. Moving to the Central Office was a wonderful opportunity. Still, I needed to overcome my fear of change. I spent several days agonizing, and then accepted the offer.

Right before I started my new job, I experienced a life-changing event that affected me for years. A day or two after I accepted the new job, the LAC hosted a day-long meeting with literacy practitioners who worked with young adults. I was to open the meeting with short welcoming remarks that would outline the day's activities and underscore why the topic was so important. Around 50 people attended, including Regina Peruggi, my soon-to-be new boss.

As I looked down at my notes and begin to talk, I suddenly felt paralyzed. I barely could get a word out. My heart was beating seemingly out of control, and I had a horrible feeling of dizziness. I thought I was going to faint. I was able to let the audience know that I wasn't feeling well and left the room to find a place to sit down and try to regain my composure. Regina followed me out of the room. She asked what was going on. Obviously, she was worried about the health of this guy she had just hired. After talking to her for a moment, I felt better and decided to return to the room and resume my remarks. But the same thing happened, the same palpitations and dizziness. This time I excused myself for good.

I subsequently learned that it was a panic attack. I wondered whether Regina, who witnessed my distress, would think that maybe she had made a mistake in hiring me and would rescind the offer. She never mentioned the incident to me. But the panic attacks followed me to the new job. For years to come, I had numerous attacks, almost all of them related to public speaking. Even the simplest of public remarks, like introducing myself at a meeting and talking about my background, could trigger the symptoms. I began therapy to better understand what was going on. I needed to be reassured that I wasn't falling apart. I learned to make sure that I was never in a position to speak publicly without scripted remarks that I could read. Almost as terrifying as the symptoms was obsessing for days and weeks before an upcoming public speaking event. My fear of having another attack became almost as crippling as the actual attacks.

Because my position at CUNY involved leading many senior-level meetings offering comments and public remarks, there was almost never a week when I wasn't afraid of having an attack—and perhaps even more devastating for me, being exposed. I didn't want to be known as the guy who had the panic attacks. I developed coping mechanisms, and they worked. Throughout the many years that I experienced these attacks I never told anyone but my wife. Over time, the attacks eased. Gradually, I became more confident that I wasn't going to fall apart while giving public remarks. Eventually, I became able to give remarks spontaneously, but I always had prepared remarks at hand just in case. Later in my career, when I shared my experiences with my closest colleagues, I was surprised to learn that none of them had any inkling of my ailment. They expressed shock that someone who seemed sure of himself was having panic attacks. On the other hand, through my experiences, I became expert at recognizing when others were having similar episodes. If they worked for me, I would try to figure out a way to let them know that I understood what they were going through and would be supportive.

The phase of my career at the Central Office of CUNY that began in October 1986 would last for the next 34 years. At the time, the Central Office building, located on the corner of 80th Street and East End Avenue in Manhattan, was a seven-story former health facility that had been modestly renovated to house the university's chancellor, most of the vice chancellors, and other senior administrators. Throughout the university, the Central Office was universally known as "80th Street" and had acquired a powerful mystique. Presidents and provosts who wanted to elude responsibility for a decision on their campus or deflect anger from their faculty would invoke "80th Street" as a signal that their hands were tied. Often, that was justified. 80th Street was where the budgets for all of the campuses was determined, where policy was decided, and where decisions about programs and personnel were approved—and rejected. Despite having worked on a CUNY campus for 13 years, I knew virtually nothing about how a system office operated, nor about the power and authority of the Central Office. All I knew was that despite the nervousness in starting a new job and having to prove myself again, it felt good to be back at CUNY. I believed in the mission of public education and felt that what we did would directly benefit people, especially those in need.

After being on a college campus for so long, it felt odd to enter a purely administrative building that had no students. I walked into my new office and introduced myself to Leslee Oppenheim. We shared a small office with an unusual bit of décor—an old hospital sink. Right outside the office was a copy machine that was in use virtually the entire day by anyone and everyone on our floor. Leslee directed curriculum and instruction for our Division of Continuing Education and, like me, reported directly to Regina. A wonderful person and a gifted educator, Leslee was creative, a terrific communicator, and funny. She was always looking for ways to improve instruction, develop the skills of teachers, and better serve students. Leslee had no real interest in being an administrator and paid as little attention as possible to that aspect of her job. Regina and I overlooked this, recognizing that almost every day Leslee suggested new ways of thinking and approaching our work. Leslee and I worked together for the next 33 years. During that time, she developed several of CUNY's most innovative, influential, and lasting programs.

I quickly came to appreciate working with Regina Peruggi. You never know how competent someone is until you work directly with them; Regina was superbly competent. Hard working, a terrific supervisor, willing to take risks, and an exceptional writer who could draft a funding proposal in a day, Regina understood the politics of the building and how to get things done in the Central Office. She was an effective advocate for continuing education with the chancellor and his senior team. Although driven, she didn't take herself too seriously. She firmly believed that it was critical to have some fun every day.

We were a small office with only six or seven full-time staff, all except Regina paid through grants. I oversaw the CUNY Adult Literacy Program, which had grown significantly with the addition of new city and state funding. As part of the new city funding, a Mayor's Office of Adult

Literacy was created, headed by Marian Schwartz and Suzanne Carrothers, two dynamic professionals. They helped fund a large network of programs administered by CUNY, the NYC Department of Education, the NYC Public Library system, and community-based organizations. Literacy funding also came to these four systems from the State Education Department, which established its own adult education office that supported our work. The expanded funding enabled us to support literacy programs at 14 CUNY campuses.

Adult literacy became the foundation for all of the program development work that came later. System-wide, CUNY as an institution was insular and tended to think of itself as unique, even among public universities. This was true at the campus level as well. Even among departments in the same academic discipline, collaboration across campuses was relatively rare. What was genuinely striking about the literacy program—and different from the rest of the university—was the close coordination among the providers of literacy instruction. This coordination included programs on CUNY campuses and outside the university, and also between the providers and the city and state government funding agencies. It was not solely a financial relationship. We all attended meetings, developed curricula, and offered staff development opportunities. We designed assessment tools to measure student progress and success. This was my introduction to working collaboratively with educators beyond CUNY and with government officials. I quickly saw how important it was to develop relationships with the government officials heading these offices and to demonstrate to them that CUNY programs were of quality. I also learned how, without being critical of the programs administered by our city partner organizations, to advocate specifically for CUNY when new funding became available.

The literacy program was the largest program in my portfolio, but I also supervised two other programs: the Youth Internship program, and the City Volunteer program, both dedicated to serving young people ages 16–24. At first, most of my time and energy was spent overseeing these programs. While Regina and I talked every day, and I often visited campus programs, I rarely interacted with senior university officials.

That was Regina's responsibility. I learned a lot by observing her as she worked to educate them on the importance of our work and the need for the university to support it. Continuing Ed was part of CUNY's Office of Academic Affairs, although at the time we were not involved in degree or credit programs. Nevertheless, Regina, like Gussie Kappner before her, demonstrated to the vice chancellor that Continuing Education should be treated as an integral part of the Office of Academic Affairs.

Joe Murphy was CUNY's chancellor when I came to Central in 1986. Murphy, the former president of Queens College, had a left-leaning political perspective and a sharp wit. He was a steadfast union supporter and an effective public speaker. Regina had established a good relationship with him, and he supported our office and the programs we administered.

Over the next few years, taking advantage of opportunities to develop new programs, we continued to grow. Administering each new program brought revenue and required additional staff. In 1986, as part of President Reagan's Immigration and Reform Act, Congress passed a companion provision with a typically unwieldy title: State Legalization Impact Assistance Grant (SLIAG). Through this provision, states were reimbursed for the costs of providing public assistance, public health, and education services to eligible "legalized aliens." Under SLIAG, CUNY received significant funding to provide citizenship education and English-language instruction to undocumented immigrants. This helped qualify them to be granted amnesty and stay in the United States legally. Our division at Central created and administered the program and distributed the funds to campuses where the instruction took place. Looking back at the ongoing failure of the federal government to develop a coherent immigration policy, as well as the rise of Donald Trump, it is ironic that in the 1980s there was a comprehensive amnesty program created by Ronald Reagan, a conservative Republican president.

During that same time in the 1980s AT&T approached us, asking us to create a program to provide career counseling to thousands of their workers losing their jobs due to changes in technology at the company. We struggled with whether we wanted to be part of a downsizing process at AT&T, which decreased the number of union jobs at the company and ended careers for many longtime workers. We ultimately decided to go ahead, concluding that we had a responsibility to help adult students/workers and that we would offer quality training that would lead to new job opportunities.

With our expanding grant portfolio, we added new staff. Deborah Douglass, a teacher at the City Tech Adult Learning Center, joined us to direct one of our youth programs, and in 1988 Regina hired John Garvey, the former cab driver who came to City Tech as a jail tutor, to be our unit's special projects coordinator. A year later, Bill Ebenstein joined our division to partner with John Kennedy Jr. to develop an Institute for the Study of Disabilities.

Regina had created a solid team. As Fannie had done at City Tech, Regina brought together people with varied backgrounds and experience. As a group, we were always thinking about our next project, ready to say yes to almost any opportunity and to seek funding from a variety of sources. Much of the rest of the Central Office was principally an administrative shop that created policy, set priorities for the colleges, and was responsible for compliance and oversight; we became a program shop as well. While we worked closely with our continuing education campus partners, at times we administered programs directly from the Central Office ourselves. With an eye to possible program opportunities, we paid careful attention to what was going on in New York City, the problems that city agencies faced, and the intersections between social policy and education.

Universities and colleges operate within complex networks of procedures and regulations, including their own policies and governance, as well as those of their accreditors. In New York, that also means the State Education Department. It can take several years to mount a new degree program because of required approvals at the campus, the university, and the state. In Continuing Ed, we were fortunate that as the non-credit arm of the university, we often received little scrutiny or even attention. We could build programs quickly and not be so bogged down by bureaucratic rules and institutional obstacles. We were not delayed by any formal program approval process either at CUNY or State Ed, nor were we restricted by formal governance regulations. Funding agencies, both public and private, began to recognize that if they needed to develop a project quickly, they should come to us in CUNY's continuing ed office.

We made sure that the chancellor and members of his senior team knew about our work. We celebrated student success by organizing public events that highlighted the students' stories—which were also CUNY success stories. The students' back stories were compelling and often moving—sagas of harrowing journeys from across the word to start a new life in America, and of overcoming illness, poverty, and family demands to secure an education. These events often featured participation by city officials, the chancellor, and members of the chancellor's cabinet. Mayor Ed Koch attended our first literacy recognition ceremony honoring the achievements of students who had either earned their high school equivalency diplomas or made significant progress in improving their reading and English language skills. The mayor, whom we honored for providing funding for the city's literacy program, read out the bios of the eight students being honored. It was hard not to get emotional while listening. Regina also created a university-wide "graduation" ceremony for the students who had earned their high school equivalency diplomas as participants in one of our campus literacy and GED programs. Held in the rotunda of the CUNY Graduate School, then located at 42nd Street in Manhattan, the elegant ceremony gave students who had dropped out of high school a formal event at which to celebrate receiving their diplomas. These were moving occasions for students, their families, and the officials who attended.

We worked closely with Jay Hershenson, then CUNY's vice chancellor for communications, in organizing the events and getting press coverage and in enticing the chancellor to attend. Jay, from the outset a huge supporter of our programs, had a keen political sense of the value of our public events. Government officials welcomed the chance to publicize the achievements of hard-working students. Local newspapers and broadcasters were often happy to publish good news.

The stakes were high for such events, and we aimed to organize them flawlessly. We calculated how many participants needed to attend to ensure that the event appeared crowded. Speeches and remarks were reviewed in advance, student speakers had to arrive on time, the technology had to work, and the event had to start on time and not go on too long, particularly if someone like the mayor was attending. Checking and rechecking the details became routine for me and my staff as the years went on.

In talking to Regina about this book, she spoke about how there was "no backstabbing in our unit, that it was safe to disagree with the boss and take risks, that almost everyone was pleasant and down to earth, and that it was fun to go to work." She also said that we "took shit when we had to," recognizing that at times we had to make friends with people we didn't really like and those who saw things differently.

By 1990, as a growing unit with an effective team, we were being recognized both inside and outside the university. Enthusiastic and optimistic, we did not anticipate the major changes soon coming to the university and within our division.

CHAPTER 6

Becoming the Dean

IN 1990, CUNY'S CHANCELLOR, JOE MURPHY, RESIGNED. MURPHY had been a strong supporter of continuing education. As the dean, Regina Peruggi had a good working relationship with him. I was hopeful that whoever succeeded Murphy as chancellor would also recognize the value and importance of our division. To us in the division, the far more consequential change, however, was Regina's announcement in the late spring of 1990 that she would be leaving CUNY to become president of Marymount Manhattan College. That was wonderful news for Regina, but worrisome for the rest of us in Continuing Education. Although her move could create an opportunity for me, it inevitably reminded me of my time at City Tech, which had ended with rejection and being passed over as Fannie's successor. Immediately, I started to obsess and worry privately about that happening again, while trying my best to keep these feelings to myself.

Regina would leave CUNY in mid-June. As that date neared, no one at a senior level had talked to me about who would replace her. This was further complicated by the fact that Regina had encouraged me to attend Harvard's Institute for The Management of Lifelong Education, a two-week professional development session run by Harvard's Graduate School of Education for continuing education administrators throughout the United States. Regina had attended the institute the previous summer, raved about it, and put aside money for me to attend. The problem was that the institute overlapped with Regina's leaving and with an event celebrating her years at CUNY. I thought about not going to Harvard, but Regina would have none of that. She pushed me to attend. And it was a life-changing experience.

Two weeks prior to the institute, participants were asked to read the book *Composing a Life* by Mary Catherine Bateson, which would be discussed at one of our initial sessions. The book featured the lives of five prominent women, including Bateson herself, and examined how each of them managed their daily lives. A key theme of the book and most relevant to me during this uncertain time in my career was to see change in your life as an opportunity rather than something to run away from.[1] Now that I was about to turn 44, it was a high time I learned to deal with change.

The Harvard program strongly encouraged participants to reflect deeply on their own lives and careers, and also to understand how important it was as a leader to build community. During my time at Harvard, I continually reflected on that theme of change as an opportunity. I also engaged any number of the other participants in conversations about how I should manage my return to CUNY after the institute concluded. By the time the institute ended, a large number of the 80 participants knew my story. These two weeks were like therapy for me.

I returned to the uncertainty of my CUNY role and simply assumed responsibility for the Continuing Education division, which now had approximately 25 full-time staff and a grant portfolio of slightly over $11 million. The Central Office itself was also in a transition period, awaiting the arrival of Ann Reynolds, who had just been named to replace Joe Murphy as CUNY's chancellor, from the California state higher education system. In an additional development, Matthew Goldstein, the president of the CUNY Research Foundation, was appointed interim vice chancellor for academic affairs.

Given the size of our division's grant portfolio, I had worked closely with the Research Foundation and had a good relationship with Matt Goldstein. He liked me and supported our division's programs and activities. Knowing that enabled me to relax a little as I took over Regina's portfolio. I still had the same title, and to protect myself from the possibility that I wouldn't be named dean, I applied and received an offer to become the dean of the Division of Continuing Education at Bronx Community College. That offer was appealing—more than a mere fall-back. Bronx had an active, high-quality continuing ed division. I was impressed with the college president, Roscoe Brown, who had served in World War II as one of the Tuskegee Airmen.

I approached Goldstein about the Bronx job offer. He advised me to turn it down, stressing that leaving the Central Office at this time was not in my best interest. I replied that I agreed with him, but that the Bronx job was a dean's title, while at Central I was still in a director position. Matthew said he would see what he could do.

A day or two later, he called me into his office and let me know that I would be appointed the university associate dean for adult and continuing education, the same title that Regina had held. There was, however, one condition to the appointment. The university wanted me to pay for my own salary through the grants we generated. While I could perhaps have played hardball and turned down that offer, assuming that they would back down, I had neither the political savvy nor the confidence to push back. In truth, I really wanted the Central Office position. I accepted the offer, and the conditions. For the next 30 years as my CUNY career continued, I would always pay my own salary from grant funds generated from my area. I guess this was my introduction to some of the Central Office politics that I would come to understand and expect. I came home from work that night to be greeted by Bonne and my two daughters, Amy, age 11 and Laura, age 8, with a big banner spread across the living room wall congratulating Dean Mogulescu. It was very exciting and touching.

I became dean at about the same time that Ann Reynolds began as chancellor. The new chancellor had strong opinions as to where she wanted to take the university, and she was said to be exceedingly demanding and impulsive. One after another, administrative assistants failed to meet her standards and were dismissed. Staff members who worked directly with the new chancellor reported that she would write you off quickly if she didn't think that you could be helpful, and it was often discomfiting to be around her.

One of my all-time favorite CUNY stories happened during the administration of Chancellor Reynolds. At the time, the chancellor lived in a university-owned residence, a few blocks west of the Central Office on East 79th Street. One day the housekeeper at the residence placed a frantic call to the Central Office, indicating that one of the chancellor's two dogs had escaped from the residence and was last seen running down 79th Street. The chancellor adored her dogs, two massive wolfhounds. It was clear that all hell would break out if the dog was not quickly found or even worse if something happened to the dog, like being run over by a car. Jobs could be at risk.

Time was of the essence. The chancellor was at an outside meeting but was expected back at her residence shortly. Almost immediately, Deputy Chancellor Larry Mucciolo dispatched a small team of high-level Central Office staff toward the house on foot to try to find the dog. At the same time, he called Gerald Lynch, the president of CUNY's John Jay College of Criminal Justice, to see if the NYPD could send police officers to search for the dog. Incredibly, at least to me, NYPD put out an All-Points Bulletin. Every police office with a radio was looking for the canine runaway. Mucciolo headed for the house, dreading the possibility of having to inform the chancellor that her dog was missing.

Just as the chancellor's car reached the corner of 79th Street, with top staff and police officers all looking, and Mucciolo steeling himself to give the chancellor the bad news, here came the dog, trotting briskly toward home. He had found his way on his own. A minute or two later, the dog arrived, and a minute or two after that the chancellor arrived, neither dog nor owner aware of the commotion. Disaster averted and a forever story to be told and retold.

I did not interact with the chancellor very often, but I did understand that we needed her support if our programs were to continue to grow. As I gained a better sense of the culture and politics of the building, it became clear to me that Reynolds relied the most on two senior administrators, Vice Chancellor Jay Hershenson, who led the university system's communications efforts, and Deputy Chancellor Larry Mucciolo. Other than the chancellor, Jay and Larry were the most powerful people in the building. Reynolds consulted with them often and listened to their advice. They also were among the few people able to calm her down when she got annoyed. Regina, my predecessor, had already established good working relationships with Larry and Jay, and I had gotten to know them some before Regina left. I built on that history and worked hard to interact with them as much as possible and keep them informed about the work of our division.

I reported to then-Interim Vice Chancellor for Academic Affairs Matthew Goldstein, although he stayed in that position for only a short time. He left the Central Office in September 1991 to become the president of Baruch College. In 1992, the chancellor appointed Richard Freeland as the new vice chancellor for academic affairs. Richard, almost Kennedy-esque in his boyish looks, was a historian who had worked at the University of Massachusetts at Boston for over 20 years in a variety of faculty and administrative positions prior to coming to CUNY. Brilliant, hard-working, and decent, Richard got along with almost everyone. As the university's chief academic officer, he built a good relationship with the chancellor though she seemed to rely more on Jay and Larry except on purely academic matters. Richard was smart enough to recognize that landscape and took care to establish good relationships with both Jay and Larry. They respected Richard as well. A few years later when Richard was named president of Northeastern University, he took Larry Mucciolo with him as his senior vice president for administration and finance.

Once again, as had happened with the corrections officers at the Brooklyn House of Detention, sports helped me get to know Larry and Richard on a more personal basis. Larry was a sports junkie who was highly competitive and loved basketball. Once he knew that I had been a college athlete, he often had me come up to his office on the seventh floor at the end of the day to bullshit about some player or team. We often shot a little foam basketball at the miniature hoop in his office. Before long we were placing small bets on the NCAA basketball tournament and arranging to play pickup hoops at John Jay College after work. We were joined by Richard Freeland in those games, along with a number of other Central Office staff. Besides basketball, we often played tennis doubles: Larry and I versus Richard and Ron Berkman, another dean in the building. I very much enjoyed those games and those guys, and I think they enjoyed it too.

This story speaks to the kind of "boys' network" that enabled me to establish personal relationships with senior university officials. Those personal relationships provided me a level of access to them that probably would not have been possible merely based on a work relationship. It was unfair, of course. But it was the reality in many offices at that time.

Soon after Ann Reynolds became chancellor, I was confronted with a problem that had the potential to severely diminish the work of our office. If not handled well, it could also place me in a vulnerable position as to my future at the Central Office. CUNY had received $3 million from New York City designated for literacy funds. The chancellor decided that she was going to reallocate the $3 million, moving it to the general operating budget of the university. If this decision were to stand, the program would have to be diminished by over 50%, with many staff losing their jobs and thousands fewer students being served. Doing so could also set a precedent for doing the same thing for future Continuing Ed programs funded by the city and state.

I immediately told Leslee Oppenheim, who directed the literacy program, about the chancellor's decision and suggested that she inform the directors of the literacy programs throughout the university. A day later Leslee let me know that the directors were planning to protest the decision to cut the funds by holding a demonstration in front of the 80th Street headquarters on the day of the next Board of Trustee meeting.

I expected the demonstration to be both large and noisy. Many of our directors were activists, and they were committed to supporting the program and the literacy students. And Leslee was a creative organizer. I also expected the chancellor to be extremely unhappy about any interruption of a board meeting; she might blame me for the protest, or at least for not stopping it. I did let Vice Chancellor Richard Freeland know in advance that a protest was planned, but I wasn't able to stop it. Richard told me that he disagreed with the chancellor's decision and agreed, as well, that we were at risk if the day went badly.

Behind the scenes, I worked closely with Leslee to organize the event. I understood the true danger to Continuing Ed's future if the chancellor's decision were to stand. I couldn't stand back. I also wanted to make sure that, however quietly, I had some input into how the day was organized.

On the day of the board meeting, I arrived at 80th Street really early, probably at around 7:30 a.m., going directly up to my office on the fourth floor. Around 8 a.m., I began to hear some noise in front of the building, soon followed by loud drums and a forceful voice speaking over a very good speaker system. Looking out the window at the street below, hours before the late afternoon meeting of the trustees, I was astonished to see hundreds of demonstrators in front of the building, many with signs of protest. The staff members of the college literacy programs were accompanied by large numbers of their adult students.

Thus began 12 straight hours of drums, speeches, music, and chants about the need to save the program. As part of the demonstration, the literacy students took turns reading passages from books they had been assigned, demonstrating the educational progress they had made in the program. The loudest noise was reserved for the time that trustees arrived at the building and the 4:30–6:30 p.m. meeting itself. I was surprised the large police presence at the demonstration never interfered with any of the activities and let the demonstration continue for such a long time and so close to the building.

During the meeting, the noise from outside was a major distraction, and it was relentless. Even after the meeting ended around 6:30 p.m., the demonstration continued until around eight o'clock. It could not have been organized better. Throughout the long day, there were never fewer than 200 people in front of the building. During the meeting itself, there must have been more than 500 demonstrators. Students and staff arrived in shifts, although some participants stayed the entire day. You could feel their passion and anger.

The next day, the demonstration was the talk of the building on 80th Street. I wasn't sure how the chancellor would react. I was surprised that I didn't hear from her for rest of the week. I finally learned that she had decided to set up a task force to assess the program and determine its future at the university. When asked who I would recommend to lead the group, I suggested Regina Peruggi. The chancellor went along with my recommendation, and Regina—my former boss, my colleague, my dear friend, who had overseen the literacy program while at CUNY—was indeed asked to chair the task force. At that moment, I could see that the chancellor was looking for a way out of the situation. She wanted to back off from cutting the program. A month or so later, the task force filed a report praising the literacy program and strongly urging that its funding be maintained. And it was.

Organizing the demonstration was a good example of how we approached our work. It was no surprise that we were able to bring out a few thousand students and staff over the course of the day. We applied the lessons learned from having run many events. For this event we knew that to have any level of success, we had to have lots of people in attendance all day, and they needed to make a lot of noise. Knowing the chancellor's personality, interrupting a board meeting and embarrassing her was a major risk. Fortunately for us, it turned out well. She must have known I was involved in helping to organize the demonstration, but she apparently decided to give me a pass. I continued to have a good, but relatively distant, relationship with Chancellor Reynolds for the rest of her time at CUNY.

In October 1997, a year after Ann Reynolds had left CUNY to become president of the University of Alabama at Birmingham, I received a letter from her. I don't think that I have ever received a better tribute or one that meant more to me. To receive it from Ann Reynolds, a person who had an imperious way of working with staff, was a pleasant surprise. The letter revealed a side of the chancellor that few people knew existed. She wrote:

> My admiration was greatest for you when because of political changes or budgetary constraints I would start down the road of tightening up on our many out-reach programs which bled money from CUNY. I don't think I was ever successful in any of those endeavors because you were always so convincing as to how important they were and to how desperate the individuals were being served by those programs. You were right, of course.

> Thank you too, for being such a consummate administrator. I always knew that any program you were dealing with would have fiscal order, that you would have a good sense of the caliber of the personnel and how best to work with and oversee them and that there would be concrete results. This is where so many people falter, and this is an especially important skill. The world does not give enough credit to first rate "bureaucrats," and you are truly one of the very best.[2]

It wasn't in my nature, and I'm not sure why, but for some reason as the dean I felt a sense of calm. I was grateful for the appointment and enthusiastic about the work. As I assumed higher level positions with greater levels of responsibility, I actually got less anxious. That was perhaps because I had greater control over my job and also because now I could rely on the support of staff throughout the entire division, and not on a limited number who were directly in my area.

CHAPTER 7

Adapting to Political Reality

Serving CUNY Students Receiving Public Assistance

BY THE LATE 1980S, CONTINUING EDUCATION AT CUNY HAD become aggressive in seeking outside funding. We began to develop relationships with senior officials from city and state agencies, including the New York City Human Resources Administration (HRA), the agency responsible for overseeing public assistance programs. As the largest social services agency in the country, HRA provides an array of services to millions of poor New Yorkers each year. In discussions with then-HRA Deputy Commissioner Cathy Zall, we developed a program for public assistance recipients attending CUNY colleges. At that time, they numbered 27,000. These students often struggled to complete their degrees. The program we developed with the commissioner aimed to provide a package of services that we believed would lead to increased retention and graduation rates. Commissioner Zall shared our strong view that obtaining a college degree was the best pathway to a life of financial independence and career success.

Named COPE (College Opportunity to Prepare for Employment), the program began in 1992 at four CUNY colleges. Students on public assistance were offered tutoring, counseling, and job preparation. Besides funding the costs for administering the program, HRA paid training related expenses to cover childcare costs, books, and other education-related expenses to all CUNY students receiving public assistance if they were enrolled in vocationally oriented associate degree programs.

In return, HRA required CUNY to monitor student attendance and academic performance.

Over the next few years, CUNY entered into additional agreements with HRA, expanding its programs to include services for non-credit students. Thousands of public assistance recipients received ESL, literacy, and GED instruction, together with work experience placements at outside agencies and organizations.

Despite the demonstrated success of CUNY's programs, the rules and support for CUNY students on public assistance changed dramatically when Rudy Giuliani became mayor of New York in 1994. No longer were students encouraged to attend and graduate from college while being supported by public assistance. Instead, to maintain their public assistance benefits, students had to work a full 35 hours a week at what were called Work Experience Program (WEP) assignments. We needed to modify our programs to meet the new guidelines in order for CUNY to maintain funding for our programs.

While it was clear that we would not be successful in opposing the work requirements established by the city, Chancellor Ann Reynolds made two requests of the mayor that we felt were necessary to enable students to stay in college while on public assistance. The first was to permit students to do their work assignments on or near a CUNY campus. The second was to enable students to count their classroom hours as part of the 35-hour work requirement. The chancellor was quite public in stating her views. She also was quietly working through the state legislative process, assisted by Vice Chancellor Jay Hershenson, to advance a bill that would codify these provisions.

What was happening in New York City was part of a national trend to reduce the number of people on public assistance. The very titles of the federal legislation made the goals strikingly clear. The 1996 bill codifying the Clinton administration's welfare reform program was titled the Personal Responsibility and Work Opportunity Reconciliation Act. It replaced AFDC (Aid for Families with Dependent Children) with TANF (Temporary Assistance for Needy Families). The federal government and the Giuliani administration were in sync with "ending welfare as we know it." It also was clear that CUNY's chancellor and the mayor of New York were on a collision course.

In 1996 Chancellor Reynolds, realizing that she had gone too far in so publicly disagreeing with the mayor, requested a meeting with him. She continued to hope for a compromise on the issue of work assignments for CUNY students receiving public assistance. She asked Jay Hershenson and me to accompany her to the meeting.

At City Hall, we were escorted into a small conference room on the first floor. I was uncertain what my role would be, but had a very bad feeling about this meeting. While we waited for the mayor, Jay and I tried to make small talk with the chancellor, who appeared anxious and distracted. When the doors opened, in walked two of the mayor's most senior officials: Tony Cole, senior adviser to the mayor, and Randy Mastro, Giuliani's chief of staff and a deputy mayor from 1994–96. Cole informed us curtly that the mayor would not be attending the meeting. He expressed the mayor's unhappiness at the chancellor's public comments on the issue of student work assignments. Chancellor Reynolds asked what she could do to resolve the situation. The mayor's aides both declared that it was too late. Flustered and upset, she again asked what she could do, perhaps a joint press conference or written statement to the press? Dismissively, Cole reiterated: Too little, too late. He abruptly ended the meeting. As we walked out of City Hall, I really didn't know what to say to the chancellor. A proud, accomplished woman had been embarrassed and humiliated.

Not long after the meeting, the chancellor announced her resignation to assume the presidency of the University of Alabama at Birmingham. The dispute with Giuliani was only one of the many problems Reynolds had; it also appeared to me that she also had lost the support of the CUNY trustees.

For me and the program directors, the immediate challenge presented by the mayor's policy was how, within the mandated framework of work assignments and job placement, we could maintain HRA support for what was now a number of multi-million-dollar programs that supported CUNY students on public assistance. That challenge was further complicated by the fact that HRA Deputy Commissioner Cathy Zall, our most ardent supporter, had been summarily fired. In 1997, Giuliani brought in Jason Turner as the new HRA commissioner. Turner had worked for Governor Tommy Thompson in Wisconsin on welfare-related issues. A staunch believer in the new federal welfare reform regulations, Turner committed to a quick reduction in the number of city residents receiving benefits.

To save our programs, the first compromise we made concerned our request that HRA permit CUNY students fulfill their work requirements on or near a campus. We reluctantly agreed to have an outside organization, the Jewish Community Council of Greater Coney Island, administer the program. Rabbi Moshe Weiner headed the JCC, a multi-service agency with a long history of serving the poor of Coney Island and beyond. We didn't know what to expect, but fortunately we developed a strong working relationship with Rabbi Weiner and his staff. The agency was committed to helping CUNY students find the best possible work placements and to supporting the students when problems arose. Deborah Douglass, the CUNY administrator responsible for overseeing most of our programs for welfare recipients, became a close colleague and friend to her JCC counterpart.

Equally important, Cathy Zall's replacement at HRA, Seth Diamond, was committed to working with us. Seth was one of those rare public figures able to survive multiple New York City mayors, serving as the executive deputy commissioner at HRA for both the Giuliani and Bloomberg administrations and later as the commissioner of homeless services for Mayor Bloomberg. Over these years, together with Seth and his staff, we developed further initiatives for CUNY students receiving public assistance, almost all related to finding employment for students while maintaining their ability to stay in college.

The change in federal and state welfare policies had a huge impact on the number of public assistance recipients receiving benefits overall in New York City. According to Mayor Giuliani's press release on December 28, 1999, public assistance cases dropped from 562,000 in March of 1995 to 276,000 by the end of 1999. At CUNY, where 27,000 students had received public assistance in the late '80s, the number had shrunk to slightly more than 10,000 by fall 1998.

The funding CUNY received from HRA to support existing and new programs did not change during this time. It subsequently increased significantly during the Bloomberg and de Blasio administrations. We were able to continue to serve our students by adapting to the changing rules, establishing good relationships with our HRA colleagues, and administering quality programs that almost always met required program milestones. For a time, we were required to enter into performance-based contracts. These paid us a set amount based on established performance indicators, usually related to job placement, and rewarded us if we over-achieved. Such agreements are risky. If you fail to meet your milestones, you can end a fiscal year in deficit, having spent more money than you brought in. To avoid that, we worked closely with HRA staff to create agreements that set reasonable targets. Often, we ended a program year with a budget surplus that we were able to keep and use for other purposes.

I can't overestimate the value of both establishing close relationships with agency officials at the most senior levels, but also of working closely with line staff as well. We were fortunate that Seth Diamond assigned Mia Simon and Abi Morrison to be our program contacts at HRA. While following HRA polices and the emphasis on work, they shared our belief that college access and success was important. They helped us figure out how to develop programs that complied with the HRA requirements, while ensuring that students on public assistance could stay in college. They approved milestones that were reasonable and doable. They were as committed to our students as we were.

Through the Giuliani and Bloomberg administrations, our programs with HRA continued to grow although the number of CUNY students receiving public assistance continued to decrease, consistent with national and local welfare policy. By Fiscal Year 2005, we were administering seven programs funded by HRA with a combined budget that totaled almost $30 million.

With the election of Bill de Blasio as mayor in 2014, HRA policies for

CUNY students receiving public assistance changed again. The mayor selected Steve Banks to become commissioner. Banks had been the Attorney-in-Chief of the NYC Legal Aid Society, where he had often fought against many of the welfare policies enacted by the Bloomberg and Giuliani administrations. While I didn't know Commissioner Banks personally, I was familiar with his background and confident that he would bring a new attitude about the value of a college education as perhaps the best path to permanent self-sufficiency.

I was not disappointed. Soon after Banks was named commissioner, we began a series of meetings with his team to redesign the programs we were already offering with HRA support to CUNY students receiving cash assistance. The COPE program was renamed CUNY EDGE (Educate, Develop, Graduate, Empower). While the EDGE program retained some of the original components of the COPE program such as advisement, tutoring, job readiness seminars, and limited financial assistance, it counted classroom and instructional hours as meeting work requirements and expanded the program to include support for students enrolled at all CUNY campuses. It also provided benefits for students in liberal arts programs rather than restricting participation to those enrolled in vocationally oriented degree offerings. Finally, the program provided funding to pay students for their work assignments—dollars that would be added to the money they presently received as part of their public assistance allocation. For the most part, forced work experience was eliminated and college graduation became the program's foremost priority.

The HRA story demonstrates our ability to sustain a major program throughout four different administrations that enforced opposing philosophies about public assistance. Through judicious compromise and building effective relationships within city government and other agencies, we were able to continue the program that reflected our values and commitment to serving the most economically disadvantaged CUNY students.

CHAPTER 8

The CUNY Language Immersion Program

We Enter the Mainstream

HISTORICALLY, ADULT AND CONTINUING EDUCATION AT CUNY served only adult, non-degree students and had little or no direct involvement with matriculated students seeking college degrees. This was the case at almost all CUNY campuses. No rules or regulations prevented Adult and Continuing Ed from serving degree students. It was simply part of the CUNY culture and generally accepted throughout the university that ACE was its non-credit arm. Degree programs were the responsibility and purview of the faculty and academic side of the house. Instead of college faculty, CUNY Adult and Continuing Education, as stipulated in the union contract, employed continuing education teachers (CETs) to teach its courses. CETs did not have the same status as regular faculty. They were paid less, had little job security, and were rarely full-time employees. Although this division between credit and non-credit seemed natural within CUNY, it was actually atypical in higher education. The vast majority of colleges and universities throughout the country, including many of our nation's most elite schools, have vibrant and successful degree programs administered and taught by continuing education divisions. CUNY was an exception.

In the early 1990s, engagement with credit or degree programs was not a priority of our division. We were focused on expanding our outreach to low-income adult students poorly served by the traditional educational establishment. We concentrated on two key areas: adult literacy, language skills; and GED instruction and workforce training. To accomplish this work, we had become increasingly successful in seeking outside funding and had begun to develop productive working relationships with senior city and state officials.

In 1995, we had an opportunity to broaden our mission to include working with degree students. From its outset, CUNY has been a university that served immigrants, first-generation college students, and poor and working class New Yorkers. In the early 1990s almost a third of CUNY students were first-generation college students. For close to 40% of CUNY students, English was not their native language. As a result, many first-year students needed to improve their English proficiency in order to be successful in college. They were required to take non-credit courses in English as a Second Language (ESL), in addition to all of the credit courses needed for their degrees. Almost all of CUNY's colleges offered ESL courses. Students enrolling with the weakest English language skills were mandated to take a series of courses until they were deemed proficient. Because students didn't earn academic credits for these courses, the lengthy period of time students spent taking them extended the time to graduation and often used up financial aid. This, in turn, caused some students to leave school long before earning a degree. On top of it all, the second-language courses, generally anywhere from 3–6 hours per week, were not intensive enough for typical students to become language-proficient. For non-native speakers, the path designed to help them start earning a degree often became a major obstacle.

Chancellor Ann Reynolds understood this problem and began discussions with our division to see if we could develop an alternative program. We had many years of experience teaching ESL through our literacy initiative, and Leslee Oppenheim and her team had spent years developing curriculum and training teachers. In response to the chancellor, they developed a new program called the CUNY Language Immersion Program or CLIP. We began a pilot program in 1995 for 90 students in the building that formerly housed the Theresa Hotel on Adam Clayton Powell, Jr. Boulevard, between 124th and 125th streets in Harlem.

As Chancellor Reynolds had requested, CLIP presented an alternative to the standard ESL courses the university campuses had been offering. To enroll in CLIP, students first had to be accepted by a CUNY college as degree students. Then they would agree to defer their formal enrollment in college coursework to focus first on becoming language proficient. Participation was voluntary. The program was targeted to those students whose limited English language proficiency was "likely to be a barrier to their academic success."[1]

Several important features distinguished CLIP from the college ESL programs. CLIP was intensive, designed to bring students to an adequate level of proficiency in English in one year or less. Students in CLIP received 25 hours of instruction in English-language skills per week, up from 3–6 hours in college ESL. Unlike most although not all of the campus ESL programs, which taught reading, writing, and speaking and listening in separate courses, the CLIP curriculum integrated the language skills. It also taught language skills in the context of themes that helped prepare students for college course requirements, incorporating materials from content courses such as history, sociology, psychology, and literature.

Courses were taught by continuing education teachers (CETs) with each teacher responsible for a single class of not more than 25 students. At first the teachers were paid on an hourly basis even though they worked full time: 30 hours a week (25 hours of teaching and five paid hours for preparation). As the program expanded over the next few years, the faculty union, the Professional Staff Congress, strongly advocated for CLIP teachers to receive full-time status with accompanying benefits. From the beginning, Leslee and I agreed with the union. We worked quietly at the Central Office to push for that to happen. That process was not simple, however, because it was part of collective bargaining. In 2017 after many years of discussion, CLIP teachers got the full-time status that we long believed they should have. It was a classic illustration of how complex an apparently straightforward decision could be at CUNY, even when all parties wanted the same outcome.

From the pilot program with 90 students in 1995, CLIP grew quickly. The following year, the Harlem program, administered by Borough of

Manhattan Community College, expanded to an enrollment of 220 students. New sites opened at Kingsborough Community College, LaGuardia Community College, York College, New York City Technical College (now called New York City College of Technology), and Bronx Community College. During the 1996–97 program year, 1,495 students enrolled. Students accepted for admission at any of the 17 undergraduate CUNY colleges were eligible to enroll, although the vast majority were from the community colleges and the two senior colleges, York and Lehman, that had campus CLIP programs.

Over the next ten years the CLIP program became fully integrated into the mainstream of the university. CLIP's annual enrollment increased to approximately 3,000 students. In addition to the initial campus programs, the College of Staten Island and Queensborough Community College were added. The beginning level ESL classes, offered for so long at CUNY, were gradually replaced by CLIP, as were intermediate-level courses. Eventually only the highest-level courses were maintained by college faculty. All of the programs except the one at York College were administered by the respective college continuing education program. Funding provided by the Central Office paid for all program costs, including a full-time CLIP director at each campus. Almost all of the directors had both administrative and teaching experience. Our division in the Central Office administered the program for the university, with Leslee and her team responsible for overseeing the curriculum and instruction. They built a strong CLIP community that included a university-wide Council of CLIP Program Directors, a full array of staff development activities, all-staff days, a CLIP teacher and staff listserv, and many other support activities.

Because CLIP provided what the state called "non-credit remedial courses," it qualified to receive state aid for CLIP programs offered at the community colleges. That aid more than paid for CLIP, and we provided the program at a nominal cost for students: $100 for 14 weeks of instruction. It was critically important, too, that CLIP students did not have to use their financial aid for the program; they could reserve that money for their degree programs. I was forever arguing with the university budget office that CLIP actually produced a surplus of dollars that should have been returned to the campus programs. I had little success in convincing them.

CLIP demonstrated conclusively that our unit at Central and the campus adult and continuing education programs had the expertise to administer quality instructional programs for regular degree-seeking students. That recognition served us well as we began to challenge regular remediation at the university and what we believed was its lack of success. We began to build an infrastructure of serious educators dedicated to reversing CUNY's low graduation rates. They believed the university needed to do better. The intensive instruction provided by CLIP was a big step in the right direction. CLIP introduced students to the demands of college-level study. Students responded by going on to complete college successfully. The CLIP staff has been justifiably proud that a number of students who began their college careers with CLIP have gone on to receive their degrees with honors and even become campus valedictorians.

CHAPTER 9

Louise and Matthew Arrive

Anything Is Possible

IN ONE OF HER LAST ACTS BEFORE LEAVING FOR ALABAMA IN 1997, Chancellor Reynolds appointed Louise Mirrer as vice chancellor for academic affairs. Louise came to CUNY from the University of Minnesota-Twin Cities, where she had been the vice provost for arts, sciences and engineering. She arrived at a time of turmoil at CUNY. Christoph Kimmich, the provost of Brooklyn College, was about to be named interim CUNY chancellor; Governor Pataki had appointed Anne Paolucci as the new board chairperson, replacing Jim Murphy, who had been chair since 1980; and Mayor Giuliani had intensified his scathing public criticism of CUNY. On May 6, 1998, the Mayor announced the creation of the Mayor's Advisory task force on The City University of New York to examine the state of the university.

The announcement of the task force generated fear and anger across much of the university community. There was widespread belief that the investigation and ensuing report would reflect Giuliani's previous criticism and attack CUNY unfairly. I worried about the membership of the task force. It would be headed by Benno Schmidt, former president of Yale and founder of the Edison Project, a for-profit educational organization. Other task force members included the Manhattan Institute's Heather MacDonald, who had written bitingly critical articles about CUNY; Richard Schwartz, a former senior advisor to the mayor; and Herman Badillo, a long-time member of the CUNY board and soon to be board chair. Badillo had once been a liberal Democratic congressman representing the Bronx and deputy mayor under Ed Koch. He subsequently switched to the Republican Party and became a member of the Giuliani administration.

The task force spent a huge amount of time talking to different CUNY constituencies. It held hundreds of meetings—with the chancellor and other senior administrators, many faculty and staff, college presidents, city and state officials, and outside higher education experts (107).[1] Roger Benjamin, executive director of the task force, was smart and fair-minded, and the full-time staff and consultants hired to assist in the process asked good questions and listened carefully to all points of view.

The report was released in June of 1999 under the inflammatory title "The City University of New York: An Institution Adrift."[2] Faculty leadership, the union, and more quietly, campus administrative leaders objected. As I read and then discussed the findings and recommendations with our division staff, we found somewhat to our surprise that we agreed with at least some of the recommendations. We saw them as pointing up needed change at CUNY. We were pleased that up front the task force report stated that "it wishes to emphasize its absolute commitment to CUNY's historic mission: to provide access to first-rate college and graduate-degree opportunities for all New Yorkers ready and able to take advantage of community and senior college education in the liberal arts, sciences and the professions" and "applauds CUNY's special commitment to students who, by reason of jobs, family responsibilities, or lack of financial means, must struggle to avail themselves of higher education opportunities."[3]

A key recommendation in the report concerned changes to the remediation policy. The report recommended that remedial classes continue to be offered, but only for students entering community colleges/associate degree programs. To enter senior colleges or baccalaureate programs students would have to demonstrate through SAT scores, New York State Regents exam grades, or CUNY's own placement tests that they did not need any remedial work in English or math. That change had already been decided upon by the Board of Trustees at its January 1999 meeting. Their 10–6 vote had been preceded by bitter fighting between faculty and the trustees. The meeting where the vote took place was at LaGuardia Community College and was perhaps the most contentious in my years at CUNY. Hundreds of people attended, almost all of whom opposed the resolution, and it was next to impossible to hear any of the trustees talk. The level of noise in the auditorium went from loud to louder, with constant interruptions, shouts, and displays of outrage.

One of the concerns raised, and it was a legitimate one, was that ending remediation at the senior colleges would bring about a significant decrease in the number of Black and Hispanic students attending those schools. At one of the earlier public hearings held by the trustees to discuss the issue, my former dean and hero, Fannie Eisenstein, joined people such as playwright Tony Kushner in testifying. They argued passionately that ending remediation would be a huge mistake. They warned that it would deny thousands of students of color access to CUNY. They said it was racist. Listening to Fannie's eloquence, I smiled, recognizing that few people knew who she was. Still, while hating to align myself with politicians and board members who didn't share my political background and beliefs, I didn't fully agree with Fannie that ending remediation for the baccalaureate programs would be a disaster. Remediation had not succeeded in erasing the disparities in graduation rates and should be reconsidered.

Over the next ten years, Black and Hispanic enrollment did decrease at some CUNY senior colleges like Baruch, Hunter, and City College, which had added a requirement for higher SAT scores, but the number of minority students at CUNY overall increased significantly. On the other hand, nationwide, remediation began to be viewed as an obstacle to progress and success for many students. By 2020, remediation as we knew it was virtually eliminated throughout CUNY. Our division had a role in that process with the creation of the CUNY Start program in 2009, providing a more effective means to ready under-prepared students for college work.

In addition to the remediation issue, the report recommended a strengthening of the relationship between CUNY and the New York City Department of Education, placed a priority on appointing a strong chancellor empowered to "reconstitute CUNY as an integrated university," improve its budgeting and financing processes, invest further in a "university wide technology infrastructure," and work to make CUNY function as a university and not a "confederation of individual colleges."[4]

I disagreed with many things in the report and considered the title unfair. Yet I felt that overall, its analysis of the state of CUNY was largely correct. It was true that what the report described as "a loose federation" of colleges, especially in the absence of a strong chancellor, was an outmoded model that kept the university from moving forward or addressing some of its problems. An integrated university with a chancellor empowered to lead would be a very different institution. Fortunately, the report had avoided any recommendations that would threaten CUNY's future as an autonomous university. And the report's recommendations provided a blueprint a new chancellor could follow.

The next priority of the trustees was to select a new chancellor. To my pleasant surprise, the board selected Matthew Goldstein, effective September of 1999. They also made a critical change in the chancellor's authority: the college presidents would report not to the Board of Trustees but directly to the chancellor. It was a big and positive step toward the integrated university that the Schmidt report had called for.

Matthew Goldstein knew CUNY from the inside. After leaving the presidency of the Research Foundation, he served as Baruch College president from 1991–98, and then assumed the presidency of Adelphi University in Long Island. I knew Matthew well and couldn't have been more pleased with the appointment. Matthew had invited me to join his senior team at Adelphi, an offer that I considered but turned down. I was committed to the CUNY mission. His return so soon turned out to be fortuitous.

Matthew came to CUNY with ideas and vision. He fully embraced Louise Mirrer as his partner and the second most important person in the university. To have the academic vice chancellor with that kind of status sent a message that change was coming, that the future agenda for CUNY would be driven by the academic side of the house. Other senior leaders, even Jay and Larry, though still important, would not dictate policy and budget considerations. Matthew made Louise's status clear in both direct and subtle ways. For all Chancellor's Cabinet and other high-level meetings, the Chancellor's administrative assistant would bring the Chancellor and Louise tea or coffee in real China cups while everyone else at the meeting would be sipping out of Styrofoam.

Advancing Louise and making her status and power explicit was a critical first step to Matthew's success. She was a brilliant, tenacious, and no-nonsense leader, willing to take risks. She also brought academic credibility to the position. I had reported directly to Louise since she arrived in 1997. By the time Matthew arrived as chancellor, Louise had gotten to know me, my top staff, and the work of our unit. She had confidence in us. She and the chancellor began to set the stage for our unit to become the innovative arm of the university. At the end of virtually every day, I would be in Louise's office talking about CUNY, suggesting new programs, listening to her challenges, and helping her figure out strategy. She quickly understood how our division could help conceive and implement many of the new concepts brought forth by the chancellor. Louise soon promoted me to the position of university dean for academic affairs and deputy to the vice chancellor. The lack of formal academic credentials for me and many of my staff was not an issue for either Matthew or Louise.

Although I had seen only glimmers to that point, Matthew Goldstein had a broad vision for CUNY. He would become the most influential chancellor in my long history at CUNY. Going forward, he brought opportunities for our unit to become involved in the development of programs that would dramatically change CUNY and the city.

PART 2

So Much More Ahead

Expanding Our Vision, Making Connections, and Creating Partnerships

With the battle over remediation behind them, Matthew Goldstein and Louise Mirrer could focus on moving the university forward. While I had worked with the chancellor before and thought that I knew him well, I had no idea how bold his plans for CUNY would be. Or how driven he was. Matthew was not a charismatic leader nor was he an inspirational speaker, but he was incredibly smart and astute. He had a relentless focus on what he wanted to do and an engaging way of getting support for his ideas from influential people both within and outside the university. He understood politics. But he also had courage and was willing to stand his ground when he thought he was right, even if it occasionally irritated people in power, including elected officials. He was charming one-on-one and could make almost anyone believe that he was in their corner. In 2003, Benno Schmidt was appointed as the CUNY board chair. Benno and Matthew developed a close relationship. Although I had no idea as to the nature of their private conversations, it certainly appeared that Benno supported almost everything Matthew wanted to do.

Matthew also knew how to wield power. Before he became chancellor, the CUNY college presidents reported to the Board of Trustees rather than to the chancellor. Matthew was able to convince the board that, as a condition of his employment, the presidents should report to him. The board passed a resolution to that effect. That resolution sent an early message to the presidents that the chancellor was fully in charge. Although he treated the presidents with respect and publicly praised almost all of them, he was more than willing to call them out or have one of his senior staff make it known privately that the chancellor was not happy. Matthew believed in the importance of establishing an integrated university, with its agenda driven by the Central Office.

The chancellor had a fairly large cabinet of senior university officials, but those closest to him and whom he relied on the most included Louise, Jay Hershenson, Allan Dobrin and Rick Schaffer. Allan and Rick were early hires, Allan as vice chancellor for finance and administration and chief operating officer, and Rick as vice chancellor for legal affairs and general counsel.

Because I knew Matthew pretty well and had already established a very good relationship with Louise, I was confident that our division would thrive. As the university dean for academic affairs and deputy to the executive vice chancellor (Louise), I also was gaining status throughout the university, both at the Central Office and with the college presidents.

Even so, I could not have anticipated that during Matthew's 14 years as chancellor, our unit would lead some of the most significant and lasting initiatives in the university's history. Almost every year we started a large new program, often more than one, with many beginning small and then scaling up. Nor did I envision that the staff we brought in to lead the new projects would go on to hold major leadership positions at CUNY and throughout the country.

I. PARTNERING WITH CITY AGENCIES

As our office grew, partnerships with government agencies, nonprofit organizations, and private foundations were central to expanding and accomplishing our work. These partnerships were a major source of funding. They also led to our growing reputation for dependable, creative, and timely performance. In the earliest days when adult literacy was the core of our operation, we had learned how to work collaboratively with funders—then largely the mayor's office and New York State Education Department—and quickly recognized the benefits. Collaborating with the Human Resources Administration to coordinate work requirements for students receiving public assistance had required us to establish mechanisms to manage funds in compliance with city, CUNY, and Research Foundation policy. In all, we probably developed many dozens of projects with city agencies, not counting the NYC Department of Education, which in itself accounted for a huge portion of our work. The four projects discussed in detail here illustrate different aspects of that work, some of the many forms it took, and the varied challenges and issues to be solved.

CHAPTER 10

Streetwise

Working with the NYPD

IN THE SPRING OF 1997, I ENTERED ONE POLICE PLAZA, THE 14-story headquarters building of the NYC Police Department (NYPD) with Leslee Oppenheim, my in-house expert on language and curriculum development. Greg Donaldson and Doug Muzzio, CUNY faculty experts on police, city politics, and urban life, joined us. The vast, imposing building, located on Park Row in lower Manhattan at the foot of the Brooklyn Bridge and steps away from City Hall and the Municipal building, houses the police commissioner and many of the department's highest-ranking staff. We showed our CUNY identification at the reception desk and were escorted to the office of Deputy Commissioner for Community Affairs Yolanda Jimenez, who had invited me.

Because neither Leslee nor I had ever worked with the NYPD before, I had asked Greg to join us. Four years earlier Greg had published an award-winning book about cops, entitled *The Ville: Cops and Kids in Urban America.*[1] His book, highly praised by law enforcement officials, including former Police Commissioner Bill Bratton, followed the lives of a young black housing cop and a male teenage housing project resident in the Brownsville section of Brooklyn. To write it, Greg spent two years in Brownsville accompanying cops as they did their jobs. He knew police and policing and New York City. Cops respected him—not quite as one of their own, but close. Doug, a professor in the Baruch College School of Public Affairs, was an acclaimed journalist and pundit with deep knowledge of city life and its politics. He knew and understood police and policing, too.

Deputy Commissioner Jimenez explained that the department felt the need to improve community-police relationships and that they wanted CUNY to help them achieve that goal. The NYPD had no preconceived notion about what the project should look like. She saw this as a joint project and welcomed all ideas as to the format and content. She said that whatever department staff we needed would be available to work with us.

I was struck immediately by the intelligence, candor, and commitment of the deputy commissioner and her team. I had come into the meeting with my own negative stereotypes about the mindset of police brass, particularly those appointed during the Giuliani administration. By the end of our first meeting, however, I recognized that my views were off the mark, at least for the NYPD Office of Community Affairs.

Thus began a series of meetings where we developed a framework for the project. We expanded our CUNY team, and the department added some other members, including a few experienced officers who had joined Community Affairs after many years working in a precinct.

At one of our first meetings, Greg suggested that we name the project Streetwise. He felt it was essential to give the project a name that wouldn't sound academic and would relate to street cops. Everyone agreed. We subtitled it "Language, Culture, and Police Work in New York City." Our goal was to prepare recent graduates of the Police Academy "to employ knowledge of language and culture as an important tool in New York City." We developed curricula around some of the largest ethnic communities in the city, with an understanding and belief that "police officers who know about language and culture in the communities they serve equip themselves with powerful tools for protecting the safety and well-being of themselves, their colleagues and the public."[2] We hoped that the training we delivered would lead to a greater degree of trust between community members and the police. We also hoped to develop a more community-oriented way of policing. The communities we selected to highlight included Chinese, Haitian Creole, Hispanic, Russian, South Asian, and African/Caribbean-American. We also included a unit on what was then called the LGBTQ community.

To complement the written material, we made a series of 7–10 minute videos that illustrated the work of cops as they interacted with residents in each of these communities. We hired two young filmmakers, Bill Bixby and Bill Thierston, to produce the films. We chose cops well regarded by the department to be featured. The videos, though brief, were engaging and informative. Our respective teams went through an extensive editing process; we challenged the filmmakers and ourselves about the realism of the videos and whether they were free of stereotypes and bias. I remember screening the videos the first time. I smiled as I watched a seasoned beat cop walking the streets of Chinatown greeting the residents and merchants with phrases in Cantonese, Mandarin, and Fukienese. Looks of surprise and appreciation appeared on the faces of the community as they heard a cop of Italian heritage speaking their language. I was equally impressed as I watched the African/Caribbean-American video and listened to a detective explain how to act when arresting a suspect in that person's home surrounded by family. He spoke of the need to enter the house cautiously, but with humility, understanding that you are the police and that you come with power. There was no need to disrespect family members or the person being arrested, the cop advised; being arrogant and abusive just made a difficult situation worse and also could lead to a lifetime of ill-feeling from children seeing their father or mother arrested.

It took about eight months to produce the videos and written material. They would be shown first at a staff day for 2,100 recent graduates of the Police Academy who were newly assigned to precincts all over the city. We would hold the training at five different venues, one in each borough, with about 400 cops participating at each site. As part of the preparation, Doug and Greg trained cops to lead workshop sessions. Being a workshop facilitator is not a simple task. It was important to select officers who bought into the value of the training, something that was not the case with everyone we picked initially. Fortunately, Greg and Doug were exceptional teachers who also related well to the cops. In fact, many of the participating police officers assumed that Greg was a cop, too. Greg was fine with that. When they learned that Greg was actually a CUNY professor, the participating officers were surprised—and pleased. Doug also was popular with the police because of his personality. He was a character. The most animated of people, Doug was outspoken, dynamic, and loud. He talked with his whole body, swinging his arms constantly and engaging his audience through his exuberance and energy.

We approached the staff day as we would any other conference we were organizing—taking nothing for granted. We visited each site to make sure that the technology worked. We checked with the trainers to confirm they had the schedule down. We also assigned staff to facilitate the day's activities at each site. I moved from venue to venue to watch the proceedings and get a taste of how the day was going.

Despite all our care, we did have one glitch at the Brooklyn site. The Borough Commander was supposed to give greetings, welcome the participants, and give an overview of the day. But the chief cancelled at the last moment. Fortunately, this was the location where Greg was assigned. Greg smoothly filled in, with the talk and body language of a chief. The participating officers thought he was a boss cop, and Greg never told them different. His performance that day gave him a story he could tell over his lifetime.

Later in the day, though, we had a more serious issue that left with me another of my favorite CUNY anecdotes. Soon after I got back to the office, I received a call from a *Daily News* reporter working on a story about the training. He had read our press release and needed me to clarify one point. In the curricular materials for the "Say the word in Spanish" unit, in the small section "Well-Known People," we listed prominent figures such as Cesar Chavez, Chita Rivera, Roberto Clemente, Gloria Estefan, Jennifer Lopez, and Geraldo Rivera. And Juan Valdes. The reporter asked whether that was the fictional Hispanic person who sat on a donkey in the television and print advertisements for Colombian coffee. "Oh boy," I thought to myself, "this could be a big problem." I suspected the reporter would like nothing better than to embarrass us for including a fictional, stereotypical person in our listing of prominent Hispanic people. "I'll get back to you," I said.

I went immediately to Leslee Oppenheim, who had overseen the curriculum development. "Leslee, is Juan Valdes the donkey guy?" She sheepishly responded that yes, that was the guy. She had included him because everyone had seen the commercial and would recognize the name. She hadn't given a thought to any other implications. Leslee is amazing, and certainly at the moment I didn't want to criticize her, but I needed to figure out how to respond to the reporter. We did a quick search on the internet to see if there were any other famous people by the same name but came up empty. I swallowed hard. I needed to tell Louise Mirrer, who would need to alert the CUNY communications people that trouble was coming.

Louise listened, and then produced one of the better examples of the many times I benefitted from working with people who are better educated and more highly cultured. She thought a moment, then said, "I think I have a solution." There was a famous Spanish neoclassical poet named Juan Valdes. She also pointed out that the spelling of the man on the donkey in the advertisement ended with the letter z rather than an s, as our material had done. I called the *Daily News* reporter, informed him that Juan Valdes was a famous Spanish poet and added that I was surprised that he had not heard of him. I didn't imagine for a second that the reporter believed me, but I assumed that being on deadline he had dropped the matter. I've retold this story many times but only recently read the actual news story. It states, "The diversity lesson plan also contains some curious information about ethnic and racial communities." Observing that the examples of people from Hispanic culture were chosen largely from sports and entertainment, it goes on to say, "The lone exception was Juan Valdes, who reporters originally thought referred to the Colombian coffee pitchman but who turned out to be a 16th century Spanish author."[3]

That evening, Deputy Commissioner Jimenez and I had arranged for the CUNY and NYPD teams to meet at a Midtown restaurant for what we'd hoped would be a celebration. We were not disappointed. Our organizers and site leaders came directly from their boroughs, each exuberant at how the day had gone. We had spent eight months preparing, and it was a wonderful success. Giddy with excitement and pride, we spent a long evening sharing stories. We had become colleagues and friends with the members of the NYPD. At the time, the department was beginning to become more diverse regarding both race and gender, a trend that has continued since then. The cops we worked with represented the department well, exhibiting almost none of the negative attitudes that we had seen among many experienced cops at the precinct level. The officers we worked with accepted the members of our team. They seemed impressed with how much we knew about running good programs, and that we were flexible in our thinking, listened to criticism, and were humble and respectful.

We moved on to a second phase of the project, integrating the Streetwise material as a permanent component of the Police Academy's curriculum. That took additional months of work. As with all of our city programs, Streetwise was supported by city funds generated through an intra-city agreement between CUNY and the NYPD. In fiscal years 1999 and 2000, an additional 4,800 new graduates of the Police Academy were given the Streetwise training.

When the project was completed in 2001, the top brass of the NYPD honored us with a ceremony. Although I did not know it, my time working with the NYPD was not over. Shortly, I would be asked to become part of a new police initiative to assess the NYPD's overall training.

Streetwise was a true team effort. Doug and Greg led our training team, and Leslee oversaw the curriculum development and video portion of the project. Gifted communicators and teachers, they brought skill, humor, and sensitivity to the training and were able to relate to the rank and file police as well as to the police brass. Streetwise once again demonstrated the importance of selecting the right staff to lead challenging projects. In March 2023 I attended a retirement celebration for Doug. I hadn't seen him in a long while. As I greeted him, he gave me a big hug and shouted out that participating in the Streetwise project was the single best experience of his long CUNY career. For other members of the Streetwise Team, that was true as well.

THE NYPD BOARD OF VISITORS

As we approached the conclusion of the Streetwise Project, Commissioner Jimenez asked to meet with me in her office. She told me that NYPD Commissioner Howard Safir was establishing a Board of Visitors charged with reviewing all aspects of Police Department training, including both the Police Academy and ongoing, in-service training. The board would include members from the media, nonprofit organizations, the clergy, higher education, and the military, as well as former members of the department. They would have full authority to examine all aspects of police training and would submit an independent report on the findings. She invited me to become a member of the board.

I must admit that I was surprised that the NYPD, with the certain approval of the mayor, would establish an outside board to assess its training. For an organization so protective of its image and proud of its training, this seemed like a bold and somewhat risky step. Clearly, the establishment of the Board of Visitors was at least in part a result of two recent horrific incidents involving police. In August of 1997, Abner Louima, who had been arrested earlier in the evening after a fight broke out at a Brooklyn nightclub, was viciously beaten and sodomized with a broomstick by police officers after being brought to the 70th precinct. The second incident happened in February of 1999 when Amadou Diallo, an unarmed Guinean immigrant, was shot and killed by four NYPD plainclothes officers in front of his Bronx apartment house. The officers fired 41 bullets at Diallo, hitting him 19 times. The officers claimed that they were looking for an alleged serial rapist and mistakenly believed that Diallo was reaching for a gun when they began shooting. Each of these incidents set off a wave of protests within the city and beyond. The reputation of the NYPD was severely damaged, and much of the criticism was directed at the training that police received.

After checking with the chancellor, I agreed to join the board. I was flattered to be asked by the deputy commissioner and trusted that if she was involved the board would function as an independent entity that would reach its own conclusions about police training. During Streetwise I had learned a lot about the training at the Police Academy and the general culture of the Department. But I knew little about the many aspects of in-service training.

The fifteen-member Board of Visitors was officially established by Commissioner Safir in May 1999 and started meeting almost immediately. While I didn't know any of the members personally, I recognized some of their names, including Ralph Dickerson, president of the United Way of NYC; Lorraine Cortez-Vasquez, president of the Hispanic Federation; Stanley Crouch, a columnist for the *Daily News*; Richard Green, CEO of the Crown Heights Youth Collective; and Thomas Reppetto, president of the Citizen's Crime Commission.

Four separate committees were established to drive our work: In-Service; Firearms and Tactics; Leadership Training/Recruitment and Retention; and Recruitment/School Safety. Each committee had a chair. I was assigned to the In-Service Committee. While attendance at the meetings was good and all of the committee members seemed engaged, the conversations were often dominated by a handful of members. Initially, we did not select a board chair, and board meetings often rambled. It was difficult to focus on our assignment. Soon, however, several members suggested that we select one of the members to chair the board. The group turned to me, perhaps because I was relatively little-known. I actually was glad to assume that role; I hated meetings that lacked a focus. I was comfortable pushing people to arrive on time. I was happy to draft meeting agendas. The position also gave me some control as to the direction of the group and the need to make progress.

I was responsible for making sure that the committees did their work and met the deadlines for delivering reports. Even though the board members were all pretty distinguished and leaders at their organizations, I didn't mind nudging and bothering them if a committee didn't seem to be progressing fast enough. The department had given us a relatively short timeframe to complete our initial report, and I was determined to meet their deadline.

As chair, I had the opportunity to observe and visit training sites related to the work of all of the committees. That was a fascinating experience. I received an NYPD ID giving me entry to all precincts and training facilities. At almost every location I visited, I was greeted respectfully by police officers and their commanding officers. Watching the tactical and firearms training up close was eye-opening. I tried to put myself in the shoes of a rookie or inexperienced cop going through role playing and actual training simulations where an inappropriate use of a firearm could lead to the injury or death of a suspect or bystander. On the other hand, failure to respond could lead to injury or death to oneself or a fellow officer. The simulations were realistic and well done.

My many visits to precincts were revealing. Some precincts were located in old buildings in need of renovation, while others had newer, more modern facilities. Apart from the training, I observed how the precincts appeared to function. In some precincts, phones were answered quickly and cordially. At others, the phone would ring many times before being answered, and citizen requests for assistance were met largely with indifference. Similarly, upon arrival at a precinct, I might be greeted by a cordial front desk officer or one who barely noticed my arrival.

The variance in what I would call customer service at the precincts was not surprising. I had often seen the same thing in my days working at the Brooklyn House of Detention. Or for that matter, when I visited a CUNY campus or tried to call a particular campus office. I would trace this back to a failure of leadership and an unwillingness to set standards and supervise staff. Creating an office environment that is friendly and available to its constituents is not hard to do, but incredibly important. I learned that from Fannie Eisenstein and tried to create such an environment throughout my career.

As the due date for the committee reports approached, I had to push the committee chairs to get them in on time. Two of them failed to meet the deadline, but after some intense nudging, they finally submitted their reports. Unfortunately, three of the four reports were not written very well, or findings were not comprehensive enough. Given the short time frame to deliver the report to the department, I turned to my own staff to translate the committee reports into a coherent, single document. Leslee took the lead here. She was a gifted writer, knew a lot about the police through Streetwise, and was always willing to accept new and important tasks. When I let the committee chairs know that we were seriously editing their reports, they seemed grateful for the help. None objected.

The report delivered to Commissioner Safir in June 2000, a year after the board was established, was comprehensive. While generally positive about the overall effectiveness of the training provided at the Police

Academy, it criticized the precinct training. At the precinct level, the subcommittee found that the "training is not effective and needs substantial review and revision. What was observed was not training, but simply the passing on of information." At the precinct level, much of the training took place for 20 minutes as part of the briefing/roll call of officers prior to a shift. The training sergeant often struggled to get the attention of the officers, particularly more experienced officers who felt that they had nothing to learn, at times talking through the training and giving off negative body language throughout.[4]

Two months after we submitted the report, in August of 2000, Commissioner Safir resigned and was replaced by Bernard Kerik. The board met with the new commissioner twice to discuss our recommendations. We continued to meet as a group for the next year or so. But nothing else happened. We never did learn whether the recommendations led to any real change within the department. With the election of Mayor Bloomberg and his appointment of Ray Kelly as police commissioner, the board was eliminated.

For me, being on the board and becoming its chair was fascinating. I learned a great deal about the police department and how it functioned: how a large and vitally important city agency operated, how it handled political pressure and intense criticism, and how open or not it was to change. I got to know some of the board members really well and maintained relationships with them for years to come, talking about our jobs, sharing stories, and asking for advice.

As a board we were proud of the report we delivered. Still, we recognized that while the report may have led to some small improvements in the quality of the training provided by the department, it did little to change the overall culture of the force or improve community-police relations. Over the next 20 years meaningful police reform remained elusive as the nation was confronted with the dilemma of figuring out how to combat periodic spikes in crime, while also confronting horrifying incidents of police abuse, most poignantly demonstrated by the brutal killings of George Floyd and Tyre Nichols, and the need to change police culture and hold "bad" cops accountable for their actions.

CHAPTER 11

NYC 311

Assisting New Yorkers

"THERE'S A DEAD RACOON IN THE MIDDLE OF THE STREET." IN the summer of 2008, after a morning walk in Prospect Park, my wife Bonne came back into our Brooklyn house and let me know that right in front of the house on our busy street was a large and apparently dead animal. This was a first for us after 30 years in that house. Bonne called 311. Within an hour, a Health Department employee arrived to remove the racoon. Soon after that, a 311 call representative phoned to let us know that the racoon had been removed. I turned to Bonne and commented on how the 311 service had added so much to the New York City experience in the five years since it had been established by the Bloomberg administration.

By the time of our raccoon, the 311 hotline had received more than 100 million calls and was receiving 50,000 calls a day. Everyone in the city uses 311. What perhaps is less known is that CUNY had an important role in the development of the system and since it began operation, in ensuring that the 24-hour system was fully staffed.

Within a month of assuming office as mayor of New York City in January of 2002, Michael Bloomberg announced that one of his major priorities would be establishing a 311 system. The system would be administered by the NYC Department of Information Technology and Telecommunication (DOITT). Vice Chancellor Allan Dobrin, CUNY's COO, had served as DOITT commissioner in the Giuliani administration. Soon after Mayor Bloomberg's announcement, Allan asked me to assume responsibility for a new project. He didn't go into detail other than to indicate that we would be assisting the city in establishing the new 311 call center.

A few days later, I entered 59 Maiden Lane, a large office building in downtown Manhattan and went to the fourteenth floor and the new 311 call center and headquarters. I was astonished by its size and design. The space seemed as big as a football field, but except for a few offices and conference rooms, it was mainly divided up into workstations. From here, 311 representatives would answer calls and respond to the daily needs of New Yorkers. Brian Peterson and Abi Morrison, two members of a new team I had put together, accompanied me to meet the leaders of the project and to learn what they needed from CUNY.

The city wanted CUNY to select, train, and hire CUNY students to become part-time call center representatives (CCRs), to complement 311's permanent full-time staff. The students would work shifts that regular city workers preferred not to take—late nights, overnights, and weekends. Shifts would be arranged around student class schedules. Students, undergraduate or graduate, would work a maximum of 18 hours per week, with the opportunity for additional hours during school breaks. Hourly pay for undergraduate students would be $11.98/hour and graduate students $14.98. That was well above the minimum wage of $7.15. The DOITT staff stressed that we would need to recruit, hire, and train the students quickly.

I immediately accepted the challenge of establishing a CUNY 311 project. Not only was this a good opportunity for our students, but it was also a priority project of a new mayor. I asked Abi Morrison to oversee the project and given its urgency added a few other staff from our unit to assist in the development process. In addition to a project director, Abi and I hired other staff, including a payroll coordinator, trainers, and student recruiters.

As I had learned to do when working with the city's Human Resources Administration, I entered into a new intra-city agreement with New York City. The agreement would provide funding for project staff as well as pay student salaries, resulting in an overall annual budget close to $2 million. Because it would take time to complete the intra-city agreement, the CUNY Research Foundation needed to forward fund the project, almost always the case with "urgent" city and state projects. The RF staff never liked to start programs without signed agreements, but they had learned that they could trust my unit's track record, and they understood the importance of this project. Nevertheless, they took care to remind me that, in the event funding was not received from the city, the RF would charge my earnings account. Fortunately, by 2002, my unit had received dozens of prior grants, totaling over $60 million. The indirect costs earned through those prior grants had accumulated in what was called an earnings account at the Research Foundation. My unit's earnings account was now large enough to offset any losses from the 311 project. In Margaret Panciera, our unit had a gifted budget director who kept track of our many projects and the earnings account. Margaret knew when to tell me that I was taking too big of a risk. I trusted her advice and almost always listened to her.

Our team immediately began to work with our campuses to publicize the program, developing a recruiting and screening process for accepting students into the 311 project. Collaborating with city 311 staff, we developed a training protocol. The training was rigorous, demanding, and comprehensive. Students who missed a class, came late, or couldn't adapt to the demanding work rules were asked to leave. These strict guidelines seemed harsh to me, but we were preparing students for hard jobs. They would be interacting all day with New York City residents, nearly all of whom were calling because they had a problem. A large number of callers would be extremely unhappy and upset about things like having no heat or hot water in their apartments.

DOITT provided CUNY with its own training room at the Maiden Lane facility. Within weeks, Abi and her team had accepted the first group of students and began training. With many more applications than open slots, we had to turn down any number of qualified applicants. The CUNY students accepted into the program came from all of the CUNY colleges.

As the start date neared, we were confident that the students had been well trained and would do their jobs effectively. We did worry a bit about whether the students would be accepted by the regular full-time city employees working at the call center; there had been some initial criticism about using lower-paid CUNY students instead of full-time, union-represented city workers. Once students began, however, most of the criticism went away, as the city workers acknowledged that for the most part CUNY students were filling late evening and weekend time slots that the regular workers did not want.

Larger problems had to do with who supervised the students, and with job security. We had established rules for hiring, maintaining, and terminating students for non-performance, but our staff and the DOITT staff did not always agree on how best to interpret the rules. The students were paid by the CUNY Research Foundation and bound by its work rules. Yet the students' on-site supervisor was a DOITT employee. Who was responsible for disciplining students who did not comply with the rules? Who should determine that it was time to terminate a student? It took a while for CUNY and DOITT staff to understand each other. Over the first few years of the project there were disagreements over how to handle these student issues. Together with one of DOITT's senior staff, I attended several of the many meetings convened to resolve the matter. Eventually, we found a way to handle discipline collaboratively.

Being a call center representative was terribly hard and stressful. It was not for everyone. Often students who were unhappy with the job simply stopped coming to work. On a positive side, the job offered students the opportunity to see how a large organization worked and to learn about the array of agencies and services provided by the city. The 311 service was an extremely efficient operation and was welcomed by most city residents. The students recognized that they were an integral part of something important and that they could do a complicated job well.

Over the first six years of the CUNY 311 project (2003–2009) almost 3,600 students applied for positions. Nearly 900 CUNY students completed the training and began working as CCRs. Approximately 10 percent of them were later hired as full-time city employees at the call center. The project provided millions of dollars in wages for CUNY students while offering them an interesting job vital to the interests of city residents. CUNY's involvement with 311 has now become institutionalized, with the agreement with the city continuing through the years of the de Blasio administration and the beginning of the Adams administration.

Whenever I call 311 and particularly during weekend or late-night hours, I ask the person picking up the phone if they are a CUNY student. They often say yes, which always gives me a sense of accomplishment and pride. This is a program that was complicated to create under enormous pressure, and one that we did well. The CUNY students hired as CCRs represented the university and their respective colleges well. CUNY became an integral part of one of Mayor Bloomberg's most successful initiatives.

But the raccoon remains our most memorable 311 call.

CHAPTER 12

We Are New York

Making Movies and Winning Emmys

IT IS SUNDAY, APRIL 18, 2010, AND I AM SITTING AT A TABLE AT the Marriott Marquis Times Square hotel with colleagues from CUNY and the mayor's office attending the Regional Emmy Awards ceremony. We are anxiously waiting to hear whether we have won in any of the three categories in which we have been nominated. As the announcer begins reading the nominations for the Writing Category, I think to myself, "What are we doing here?" At that very second, I hear first Leslee Oppenheim's name. Then David Hellman, Kayhan Irani, Sandra Poster, and Anthony Tassi. We have won! We collectively begin shouting, and Leslee goes up to the stage to accept the award on behalf of CUNY and the Mayor's Office of Adult Education. With a wide smile on her face, Leslee gives the perfect acceptance speech. Like a seasoned producer or actor who has done this many times before, she starts by thanking the Academy, thanks her colleagues who helped create the show, and ends by accepting the award on behalf of the 1.5 million immigrant New Yorkers who make our city a better place.

Almost three years earlier, Leslee had approached me with an idea to try to get funding for the development of a TV series. Her idea was to help immigrants with limited English improve their language skills, while also providing information on how to access city services. The New York State Education Department had turned down her request to fund the project, but she had another possibility. Anthony Tassi, executive director of the New York City Office of Adult Education, had expressed interest in Leslee's idea and thought the city might fund it. I had worked closely with Anthony over the past years. He was tenacious, and he understood the need to expand services for the 2.5 million New Yorkers who had limited English or lacked a high school diploma. Developing a quality TV series geared to immigrant adults was of particular interest to him because the longest waiting lists for free adult education classes were those for English language instruction.

Anthony went about trying to convince senior city officials that funding a television series not only made sense but was consistent with Mayor Bloomberg's education agenda and interest in expanding services for immigrant New Yorkers. While I never believed that Anthony could pull this off, before long he had secured a commitment from the city to allocate $5 million to CUNY to develop the series. This was incredibly exciting news, but there was one problem. We didn't know a whole lot about how to create television shows.

I did have great confidence in the creative brilliance of Leslee and knew that she would put together a talented team. I also understood that, as we had with many of our SUD unit's prior successful projects, we would figure this out. That didn't mean that I wasn't worried, however. Five million was a lot of dollars, and this project was not going to be easy.

Our first challenge was to find an experienced filmmaker to lead the project. We approached Bob Isaacson, the head of CUNY TV for a recommendation. He gave us a name of an experienced director; we met the director and offered him the position. One of his first decisions was to hire several writers to develop scripts for the shows. Although the writers were professionals with experience writing for television, neither they nor the director fully understood the implications of script writing for a population of immigrants with limited English language proficiency. This was to be an educational TV series, and they couldn't conceptualize what that meant in practical terms. Plots needed to be straightforward and language accessible to English language learners. Because the target audience represented many diverse cultures, it would be especially important to respect cultural sensitivities. The ESL educators on our staff attempted to work with the filmmaking team. The film professionals seemed to be listening to our ESL experts, but they either failed to absorb or simply ignored their suggestions.

A few months later, we all gathered in a local theater to view the pilot episode. The entire project staff was invited, as were a large number of outside folks, including representatives of immigrant populations, city officials, and other CUNY staff. As we watched, it was clear that while the actors were talented, the pilot was not merely horrible but downright insulting to one of the immigrant groups represented. The show also included gratuitous violence. The filmmakers had totally missed the point that this was to be an education program teaching its viewers language skills and how to access city services.

As I left the theater I glanced at Anthony Tassi, whose face was red with rage. We had a huge problem. We had spent several hundred thousand dollars putting the team together and developing the pilot. And we had nothing to show for it. I wondered whether we would all be on the cover of the *New York Post* for squandering tax dollars.

Leslee, Anthony, and I agreed to meet the next day to come up with a plan to salvage the project. Fortunately, Anthony had calmed down some. We all agreed that the pilot was awful and that we needed a new team. The next day I met with the director to let him know we no longer needed his services. He tried to argue with me, forcefully stating that we didn't know anything about filmmaking, but I held my ground. We were back at the beginning.

Our solution was to approach the chairperson of the film department at City College and ask him to take over the project. Andrzej Krakowski was a seasoned filmmaker who had directed a number of movies. After hearing our predicament, he agreed to do it. He hired Bob Perkis, who had worked closely with him on some of his films, to be the show runner. I still had one problem. Andrzej was already a full-time faculty member at CUNY, and he didn't want to take a leave from his faculty job. Instead, he wanted to be paid for both. Although I did push the boundaries of what CUNY would allow, I was desperate. I figured out a way to pay Andrzej through the use of summer salary differentials and payment for faculty overload activities.

We made one more crucial decision, which was to write the scripts in-house under the leadership of staff member David Hellman. We invited Sandy Poster, a faculty member at BMCC, and Kayhan Irani, a community activist and immigrant, to become members of the writing team. Writing the scripts in-house turned out to be a terrific decision. Besides having the necessary linguistic and cultural knowledge, the team could create situations that were relevant and believable. Perhaps inevitably, as the project evolved, tension between filmmakers and educators continued to bubble up, but it never reached a total impasse.

The team immediately began work on a new pilot and on planning additional episodes. Andrzej and Bob began to put the crews together to film the first episode, and the writing team started drafting several more. Because union rules demanded that we pay the actors and technical crew almost on a daily basis, we worked with Research Foundation lawyers and contract staff to form our own production company to handle the project's expenditures and cash-flow challenges. We called it ESL Productions. Our Senior University Dean unit now included a film company.

A few months later, we gathered once again to watch a pilot. This time, we would be viewing an actual 25-minute video. Titled "New Life Café," the episode highlighted a middle-aged Dominican woman named Rosa. Just as she was about to realize her lifelong dream of opening a Dominican café in the city, Rosa ran into personal difficulties. As the guide for the pilot stated, "But when her lab tests come back and the doctor tells her the bad news, her dreams are over. Or are they? A heart-warming drama about family, friendship, and coming to terms with diabetes."

We all loved the pilot. Although some edits were in order, we were back on track. While I would like to say that everything went smoothly from then on, I would be lying. We ultimately produced eight additional episodes, with the process alternating between exhilaration and exhaustion. The writers and filmmakers rarely agreed, engaging in frequent squabbling. Anthony Tassi had strong feelings about the content of each episode and was given to occasional verbal outbursts. Leslee, too, was never quite satisfied with what we thought was a final product. Many meetings were held to talk about tweaking some parts of every episode. The filmmakers pointed out that reshooting scenes was time-consuming and costly.

Always acutely aware of the dollars we were spending and our time deadlines, I tried to persuade or push everyone to accept what might not be a perfect final version but was still very good. Sometimes I was successful, but not always. Often, I wound up shouting at Leslee, which was not helpful. It also was true that the filmmakers, Anthony, and the CUNY team were all strong personalities, none of whom could understand why any reasonable person would disagree with their point of view.

After approving the pilot, we spent the next few months writing, filming, and editing the episodes. Amid all the drama within the drama, there were some wonderful moments. I often visited the many different sets. The professionalism of the union-hired film crew was amazing. They were incredibly efficient and competent. I watched as they closed down streets around the city, filmed in parks, built sets both indoors and out, and dressed the actors in appropriate costumes. The actual filming was astonishing to a novice like me. I listened as "quiet on the set" was shouted, followed by "action." In a moment the actors were transformed into episode characters.

Each episode told an intimate story of the lives of immigrants, highlighting their strengths along with their challenges. The characters were real and believable. The stories were poignant and humorous. Each show also highlighted a city service, including episodes on smoking cessation, financial management, stopping domestic violence, education, and parenting. Before finalizing an episode, we previewed it with groups of prospective viewers from many different immigrant communities. That included adult New Yorkers who were not yet English-proficient as well as staff from agencies serving immigrant populations. The response was overwhelmingly positive. We were ready to go.

We called the series "We Are New York," and it went live on June 27, 2009. It was shown several times per week on the city's educational cable television channel.[1] The show was widely publicized by the city throughout its many immigrant communities, and DVDs were made available to agencies and schools that wished to show any of the episodes. The education team had also developed curricula and instructions on how best to use the series for language instruction. By the second year of the series,

Leslee and her team had trained hundreds of volunteers to establish study and conversation groups throughout the boroughs to enable thousands of immigrants to view and discuss the videos.

All of us who had worked on the project felt proud of what we had accomplished and assumed that the project was finished. But Bill de Blasio's Office of Immigrant Services funded us to develop eight new episodes. While they renamed the series "We Speak New York," the episodes followed the same format as those produced earlier. Episode themes included food insecurity, career preparation, worker rights, elder care, immigration legal help, pre-K resources, mental health, and the Census.

"We Speak New York" was shown on New York City's Cable Television channel and was used to supplement instruction in ESL classes. Its website presented study guides and other curricular material, including lesson plans. The program also continued to train volunteers on how to lead conversation groups. In May 2019, now called "We Speak NYC," the series received an Emmy for its episode, "Rolando's Rights." That was the third Emmy for the program, adding to the two received for the original "We Are New York" series. In 2021, a new episode, "Shola's Voice," examined the importance of voting. It also helped New Yorkers understand the new Ranked Choice Voting process that would be used in New York City's upcoming primary election.

It is difficult to track how many thousands of immigrant New Yorkers have benefitted from the 18 episodes in the series. Between the actual TV episodes, the conversation groups, and the use of the instructional materials in classrooms and immigrant serving agencies, my guess would be that since the series premiered in 2009 to the present, hundreds of thousands of immigrant New Yorkers have been introduced to at least some aspect of the series.

What seemed like a crazy idea when Leslee first proposed it—that we would produce a widely seen and quality television series to teach English and show viewers how to access city services—came to be. Our team learned to make "movies" and provided a valuable service to the many immigrant communities of New York City. It was a special project. We have Emmys to prove it.

CHAPTER 13

The CUNY Service Corps

ON OCTOBER 29, 2012, HURRICANE SANDY BROUGHT WIDESPREAD flooding and destruction to New York City. Homes and businesses were severely damaged, with many destroyed. Subway stations were flooded, and millions of New Yorkers lost power. Particularly hard hit were waterfront and coastal neighborhoods in Brooklyn, Queens, and Lower Manhattan. There were billions of dollars in damage, and more than 40 New Yorkers lost their lives in the devastating storm.

As the city began the long clean-up from Sandy's destruction, I attended a regular meeting of the chancellor's cabinet. Putting aside the agenda, Goldstein talked about the impact of Sandy on the city and the need for CUNY to demonstrate its commitment to helping New Yorkers. He turned to Matt Sapienza, the vice chancellor for budget and finance, and asked whether he could free up $5 million of CUNY operating funds to support a program to provide paid service opportunities for CUNY students to work on an array of service-related projects. The chancellor was vague on details other than to emphasize that the project would need to be developed quickly. Matt Sapienza said he could find the money.

As the chancellor was finishing his comments, Executive Vice Chancellor Allan Dobrin caught my eye and motioned for me to step outside the room with him. Outside in the corridor, Allan smiled and asked me if I would lead the project and put together a team to create it. I immediately said yes. Our conversation lasted maybe a minute. We returned to the meeting, Allan announced to the cabinet that "John and his team" would oversee the project, and the chancellor thanked me for taking it on.

Later that day, I informed my senior team. By then, having been recruited to address the needs of students on public assistance, develop training for the NYPD, and help create 311, among many other projects, team members were rarely surprised when we were asked to respond to a pressing need, especially if there was a tight timeframe. Everyone in the room had experienced the force of Sandy, and many had suffered damage directly. These were also people who liked challenges. To a person, they expressed excitement, offering to help and volunteering to free some of their existing staff to build the program.

The first and most important decision was to select a project leader. Given the urgency, there was no time to conduct a formal search for a director. Suri Duitch, then the university associate dean for adult and continuing education and my deputy, recommended that we ask Rachel Stephenson, who had been working in our workforce area, to assume the position. I met with Rachel, and 10 minutes into the meeting understood why Suri had recommended her. Rachel had all kinds of ideas for the project and fully embraced its goals. She was an excellent communicator and had an infectious personality. We had our director.

Rachel immediately formed five committees to take responsibility for building the different components of the project. Student participants had to be recruited, selected, and trained. We also had to recruit and select partner organizations where the students would be placed. Once the students and partners were in place, we would need to monitor participation and ensure compliance with funding guidelines. We also needed to establish metrics to evaluate both the student and partner performance.

Many staff in the office of the Senior University Dean (SUD) were assigned to specific committees, as were other staff from throughout the Central Office and from the colleges. Given the high priority the chancellor had set for the project, we were able to fill each committee quickly with committed faculty and staff. People wanted to be part of a project that was important to the university and to the city. We also formed a program advisory board consisting of senior staff from both the Central

Office and the campuses. The initial name the chancellor gave the project, CUNY HELPS, was soon changed to the CUNY Service Corps.

Rachel quickly developed a concept paper for the program. Its introduction stated that CUNY proposed to establish "a new student service corps that will mobilize CUNY students and faculty to work on projects that improve the short and long-term civic, economic and environmental sustainability of New York City and of its residents and communities."

We opened the program to all CUNY campuses and asked campuses interested in participating to respond to a request for proposals (RFP). In early April, after a careful review process, we selected seven campuses: two community colleges (Kingsborough and Borough of Manhattan), two comprehensive colleges (Staten Island and New York City College of Technology), and three senior colleges (Lehman, John Jay, and Queens).

We then turned our attention to recruiting, selecting, and training student participants and identifying partner organizations. The response was robust in both areas. More than 1,900 students from the seven colleges applied, as did 160 nonprofit organizations. The student applicants completed an online application requiring short essays and a reference, and they participated in a group interview at their college. Their scores were tabulated and reviewed by selection committees that included staff from the campuses and Central. Eight hundred students were selected as members of the first cohort of Service Corps members and 96 partner organizations were chosen. Corps members would work 12 hours per week for 24 weeks throughout the academic year and be paid an hourly stipend of $12 per hour, on par with the 311 program. Like 311, this was higher than the minimum wage at that time ($7.15) and more than students could get at most part-time jobs.

Next came two special events. The first was a matching fair held in the gym of John Jay College. Walking into that gym was exhilarating. Each partner organization had established a booth stocked with material explaining the services they provided. The students were asked to move throughout the gym, introducing themselves to the organizations' representatives, learning about the services of the organizations, and trying to determine which would be a good fit. At the conclusion of the day, the students completed a form indicating their first three choices for possible placement.

Rachel and her team organized the event with care and sensitivity. Like proud but slightly anxious parents, our staff observed the CUNY students as they approached the booths. We hoped that they would represent the university well and demonstrate to our partner staff the quality and diversity of CUNY students. Our hope was rewarded. The students' maturity, professionalism, and enthusiasm delighted us.

The second event, a program kick-off at Borough of Manhattan Community College, was equally exciting. The chancellor, college presidents, partner organization staff, and various dignitaries joined the new Service Corps members for an event that was the closest thing I had ever seen during all my years at CUNY to a college basketball pep rally. The corps members, wearing Service Corps shirts, were seated by college. When I entered the auditorium, the noise from each school was deafening, as the students chanted their school names and slogans. The spirit in the room was unmatched by any CUNY event I had ever attended. The actual program for the event built on the excitement, with each college performing an original cheer celebrating its institution. The students clearly had spent time preparing creative cheers and delivered them with energy and exuberance.

I left the building confident that the Service Corps would be successful. In a few months, in response to the chancellor's charge to create a student-led service program, our Central Office team had built a coherent and innovative program. The logistics, involving seven campuses, dozens of partner organizations, and many components of the Central Office, were complex. Just the process of keeping the students' time at their agencies and getting them paid involved creating systems, negotiating across different agency cultures and processes, and navigating myriad rules and regulations. As we had learned from prior projects, establishing respectful relationships between CUNY staff and their counterparts at the partner organizations was not always easy but always essential. So was constant, responsive communication. Campus Service Corps directors were a critical element, providing the vital interface between the university and the partners and between the students and everyone else. Once again, our unit, with the help of our campus partners and other Central Office staff, had demonstrated that even large and bureaucratic organizations could respond quickly and competently if the right people were selected to lead, given the freedom to be creative, and buoyed by the support of the CEO.

In the early fall of 2013, the CUNY Service Corps officially began. All over the city, students started their agency placements. They worked in after-school programs, arts organizations and museums, government agencies, criminal justice and prisoner re-entry programs, health related facilities, libraries, K–12 schools, parks/wildlife organizations, and many other placement areas. The 96 partner organizations included the American Museum of Natural History, the Brooklyn Navy Yard, the Center for Court Innovation, New York Presbyterian Hospital, the Federal Reserve Bank of New York, the Wildlife Conservation Society, and Good Shepherd Services. The Corps members were supervised by agency staff, but continually interacted with college and Central Office Service Corps staff as well. Throughout the year, students attended professional development activities, which provided them the opportunity to reflect on their work experience. Service Corps staff also made site visits to the partner agencies to observe Corps members in action.

Our end-year evaluations showed that over 95% of the students who began the program in Fall 2013 reenrolled in a CUNY college in the spring of 2014. Over 90% of the students who started the program completed their placements in good standing. Also, 91% of the students rated their placement experience as either good, very good, or excellent. We were pleased with the high grade point averages of our students during the year and the average number of credits they earned. Placement attendance was exceptionally good, and our partner organizations raved about the quality of the CUNY students, often noting that they were every bit as good and far more diverse than students placed at their organizations from more so-called elite colleges.

One of the most positive results of the program was that close to a quarter of the students who completed their work assignments were offered jobs by their placement sites. It is interesting to note that in the first year the Federal Reserve was reluctant to take more than one or two CUNY students. The Fed worried that CUNY students would not be able to compete with their usual interns, who came largely from Ivy League colleges. By the third year of the program, the Federal Reserve staff had reversed that position and greatly expanded the number of CUNY Service Corps members placed there.

In early May of 2014, we held a full-day event at Lehman College to celebrate the inaugural year of the program and the achievements of the students. Like the kick-off ceremony, this too was joyous. The students showed enormous pride in what they had accomplished. Many of our partner organization staff attended. Interim Chancellor Bill Kelly spoke eloquently about the value and importance of the program, thanking both students and staff. The final speaker was Scott Kennedy, a Service Corps student attending Lehman College. Scott talked poignantly about his upbringing in Yonkers, New York:

> Like many of those who know economic hardship, as a teen I became quite familiar with bouncing from one temporary housing place to another, watching as violence hurt the innocent, watching as poorly handled disputes led to the incarceration of the angry and sometimes the death of others, watching as unstable families and insufficient resources led to hunger, domestic violence, sexual abuse and a range of other ailments and horrors to which no person deserves to be subjected.

Scott then went on to thank his mother, describing her as a hard-working single mother who offered him, "the invaluable support and the unconditional love that empowers one to do well." In so many ways, Scott was a typical CUNY student.

Scott was placed at Year Up New York, a nonprofit providing young adults, ages 18–24, a yearlong intensive training program with hands-on skill development, opportunities to earn college credit, and corporate internships. Scott assumed the role of a teaching assistant. He ended his remarks with an account of what he had gained:

> The past few months have been the most character-building and educational of my life. This is only the beginning of something so much bigger than each of us, and for me happiness may rightly be defined as willingly being a part of a process that benefits you, those around you, and leaves a positive impact during the one life you get. There's something vast in that, something of depth and gravity, and it leaves one with a feeling that in spite of any struggles faced by our communities, we succeeded in working together to do something significant to meet the challenges of our time and serve those of the present and future.[1]

Scott's speech concluded the ceremony and brought the first year of the Service Corps to a close. The audience gave him a standing ovation. Those of us there who had created the program were teary and emotional, as we had felt in many prior projects. The Service Corps introduced CUNY students to the larger New York community in ways that were new and revealing. It also demonstrated their own resilience, intelligence, and commitment to make the city a more livable and equitable place.

As for Scott, after graduating from Lehman and then CUNY Law School, he now works as a litigation associate at the prestigious New York law firm Paul, Weiss, Rifkind, Wharton, & Garrison—the only CUNY Law graduate out of over 1000 lawyers at the firm.

Over the next four years, the Service Corps continued to support between 700 and 800 students and gained a city-wide reputation as an exceptional program that addressed some of the city's most pressing needs. In 2014–15, Medgar Evers College in Brooklyn became the eighth CUNY Service Corps campus. The program was awarded a $1 million grant from the Jewish Foundation for the Education of Women to support summer extension programs in 2014–2016.

In 2016, the New York City Department of Cultural Affairs and the Rockefeller Foundation provided funding to establish a CUNY Cultural Corps, a program modeled after the Service Corps. The Cultural Corps provided paid internships for CUNY students at New York City arts and cultural organizations. Its aim was to create a pipeline for CUNY students to pursue careers in cultural organizations, and in doing so begin to help diversify the staff of these historically overwhelmingly white organizations. The Cultural Corps also became part of our SUD (Senior University Dean) unit and was administered in coordination with the original Service Corps program. By 2021, the Cultural Corps, which continued to receive city finding, had grown to include 83 partner cultural organizations, and supported 215 student internships.

While the Cultural Corps was supported by outside funding, unfortunately the Service Corps was unsuccessful in generating outside funding. It had to rely on the money provided through the operating budget of CUNY. From Fiscal Year 2016 on, the annual funding for the program was reduced each year by the CUNY budget office. I always expressed my opposition to these reductions, but with Goldstein no longer the chancellor and Governor Cuomo cutting CUNY's budget each year, it was difficult to make an argument for CUNY to continue to fund the program at the same level. Thus began a steady yearly decrease in funding and the size of the program. That decrease continued after I left the Central Office in late March of 2020. By 2022, the program received only $315,000 from the budget office, and these funds were only for Central Office program staff. The Service Corps was reduced to only five campuses; the program moved to placing students in regular internships in the private and nonprofit sectors. It served fewer than 200 students and was supported through Federal Work Study funds instead of from the CUNY operating budget.

The story of the CUNY Service Corps is one of only a very few examples of a large successful program started by our SUD unit during the period from 2003–2020 that was not fully institutionalized. This was a real disappointment. The program had a wonderful track record in providing important work experience for CUNY students—experiences that often led to full time jobs at partner organizations and with other NYC nonprofit and private employers. It also introduced a large number of city organizations and agencies like the Federal Reserve to the quality of CUNY students and overall raised the image of CUNY. Clearly, the program's loss of funding had nothing to do with its operation or the benefits it provided. My best guess is that it simply got lost in the political landscape.

There is a postscript to the Service Corps story. In 2017, Puerto Rico was hit hard by two hurricanes, Irma and Maria. Governor Cuomo decided to tap CUNY and SUNY to create what he called the NY Stands with Puerto Rico Recovery and Rebuilding Initiative. As soon as the governor made his announcement and let CUNY know of his intention, I received a call from Marc Shaw and Gayle Horowitz, two powerful CUNY officials, to meet with them to discuss the governor's request. Marc was the interim executive vice chancellor and chief operating officer at CUNY. Gayle was the secretary to the CUNY Board of Trustees and senior advisor to the chancellor. They asked me to quickly create a program that would select, train, and send CUNY students to Puerto Rico to help rebuild the island. They emphasized how important this was to the governor, who insisted that the program must begin in the summer of 2018, only a few months away.

Fortunately, we already had the Service Corps model in place and a staff that I knew would be excited to build the new program. Because Rachel Stephenson had already left the Service Corps to assume a senior position as an assistant vice chancellor for academic affairs, I turned to two other key Service Corps staff to head the project. Melissa Fernandez and Kafui Krakou were young, smart, energetic staff who welcomed the opportunity to create a new program and help the residents of Puerto Rico. Melissa had strong roots on the island where her mother still lived.

That summer we sent 225 students to Puerto Rico to help repair roofs and damaged homes. The students were sent in small cohorts for two-week stints. They fully embraced the chance to help and did exceptional work rebuilding homes in the summer heat. Melissa and Kafui spent many weeks on site, supervising students, managing their safety, and dealing with the politics of administering a complicated program. They were joined by a full team of college staff, who supervised teams of students and lived with them throughout their time in Puerto Rico. Governor Cuomo made an appearance on the island to observe the program.

For the students, helping rebuild Puerto Rico was a life-changing experience—an opportunity to engage in truly meaningful work and in some cases to apply skills they had learned in college. The videos that were created documenting their service were inspirational, showing not only the students' hard work in the hot, humid climate, but also the camaraderie they developed, and the appreciation of the residents whose homes were saved. Upon the students' return we once again celebrated the achievement of CUNY students. We sent two more cohorts of students to Puerto Rico, again with Kafui and Melissa supervising, to continue the work in the winter and fall of 2019.

Although the Puerto Rico program came about in response to the governor's urgent request, he never provided a penny of funding to CUNY to pay for it. Its cost, approximately $1 million, had to be absorbed by the university. When I asked Marc Shaw about this, saying that I thought it was unfair, he smiled. From his point of view, because we had responded so quickly and well, we had earned future good will with the governor and his staff that could be far more valuable than current dollars. Anyway, he indicated, we really had no choice. I wasn't going to argue with Marc, but I did say that we should at least have asked the governor's staff about funding, even if we were turned down. Again, he smiled, but did not reply.

II. PRE-COLLEGE PROGRAMS: MULTIPLE PATHS TO COLLEGE AND CAREER

During the first years of Matthew Goldstein's tenure as chancellor, CUNY's partnership with the public schools expanded and deepened. One result of this robust collaboration was a large increase in the number of pre-college students that CUNY served directly, mainly through enlarging dual-enrollment efforts and creating early college high schools. Our unit managed these projects, greatly expanding our portfolio. Besides these large-scale programs, we added several smaller projects with a more targeted focus—suggesting some of the many directions that universities might pursue in crafting a broader mission.

CHAPTER 14

Collaborative Programs

Building a Partnership with the NYC Department of Education

IN FEBRUARY 2022 I INTERVIEWED CASS CONRAD FOR THIS BOOK project. Cass had joined our CUNY Central Office team in the spring of 2004 to oversee the development of early college high schools. In this role, she became one of the leaders of our rapidly growing Collaborative Programs unit, CUNY's partnership with the NYC Department of Education. Cass was later appointed university dean for K–16 partnerships and became one of my senior staff before leaving CUNY in December of 2019 to become the executive director of the Carroll and Milton Petrie Foundation.

As we talked about her time at CUNY, Cass recalled a visit she made to Hostos Community College in the fall of September 2004 to celebrate the opening of the Hostos Lincoln Academy Early College High School located on the college campus. It was the first day of class for a group of sixth graders who would be attending the school from the sixth through 12th grades. As per the early college model, if they met the prerequisites, the students could also take college credit classes beginning as early as the 9th grade.

Cass recalled that first day as "transformative" for the students. Few had ever set foot on a college campus before, but now they were surrounded by college students. Though they shared the normal nervousness of entering a new school, the excitement in the air was positive. The school principal greeted the students and held up a poster bearing only a few words. In big letters it asked, "Where are we going?" The answer below stated simply, "College." Before long a group of what Cass described as "eyes wide open students" were chanting these few words in unison as loudly as they could. Attending college had become a goal for these students, who were almost all Hispanic and Black. But the responsibility for their reaching that goal did not lie with the students alone. Their attending—and succeeding in—college was also a promise and a commitment to them from their school and from CUNY. Keeping our promise to support their goal is the reason we invested so much in the K–16 Partnership. However, both for the students and for all of us educators, it was a commitment full of challenges.

EXPANDING OUR PARTNERSHIP

CUNY has always worked collaboratively with the New York City Public Schools, largely through its many undergraduate and graduate degree programs in teacher education. Over the years, there have also been a few select campus and university initiatives, including one optimistically named "A Seamless Transition" from high school to college. Nevertheless, in too many cases the transition proved to be anything but seamless. A large percentage of DOE high school graduates who enrolled in CUNY required non-credit remedial classes. At the same time, the dropout rate, especially for the community colleges, was high. And graduation rates were low even for students who did not require remedial work. These two sprawling bureaucracies, CUNY and the New York City Department of Education, shared a huge number of students, but they had failed to address in a deliberate, effective, or truly collaborative way the apparent gap between high school graduation and readiness for college. Too often, discussions between the two institutions took the form of pointing fingers to affix blame. This did nothing to assist students.

In the aftermath of the 1999 *CUNY: An Institution Adrift* report, which had strongly recommended an enhanced CUNY/DOE partnership, and with the arrival of Matthew Goldstein as chancellor, CUNY geared up to expand this partnership effort. Chancellor Goldstein asked me to oversee the partnership expansion, to be administered out of our

Senior University Dean unit within the Office of Academic Affairs. We began by enlarging an existing program called College Now. Begun at Kingsborough Community College in 1984, College Now enabled qualified high school students to take undergraduate classes for college credits. High school students not yet eligible for credit classes could take non-credit courses and workshops to build basic college preparedness skills. They could also attend a variety of summer enrichment programs. [1]

College Now is a dual-enrollment program. Such programs, in various forms, exist all over the country. Dual-enrollment programs operate on the premise that whether or not high school students currently plan to attend college, taking well-chosen and well-taught college courses will motivate them to persevere in high school and then continue to higher education. Students will, it is hoped, be engaged by the course content and gain confidence in their own abilities. They will also learn knowledge and skills needed for success. As a bonus, they can start college already having some credits, and will progress more quickly. The results bear out the expectations: dual-enrollment participants complete high school and go on to college at a greater rate than non-participants.

To assist in the expansion of College Now, the university allocated $10 million. Over the next two years, College Now was extended to all undergraduate-serving CUNY colleges with each receiving a small budget to hire a campus director and staff. The funding also enabled my unit to hire staff to administer the program.

With these additional resources, by 2004–2005 College Now had become one of the largest dual-enrollment program in the United States. It was serving over 20,000 New York City public high school students in credit classes, and a comparable number in basic skills or college preparatory classes. By the Fall of 2005, slightly over 30% of all New York City public high school graduates who enrolled as CUNY freshmen had participated in College Now. They entered college with anywhere from 3–12 credits. At Hunter, Baruch, and Brooklyn College, slightly over 50% of freshmen entering from the New York City public schools had College Now experience.

The expansion of College Now was only the beginning of significant growth of our work with the Department of Education. To further the expansion, we hired a small group of educators who would administer the existing programs and build new ones. Under John Garvey's leadership, in addition to Cass Conrad, we hired Tracy Meade, Donna Linderman, and Eric Hofmann. New ideas flowed regularly from each of them. They wrote proposals, sought out public and private funding, worked with the campuses to provide quality services, and built relationships with their DOE partners. They also consistently used data to measure the results of the different programs and strategies.

BUILDING THREE NEW SPECIALIZED PUBLIC HIGH SCHOOLS

In the early spring of 2002, Mayor Michael Bloomberg and Governor George Pataki approached Chancellor Goldstein with a proposal that would enable CUNY to assume a major occupancy at Governor's Island. Located in New York Harbor, a short ferry ride from both Brooklyn and Manhattan, the 172-acre island, included two former military fortifications and many historic buildings. Most of those buildings were seriously in need of repair. The island operated as a public park, although at the time it received few visitors.

In return for access to Governor's Island and possibly moving some of CUNY's programs (perhaps the CUNY Law School) there, the mayor and governor requested that CUNY provide space on its campuses to create and house three new public high schools. This was an offer that the chancellor couldn't refuse. He asked me and our unit to work closely with the Department of Education to make it happen. The greatest challenge was that the mayor and governor indicated that the schools must open for the fall 2002–2003 school year, only five months away.

A unique characteristic of this project was that the schools to be created would be what is called "specialized" high schools, thus doubling the number of these prestigious, highly selective high schools in the city. Admission to the three existing specialized public high schools—Stuyvesant High School, Bronx High School of Science, and Brooklyn

Technical High School—was based on a single exam. At the time, more than 20,000 students took the exam each year hoping to score high enough to secure one of the 2,500 slots. Stuyvesant, the most highly selective of the specialized high schools, accepted less than 5% of test takers. People familiar with the New York K–12 education system recognized how prized admission into these schools was. Parents, convinced that enrollment in a specialized high school would provide the best pathway to elite colleges, often paid for expensive tutoring and coaching to prepare their children for the test. Doubling the number of these schools would be well-received.

In mid-April, we held the first organizing meeting for the project. We had not yet determined where the schools would be. We had no students, no curriculum, no teachers, and no formal team to do the development work. How could these two gigantic systems, so often criticized for their unwieldy bureaucracies, pull this off?

Those of us involved in the initial planning understood that we would need the help of many partners. To succeed, there must be a sense of urgency, a moratorium on whining and negativism, and a belief that whatever problems we faced could be quickly overcome. At our first planning meeting, Vice Chancellor Mirrer recommended that all parties meet every Friday to discuss progress and determine next steps. An average of 15 people participated each week, including officials from Lehman, York, and City Colleges, which would house the schools; the Central Offices of both CUNY and the Department of Education; and the local district offices. As soon as principals were selected to lead the three schools, they took seats at the table as well. These meetings were tough and frank. Everyone had to be accountable. As problems arose, solutions with time frames were proposed and met. It helped that many of us knew one another, having worked for years to strengthen the collaborations between CUNY and the Department of Education.

As spring moved into summer, the schools began to take shape. Student recruitment efforts led to open houses and admission applications. Teachers were hired. College faculty joined with the new teachers to plan curriculum. Space planning and major construction took place. Having a drop-dead deadline of September made us all tense. We worried that we might fail to meet it. Still, at no time did any of us become cynical or look for excuses to fail. When time grew short and problems remained, we simply worked harder. By the end of the summer, more than 200 people had participated in the development of the schools.

In September all three schools opened on time with full enrollment. Students and parents were thrilled to be part of these promising schools. In mid-September, Chancellor Goldstein and Joel Klein, the new Department of Education chancellor, hosted a joyous celebration to thank everyone involved in the project. It was hard for us to believe that we had pulled this off.

A wonderful photograph hangs in my den of the entering class at the High School for American Studies gathered on the main green of Lehman College with a Class of 2006 sign. Thousands of students have followed them. I have often looked at that photo over the years, always taking pride in what we accomplished under the most extreme pressure. We demonstrated that even among huge bureaucracies, much good can happen when committed people are given the freedom to work together across institutional boundaries and to interpret rules and procedures flexibly when necessary, and if they also receive adequate support and resources. This was a true collaboration between an urban public university and a public school system. Now, twenty years later, although a CUNY presence on Governor's Island has yet to materialize, these three high schools are recognized as among the best in New York State and nationally. The *U.S News* 2023–2024 ranking of Best High Schools names the High School for Math, Science & Engineering at City College #1 in New York State and #22 nationally; Queens High School for the Sciences at York College ranks #3 in New York and #29 in the country; the High School for American Studies at Lehman College is #7 in New York and #55 nationally.

I have always had mixed feelings about whether New York City should even have these elite schools, often arguing that they should be more diverse. The selective high schools have been privileged places that fail to reflect the racial and ethnic composition of the New York City school system. Furthermore, I am opposed to the use of a single test as the sole admission criterion. It is disturbing that the percentage of Black and Hispanic children enrolled at the exam schools, never large to begin with, has decreased significantly since 2001. By 2021, the enrollment at the exam schools had dramatically shifted, with Asian and South Asian students becoming the largest ethnic group. Unlike the white students enrolled at the schools, who tend to come from middle class or even privileged backgrounds, many of the Asian and South Asian students are from working class families. At present a fierce battle continues in New York City about the future of these schools and the criteria for admission. Many in the Asian community strongly support the present system of admission to the schools, while many progressive educators and left-leaning New Yorkers believe that the schools need to better reflect the full diversity of the city. How this will play out is unclear at the moment. My guess is that these schools will continue to exist with similar admission criteria, specifically the single test, while at the same time new specialized schools will be established across the city, perhaps with broader admissions criteria.

Despite doubts about establishing new exam schools, I agreed to lead the project. I guess I could have turned down the chancellor's invitation, but I recognized the importance of the project to the chancellor, CUNY, and the future of our relationship with the Department of Education. Once the decision was made to build the schools, I needed to be part of the effort.

CREATING EARLY COLLEGE HIGH SCHOOLS

In March of 2002, the Bill and Melinda Gates Foundation, in partnership with the Carnegie Corporation of New York, the Ford Foundation, and the W.K. Kellogg Foundation, announced that it would put up $40 million to start 70 new small high schools around the United States. These schools would be designed to improve high school graduation rates significantly for disadvantaged students by enabling students to take college-level courses while in high school. In this way, the students could accumulate a significant number of college credits or even earn associate degrees while in high school. The schools would be called early college high schools (ECHS) and would enroll approximately 500 students at each school.[2]

Given our developing partnership with the Department of Education, the long history of operating high schools on CUNY campuses (e.g., Middle College High School and International High School at LaGuardia Community College, Hostos Lincoln Academy, and University Heights High School at Bronx Community College), and our intense interest in school reform, my senior team and I quickly decided to try to become part of this high profile new program. Over the next few months, a joint CUNY/DOE team developed a proposal for submission to the Gates Foundation requesting $6.7 million dollars to open ten new schools. The schools would be officially Department of Education schools with CUNY acting as an Intermediary organization. At the same time, using this model and in advance of a decision from Gates, the first early college high school actually opened in 2002, transforming LaGuardia's Middle College High School to an ECHS. Two more schools opened in September of 2003: the STAR High School, affiliated with Brooklyn College, and Manhattan Hunter Science High School, affiliated with Hunter College. (The latter is not connected to Hunter College High School, a selective and prestigious school, administered by Hunter College, that is not a part of the NYC–DOE).

The Gates Foundation approved our proposal, awarding CUNY the $6.7 million requested. From 2003–2006 we created and opened seven additional new schools, which together with the three schools opened in 2002–03, met the grant requirements.

The grant from the Gates Foundation provided only a portion of the funding needed to operate the proposed schools. I went to Chancellor Goldstein to make sure he understood that the university, together with the DOE, would be responsible for a percentage of the initial funding for the schools, and also that once the Gates funding ended in 2008, the DOE and CUNY would need to take full responsibility. That figure would be close to $7 million annually. The chancellor didn't hesitate to make the commitment, believing that the project was important and that we would be able to raise additional outside funding over subsequent years.

In the years to follow there was much internal conversation at CUNY regarding the wisdom of supporting these schools. Some of the concern was principally financial: support for high schools was a fiscal drain on the chronically under-funded university system. There was a deeper issue, however, between those who viewed the university's mission narrowly and those who extended that mission more broadly. Was CUNY's responsibility solely to offer quality degree programs or did it also include working to make degree programs truly available to New York's vastly diverse populace? The budget office, led by Executive Vice Chancellor Allan Dobrin, contended that the schools were not priorities of the university, and therefore that funding them should not be CUNY's burden.

In response to some of the criticism and hoping to get a better understanding of the scope of our programs with the DOE and why they were important, in June 2006 the chancellor established a working group on collaborative programs with the DOE. The mission was to "address programmatic, fiscal, and facilities issues and concerns" and to determine whether the "programs align with the core mission of the University and contribute to the achievement of our fundamental goals."[3] The working group members included several CUNY college presidents and many of the most senior administrators in the Central Office.

When I learned initially that the chancellor had established the working group, I worried that there would be pressure to limit any future expansion of our work with the DOE. The Budget Office was lukewarm, if not hostile, to the fiscal commitment needed to support the new schools. Budget office personnel also believed that funding for the schools should be the full responsibility of the DOE. When the chancellor named me to chair the working group, I was reassured that the group was not established to kill the program. I added John Garvey and Tracy Meade as members.

The final report of the working group, issued in November of 2006, stated in its executive summary that a "close study of Collaborative Programs data and attention to budget use make clear that the accomplishments of Collaborative Programs are consistent with core elements of the University's mission and have made—and promise to make still-more-significant contributions to the success of students matriculating at this University."

Two of the report's important recommendations were first, to establish "Joint University--Department of Education Committees" and second, for the university to "enter into a formal data-sharing agreement with the Department of Education." Both of these recommendations were quickly implemented and over the next years led to a far closer and strengthened relationship between the two systems. Data-sharing, in particular, provided a reliable and useful tool for planning and evaluating our efforts.[4]

Given the recommendations of the report and the strong support of the chancellor, our collaborative programs continued to grow. In 2009, the university and DOE opened the first Pathways in Technology Early College School (P-TECH). The school, a partnership between CUNY's New York City College of Technology, the DOE, and IBM, was a grades 9–14 school designed to enable students to earn both a high school diploma and associate degree in either Computer Information Systems or Computer Engineering Technology at CUNY's New York City College of Technology. The idea for P-TECH was advanced by Stan Litow, a former senior official at the DOE who was then working at IBM as vice president for corporate citizenship and corporate affairs. He promised that P-TECH graduates would be "first in line" for entry level jobs at IBM or similar firms.

IBM, as the industry partner, did not assume responsibility for the budget of P-TECH. It was a NYC public school, with its budget determined by the DOE. The principal and staff were DOE employees, and its facility in the Crown Heights section of Brooklyn was shared space in a DOE building. The college classes and other supports were paid for through New York State grants and other sources. However, in addition to envisioning the school in the first place, IBM's contribution was significant. They hired a coordinator and provided a great deal of in-kind support, including a number of summer internships, mentoring by IBM employees, and many enrichment opportunities for students. High-level

IBM managers served on the steering committee and advised the principal. IBM also publicized the school extensively and brought it to the attention of the US Department of Education and the White House. President Obama mentioned P-TECH in a State of the Union address and later visited the school and spoke to the students.

Adding an industry partner to the collaborative mix was a new experience for everyone. Despite many advantages, it also greatly complicated the planning and administration of the school. Steering committee meetings were often contentious. Differences in institutional cultures quickly surfaced. The IBM representatives were eager for results. They had their sights on a worldwide network of P-TECH schools and needed our model to generate positive outcome data quickly. On the other hand, the college representatives needed to ensure that students were adequately prepared to take college-level courses and meet prerequisites; they resisted pressure to enroll students in classes where the students were unlikely to succeed. Often, the high school staff was caught in the middle.

Further, everyone imagined that students enrolling in a high school called P-TECH would be budding techies. It soon became apparent that perhaps half the students were drawn to careers in technology. The others either had been influenced to enroll at P-TECH by parents who were enticed by the school's promise, or upon closer experience with technology decided it was not for them. Painstakingly, the partners and the students worked through the issues. P-TECH has had excellent high school graduation rates, and the school has served as a model for many other P-TECH institutions.

Over the next six years, an additional six DOE/CUNY P-TECH early college schools were opened, partnering with SAP, Montefiore Hospital, New York Presbyterian Hospital, Con Edison and National Grid and offering degrees through LaGuardia, Borough of Manhattan, Queensborough, Hostos, and Bronx Community colleges.

By 2015, there were 20 early college high schools, serving more than 7,000 students annually. In 2013, an early assessment of the original early college schools indicated that they had achieved a high school graduation rate of 84.8%, nearly 20% higher than the citywide average at that time. These high school graduates also had earned an average of 28 college credits prior to graduation. A small number succeeded in earning their associate degrees at the same time. It's notable that admission to the schools was not selective; they were open to all.

NEW COLLABORATIVE PROGRAMS

By 2019, under the exceptional leadership of Cass Conrad, by then university dean for K–16 initiatives, our collaborative programs were receiving over $35 million annually in funding, and the K–16 unit grew to a staff of more than 100. A steering committee made up of senior officials from both systems was established to examine, monitor, and assess all aspects of our partnership. I co-chaired the committee with Josh Thomases, the DOE deputy chief academic officer.

This new funding enabled us to create and administer many programs that increase college awareness on the part of young students, strengthen their readiness for college, and engage them more deeply in academic work:

- CUNY Explorers—A structured opportunity enabling every NYC public middle school student to visit a college campus at least once in grades six through eight.
- CUNY LINC—A week-by-week college-readiness advisory curriculum introducing students to college entrance requirements, college and career options, and effective academic skills and habits.
- CUNY Tutor Corps—Tutoring in math and computer science by trained and paid CUNY students at 180 middle schools and high schools.
- Graduate NYC—A college completion and innovation fund to spur innovation and adoption of policies and practices that increase college degree completion. Funds are awarded to CUNY colleges and community-based organizations through a competitive grants process.

- The NYC Science and Engineering Fair—One of the largest annual high school competitions in the country, where each year, more than 800 students submit their original research to panels of expert judges. The finals of the competition are held at the American Museum of Natural History.

The importance of these partnership programs can't be overestimated. Approximately 60% of NYC DOE college-going graduates attend a CUNY college, and nearly 80% of first-time freshman at CUNY are graduates of DOE schools. The better these students and their families understand the academic expectations and the logistical demands of enrolling and succeeding in college, the more likely they are to persist and earn their degrees. College requires a large investment on the part of the city and state, as well as the students and their families. Student success validates and rewards those investments in individual lives and in society as a whole. The College Now program alone offers opportunities for NYC public high school students from more than 450 high schools to take college credit classes at 18 CUNY colleges. Virtually all of the programs mentioned have as one of their major goals to see that more high school graduates are ready to do college-level work and make a successful transition to college.

The CUNY/NYC-DOE partnership is the largest such program in the country. Each year the programs that CUNY administers through the K–16 unit serve more than 100,000 DOE students. I have often said that these two enormous institutions, one serving close to 1 million children and the other more than 500,000 degree and non-degree college students, are joined at the hip. While the CUNY/NYC-DOE partnership has not solved all the many difficult issues facing public K–12 and higher education, our data show that our programs make a difference in the educational performance of students, providing opportunities that significantly increase students' likelihood of success.

By working together for the past 20 years, our two systems have learned much about each other and the challenges we face. At CUNY, we learned that the drumbeat of criticism leveled at the DOE by many CUNY faculty and administrators was often unfair and based on little if any knowledge. The colleagues I worked with from the DOE, particularly under the Bloomberg administration when Joel Klein and later Dennis Walcott headed the DOE, were highly competent, deeply committed, and willing to make necessary changes. I believe that we accomplished a great deal together. I am not looking to excuse either CUNY or DOE for low graduation rates or for preparing students inadequately. There remains much to criticize in both systems, and significant ongoing change is crucial. Certainly, far too many students in both systems, particularly Black and Hispanic students from disadvantaged backgrounds, still do not succeed. However, progress has been made. To sustain and extend that progress, the leadership of both institutions will need to continue to experiment, support innovation, and confront institutional biases and bureaucratic practices that get in the way.

CHAPTER 15

CUNY Prep

An Oasis in the Bronx

I APPROACHED THE COMMUNITY PROTESTANT CHURCH ON GUN Hill Road in the Bronx feeling unbearable sadness. It was the evening of May 22, 2015, and I was there to attend the funeral of Derrick Griffith. I entered the church and was handed a program for the service with a picture of Derrick on the cover and the title "Dr. Derrick Griffith: Celebrating an Extraordinary Life." I started to cry.

Ten days earlier, on May 12, Jay Hershenson had called to let me know he had been notified that an Amtrak train had crashed in Philadelphia, and Derrick was one of eight people killed. Over the next days I couldn't stop thinking of Derrick. I was filled with grief, anger, disbelief, and a host of other emotions that didn't want to go away. Occasionally, I did smile as I remembered some of the joy that Derrick brought to everyone who knew him.

I had met Derrick in the spring of 2003. He had applied for a job to become the principal/director of a school that we were about to open in the Bronx for out-of-school youth, young people ages 16 to 19 who had left the public school system before graduating. Derrick was one of the finalists for the job, and John Garvey and I were about to interview him for the position.

The idea for the school had come from John. In 2002, he approached me to ask if I would consider trying to get funding for CUNY to open a school for young adults. John's vision was that the school would prepare its students not only to earn a high school equivalency diploma, but also to attend and succeed in college. At the time, the largest share of students who received their GED diplomas and then enrolled in CUNY were registered in associate degree programs. Unfortunately, only a small percentage ever graduated.

Unlike most GED programs at the time, which provided a limited number of instructional hours, all targeted directly to the test, this school would offer a full-time, day-long program. It would offer a rigorous curriculum with an in-depth focus on humanities, math, writing, and science, and hold students to high performance standards. John hoped that the school would be a model demonstrating that even students who previously had left the public school system before graduating could thrive at a well-conceived and operated school.

Initially, John believed that the school should be operated by one of the CUNY campuses, perhaps directly on campus or nearby. He began discussions with faculty and administrators from a few campuses to explore interest. Before long, he spoke to me again, indicating that he had changed his mind about who should operate the program. Although the campuses he was talking to had smart and committed faculty, they also had their own views about what the school should look like, and those views were not consistent with his own. He said that we should operate the school directly from the Central Office out of our office.

The idea of a system office operating a school was certainly different. Our unit had collaborated on the development of schools, but we had never actually run them. Trying to operate a school would only feed into the criticism of our unit as seeking to take over roles far more appropriate for our college campuses or, in this case, the New York City Department of Education. On the other hand, I had enormous confidence in John, knowing that if we were able to get funding, we would create a new and different learning environment. Because this would be a grant-funded program administered through the Research Foundation, we would have flexibility in hiring instructional and administrative staff. That would be important to our success. In order to move forward, I checked in with Louise Mirrer and Matthew Goldstein, who quickly said to go for it. While the chancellor thought of these kinds of programs as "Off balance sheet," both he and Louise believed strongly that CUNY had to broaden its mission to serve student populations not normally served by higher education institutions. In some cases that role might take the form of creating a demonstration program or school that could be replicated by others. Part of our goal was creating models in New York City for other cities and universities to follow.

Prior to our interview with Derrick, I had reviewed his resume and wondered to myself why he was one of the finalists. Even to me, never a strong believer in the need for specific, formal credentials, on paper Derrick seemed young and inexperienced. Only 29 years old, he had worked as a social studies teacher for a few years after college before working on issues of school reform at two nonprofit organizations. He had no supervisory or administrative experience in a school.

A small, thin Black man entered the room, wearing a suit that was too big for him. Long dreadlocks covered his collar. Despite Derrick's slight stature, though, once he began to talk, he seemed bigger than life and captured the entire room. He had a wonderful smile and exuded enormous energy and passion. He was curious, warm, engaging, and filled with ideas. In a matter of moments, he won us over. He understood the challenge ahead but believed in our vision for the school. Derrick shared some of the many obstacles that he had faced growing up poor and Black in Brooklyn. He was a single parent with sole responsibility for a young son. We had our principal. I was confident that we had picked an exceptional educator and person, but in truth, I underestimated him. Derrick would prove to be extraordinary.

It was not easy to secure funding for the program. Most youth programs in the city were funded by the Department of Youth and Community Development (DYCD) through relatively small grants. We needed over a million dollars just to start the program. Fortunately, Mayor Bloomberg had just established a commission to examine issues of poverty in the city. One of the areas to be examined was that of out-of-school youth. I was a member of the commission and got to know a number of the new city agency commissioners and other key City Hall staff. We met with Jeanne Mulgrav, the DYCD commissioner, and two of her associates to present our idea. The commissioner was supportive of the program but didn't feel she would be able to provide the level of funding we needed to start a school. Nor could she give a long-term commitment.

One of the people helpful in getting us funded was Suri Duitch, who was working at the New York City Department of Employment at the time. I knew Suri from other work we were doing with the city. She oversaw the spending of federal monies coming to the city as part of the Workforce Investment Act, a portion of which was reserved for youth programs. Suri worked to convince Commissioner Mulgrav of the value of funding a large program. She also quietly got senior officials from City Hall to support our request.

We assigned Mia Simon, our unit's director of special programs, to be Derrick's supervisor. As was always the case in our unit, Mia, who had many other responsibilities, readily accepted the assignment, and soon developed a close working relationship with Derrick. Together Derrick and Mia began the task of hiring staff and finding a facility for the program.

A few months later, in the fall of 2003, CUNY Prep opened its doors to 200 16–19-year-old students at CUNY on the Concourse. This was a new facility established to provide workplace training and educational services to Bronx residents. The facility was operated jointly by Bronx Community College, Lehman College, and Hostos Community College in partnership with local 1199 SEIU/United Health Care Workers union. I had been involved in the planning of CUNY on the Concourse, one of Matthew Goldstein's first big initiatives after becoming chancellor.

Through much of the first year, the school struggled. There were constant behavior problems, many classes were out of control, and the school had its share of fights and disturbances. We had our own school security, but on a few occasions, we had to call the police for assistance. Derrick had not been given enough time to develop the school's curriculum and train the faculty and staff. He also had never been a school administrator and was feeling his way. The school did not yet have rules and regulations for students, including disciplinary procedures or academic expectations. All too often, when schools break down, the leader and staff blame the students they are trying to teach, or the social conditions that so negatively affect them. Not Derrick. He looked harshly at himself, acknowledging what he had done wrong, but remaining steadfast that things would get better.

We spent enormous time and energy addressing the problems. We never wavered in our belief that Derrick was the correct choice for principal, but we tried to support him with outside assistance. That included members of our own team and outside experts. I reached out to Greg Donaldson, a master teacher from John Jay College who had been an important member of our "Streetwise" team, to assist Derrick and the faculty. Another long-time friend, Mark Naison, a professor of urban and African American studies at nearby Fordham University, came in to provide guidance. For many years, Mark had worked closely with the Bronx public schools and Bronx community groups.

We spent much of the spring and summer working to ensure that when the school reopened for its second year in the fall, it would be a different place. It was. By the time the second year began in September, Derrick and his team had reconstituted the school around the theme of Resilience, Reflection, and Success. They established a code of respect that set rules and procedures guiding student behavior. They also listed the rights and responsibilities for both students and staff. They clearly defined disciplinary rules that ranged from verbal warnings for minor infractions to suspension or even expulsion for engaging in any kind of fighting, gang activity, or use of drugs on campus. A dress code included a uniform policy—CUNY Prep Shirts and casual dress pants; no hats or gang colors permitted. Considerable effort was placed on refining the curriculum and providing opportunities for the teachers to engage in professional development activities. Electives were added to supplement the courses geared to passing the equivalency exam, and clubs were organized. Students who were deemed eligible to take the equivalency exam were also able to enroll in college credit classes through CUNY's College Now Program. Finally, any number of fun activities were launched, including school dances and a year-end prom, field days, school trips, an Earth Day, a blood drive, talent shows, holiday parties, and celebrations to acknowledge student success.

By the middle of the second year, the school was transformed, and Derrick had established himself as an exceptional leader. When you entered the building, there was a feeling that this was a school that worked. Students were immediately greeted by public safety officers who knew their names and were given responsibilities beyond only being security guards. Students appeared relaxed and seemed to enjoy being in school. Discipline problems disappeared, and students showed each other respect. The typical teasing and bullying often seen in high school settings were absent, and more importantly were not tolerated. Derrick and the staff seemed to be everywhere, anticipating problems before they could erupt and always talking to students in a respectful manner. Staff morale soared. A community was being built.

Watching Derrick interact with students was to watch the best young adult educator I had ever observed. He knew how to talk to students, whether it was complimenting them for some achievement, telling them to take their hat off or pull their pants up, or bringing them into his office for a more serious conversation. He loved the students, and they loved him in return. In school-wide meetings Derrick could be serious, critical, kind, funny, and dramatic, all in a short period of time. He would eagerly show off his dance moves, which the students affectionately mocked. Most important, he believed in the potential of every student. I recall John Garvey telling me that Derrick's approach to young people was unique. It often appeared that he knew what they were thinking before they knew it themselves. When he spoke, they listened. When he challenged them, they responded. Because he believed in them, they came to believe in themselves.

Soon after the school's opening, the university put out a press release about it. The release was followed by a number of articles on CUNY Prep in local newspapers. An article in the *New York Post* enraged Derrick. The headline read "New CUNY school aiming to drag in dropouts."[1] From the outset, Derrick had insisted that CUNY Prep would not be using the term "dropouts" to define its students. "We are not going to define our students in any negative way," he declared. Someone from the staff suggested that we use the term "disconnected youth." Again, Derrick said no. He proposed "out-of-school youth," and that was it. CUNY Prep would be a school for "out-of-school youth."

From then on, CUNY Prep thrived. A few years after opening, the program leased its own space on White Plains Road in the Pelham section of the Bronx, where it resides to this day. I loved visiting the school and went often, interacting with the students and staff. I often brought Matthew Goldstein, Jay Hershenson, and other senior university officials to the school to meet and talk to students. They too expressed a joy in being there and watching Derrick and the staff interact with the students. Festive graduation ceremonies were held first at Hostos Community College and then at Lehman College. These events always started with the students thunderously shouting the school's slogan, "CUNY Prep is College Prep." They cheered throughout the ceremony. Parents and friends often became emotional watching their children receive their equivalency diplomas, as did the staff and guests. I did too.

In 2006, a few years after opening, CUNY Prep had to overcome a major crisis. The DYCD funding for the school, with the increase in costs for the building lease, had risen to over $2 million. DYCD said it could no longer fund it. The program was in danger of closing. I let Jay Hershenson know what was happening. He had become a strong supporter of the program, as had John Kotowski, who was on Jay's team as CUNY's director of city relations. John and Jay knew almost all of the City Council members and reached out to the Bronx members to alert them. Jay suggested that we organize a demonstration in front of City Hall to save the program. On the day of the demonstration, Derrick cancelled classes, and the entire school community, 300 strong, arrived at City Hall with "Save CUNY Prep" signs. Organized in advance by Derrick and the staff, the students were loud and spirited. Council members joined the students in supporting the school, and a few officials came out to talk to some of the students. As always, John Kotowski and Jay had done their homework and had given advance notice about the demonstration to the mayor's office.

The end result was that the city agreed to provide funding to CUNY Prep on an annual basis going forward. For the moment CUNY Prep had been saved. Nine years later, after some harrowing end-of-year fiscal moments and right before Derrick died, CUNY Prep was actually baselined into the city budget, giving it a permanent status as a CUNY-run school for out-of-school students. I recall going up to CUNY Prep to celebrate that announcement. Joy and relief were visible throughout the community. The yearly uncertainty of knowing whether the school would stay open was gone.

Derrick left CUNY Prep in 2010 to become the executive director of Groundworks, a multi-service agency in Brownsville. A few years later, he became the dean of students at CUNY's Medgar Evers College. We stayed close friends up until the time of his tragic death in in 2015. Derrick admitted to some regrets about leaving CUNY Prep. Neither of his next two jobs brought him the same satisfaction as being the principal at CUNY Prep. We named Jenny Ristenbatt, who had worked at the school as assistant principal and Derrick's deputy, to succeed Derrick. Jenny is a strong administrator, low-key and extremely competent. She is willing to push the students to fill their promise, and she has been an excellent principal. Under Jenny's leadership, CUNY Prep continues to serve the neediest young men and women from the Bronx and Manhattan.

There are lots of reasons to be proud of CUNY Prep. One of them is that it always enrolled approximately the same number of young men as young women, almost all of them Black or Hispanic. That was unusual in the Bronx where so many education programs, including college degree programs, have a disproportionate number of women students. Despite its overall success, CUNY Prep's graduates still struggle when they enter CUNY degree programs, and that remains the program's greatest challenge. The adjustment from a small, supportive community where everyone knows everyone else to a large, relatively impersonal environment at community colleges proved difficult to manage for many CUNY Prep students. While some succeeded, others did not.

The month before his death, Derrick defended his dissertation and earned his doctorate in urban education at the Graduate School of CUNY. His degree was awarded posthumously in May 2015. Soon after, we renamed CUNY Prep the Dr. Derrick Griffith CUNY Preparatory School.

Establishing CUNY Prep as a permanent school was an especially rewarding professional achievement for me. The school continues to serve hundreds of students each year, changing lives and providing opportunity to students who all too often are ignored and neglected once they leave the public school system. A mass of people attended Derrick's funeral. Foremost in the standing-room-audience were many CUNY Prep students and graduates. In my remarks at the funeral, I mentioned that while "pretty much everyone who works with me calls me John, Derrick never would, always calling me Dean Mogulescu and at times just Mogulescu. To him, it was a matter of respect. Derrick also loved being part of our unit and was so proud of the work we did." I recalled that it was with students that Derrick was happiest, and that there are thousands of them everywhere in this city and beyond who have been touched by his warmth and generosity. Conversations between Derrick and students almost always ended with Derrick giving the student a hug and adding the words, "Bless your heart." Those words are etched in the memories of all who came in contact with Derrick during his years leading the school. In ending my remarks, I quoted John Garvey. "Derrick's death has deprived the people of the city of the brilliance, the passion, and the talent of an outstanding educator and one of its finest residents."

Bless your heart, Derrick.

CHAPTER 16

Engaging Children in Theater and Music

The Creative Arts Team and the Harmony Program

CAT—THE CREATIVE ARTS TEAM

The subject was "Blood." In the late winter of 2005, in a small Baruch College theater, 25 New York City high school students performed a thematically connected series of skits. Each skit was based on life experiences of the students and captured serious aspects of teenage life, including bullying, death, family, gender identity, race, sexuality, and war. They used the theme of "Blood" to connect them—the blood of relationships and identity and the blood shed through violence. None of the performers was a professional actor, but all of them had become comfortable on stage, hardly missing a line, and performing with emotion and poise. The skits invited the audience to share the young people's thinking, as well as their raw feelings. As participants in the Creative Arts Team's Youth Theatre, they had spent the previous six months attending a free after school and weekend program. Through a collaborative process called "devising," they developed the skits. In the process, under the masterly guidance of Helen White, they were also introduced to the nuts and bolts—and the magic—of theater, learning about all of the elements of producing and writing a play, and then performing it in front of a live audience.

I had invited a group of family and friends to the performance. As we milled about in the lobby afterward, we marveled at what we had just seen—its power and timeliness, as well as the talent and bravery of the students. They had made their questions and their pain into art. The student actors, joyous and exuberant, bubbled into the lobby, being greeted by the open arms and praise of their families and friends. Larger than life on stage, now they looked like proud and happy teenagers. I learned later that Lin-Manuel Miranda participated in the Youth Theatre as a high school student, and that he has continued to be a supporter of CAT as he gained fame and recognition over the years.

The Youth Theatre was only one of many programs of the Creative Arts Team. CAT, as it was called, became part of our unit in July 2004. The story of CAT coming to CUNY and to SUD is one more example of taking advantage of an unexpected opportunity, one that came with risk, but that further defined the breadth and scope of our unit.

The CUNY chapter of the CAT story started with a phone call I received from Jack Lutz. Jack was a prominent consultant in New York City, whom I had met once or twice beforehand but didn't really know well. He had been retained by a theater program called the Creative Arts Team. Founded in 1974 by Lynda Zimmerman, CAT had been at NYU for 27 years as part of the School of Education. As Jack explained, NYU had decided to sever its ties with CAT, and Lynda was looking for a new home. For their part, CAT was ready to leave NYU. Would I meet with him and Lynda to learn about the program?

I agreed, and we got together. I was impressed with Lynda, who believed deeply in the power of theater to change lives and in the importance of CAT. Having kept the organization afloat for over 25 years, Lynda was politically astute as well as committed. She explained that CAT was self-sufficient, supported by an array of public and private grants that she would bring to CUNY. Thirty or so CAT staff, many teaching artists and experienced theater professionals, would become members of the SUD team. The CAT budget at the time was over $2 million, all of which would be overseen by the Research Foundation and our budget office. Lynda hoped to get CUNY space for CAT, and if necessary, indicated that she would pay for it.

At the time CAT's work was largely in the city's public schools, although it also worked with nonprofit organizations that served youth. Annually, CAT served close to 10,000 young people, including high school, middle school, and elementary school students. The many different CAT programs used theater as a medium to teach literacy skills, public speaking, and improvisation, as well as to lead anti-violence and anti-bullying workshops, and to address issues of health and safety. All of CAT's work was interactive, engaging students as active learners. Their workshops and classes addressed both academic issues and social issues as they affected the lives of the students. The work of CAT had a strong commitment to social justice.

Lynda and I met a number of times in the next few weeks to discuss the possibility of bringing CAT to CUNY. As part of the get-acquainted process, I also met with members of Lynda's staff. Never having been around many theater people before, I was struck by their exuberance and absolute belief that what they called "applied theatre" could not only build skills but change lives. At one of the meetings, I met Chris Vine and Helen White. Chris was CAT's overall artistic director, and Helen directed the Youth Theatre. They also were husband and wife. Helen and Chris combined comprehensive content knowledge with endless energy and the ability to communicate with their young students in ways that seemed almost magical. In the many years to follow, I was able to observe Helen and Chris in action, and their work was unfailingly astonishing.

As I analyzed the pros and cons of bringing CAT to CUNY, I concluded that it made sense. The programs and activities CAT offered, largely to low-income, young people of color in the city, were definitely consistent with our mission. The biggest question for me was whether CAT was fiscally sound, given its dependence on soft money—that is, on grants or contracts that were often short-term. My fiscal people had carefully examined CAT's major grants and contracts. While cautious about predicting the future, my people concluded that given its long history at NYU, we weren't taking a huge risk. They reminded me that given the uncertainty of grants, it was likely that CAT would have some fiscally productive years, but that others would fall short.

The final step in bringing CAT to CUNY was to get the approval of the chancellor and executive vice chancellor for academic affairs. While Selma Botman was relatively new to her position as the EVC, she had quickly grasped the value of our programs, and she gave me her approval. Chancellor Goldstein also approved, once again demonstrating his confidence in my judgment and his belief that programs like CAT were consistent with CUNY's mission.

During the next 15 years CAT became an integral part of our unit and expanded its programming to include not only activities for K–12 students, but for children in pre-K programs as well as college students and other adult populations. It also provided professional development opportunities for CUNY staff from the offices of admissions, counseling, student services, career services, and to offices serving students with disabilities. By 2020, CAT staff were offering annually more than 500 classes and workshops throughout the city at more than 100 schools, college campuses, and community sites. During FY20 CAT served more than 13,000 participants.

Among the wide range of programs CAT offered were an annual Shakespeare Festival for high school students; a Literacy Leaders program for middle school students; an HIV/AIDS prevention program; and a Workforce Readiness program with students with special needs. The CAT staff was alert to opportunities and receptive to new ideas. To increase opportunities for women in the music industry, they formed a partnership with the Mayor's Office of Media and Entertainment to create Sound Thinking NYC. They created an International Exchange program with the Kigali Institute of Education in Rwanda. To support the growth of applied theatre and train new practitioners, they established a flourishing master's program in Applied Theatre at the CUNY School of Professional Studies, with Chris Vine serving as academic director.

During these 15 years, some years saw significant fiscal growth, with the CAT budget going over $3 million. But there were also some fiscal challenges along the way. In years when grants to CAT were less robust, it was necessary to cut back on general operating expenses, serve fewer students, and even lay off or furlough some of the CAT staff. In a few years, to avoid a deficit, we supplemented CAT funding with SUD general funds. Largely those funds were in the form of "loans" that would be repaid over subsequent years. SUD budget staff and I met regularly with Lynda Zimmerman and her budget director to discuss CAT's fiscal status. In lean years, those meeting were painful and difficult, often ending with Lynda in tears as she faced staff cutbacks.

CAT was not unique in facing deficit spending years. As a grants-oriented shop, despite careful budget planning, other programs occasionally ended a fiscal year in deficit. The larger problem, however, came when grants ended. At that point, staff attached to those grants no longer had jobs. We always were upfront at the time of hiring to explain to job candidates the lack of security in grant-funded programs.

Still, I will say that while some staff lost their jobs at SUD because a grant ended, most did not. During the period from 1990–2020, our grant funding increased almost every year with new programs funded and new staffing opportunities. Many staff members who had started in one program could be transferred to another to maintain their employment. We hated to lose good staff simply because a grant ended. We rarely did. When there wasn't an appropriate position for a staff person, we sometimes provided bridge funding from our Indirect Cost account at the Research Foundation to create temporary positions while we waited for a new grant to be secured.

Today CAT continues to enroll thousands of New Yorkers in its many programs. Its grant portfolio has steadily evolved, and its FY22 budget was $2.7 million. Lynda Zimmerman retired in 2017 after having been CAT's founder and executive director from its inception in 1974. She was replaced by Jeanne Houck, who came to CAT after working as the director of foundation relations at the Intrepid Sea, Air, and Space Museum in New York. Jeanne continues to build on Lynda's legacy, and CAT continues to thrive.

THE HARMONY PROGRAM

Bonne and I walked into Public School 152 on a spring evening in 2009. We sat down in the school's auditorium to attend a short concert performed by a group of second and third grade children enrolled in the Harmony Program, a music education program that had become part of our unit. Entering the school building brought back memories of the three years I taught elementary school right after college. Even more powerful were memories of my own childhood. P.S. 152 is located down the block from Midwood High School and across the street from Brooklyn College. While I didn't attend P.S. 152, my best childhood and lifelong friend, Elliott Golinkoff, did. Elliott and I met in junior high school and quickly became friends, a friendship that continued at Midwood High School and beyond. We spent many a day playing softball, touch football, basketball, and a Brooklyn game called punch ball in the P.S. 152 and Midwood school yards. During all of those years sports had been the major focus of my life, and many fond memories of games and competition entered my head as I approached the entrance to the school. Elliott was forever telling the story of how he had spent his elementary school, high school, and college years all on the same corner, having attended P.S.152, Midwood High School, and Brooklyn College.

The first group of seven- and eight-year-olds, shepherded by their teacher, came out onto the stage. Some children beamed at their parents and the audience, while others focused on finding their seats. Finally, with their eyes glued to the teacher, they lifted their little half-size violins to their chins and placed their bows on the strings. The sounds of Beethoven's "Ode to Joy" immediately brought tears to many eyes in the audience. It was magical, watching and hearing these small children play beautiful classical music in front of their parents, relatives, and guests. They combined deep seriousness with a look of total joy. As each group bowed after completing their pieces on the violin, viola, flute, trombone, clarinet, or trumpet, the applause rang out, and the adults' tears continued to flow. I thought that if the children had learned this much in a very short time, this program had incredible potential.

The Harmony Program did not appear to be a natural fit in our unit. In the early years of Harmony, the children were far younger than the participants in any of our programs. It felt like a stretch for me to come up with a logical reason why I had embraced it. At times, I made decisions like this based on instinct and on the sense that a program would provide educational opportunity for students who often did not get many such chances.

A year or so earlier I had hired Anne Fitzgibbon as chief operating officer of our unit. Anne had been a policy advisor in the administrations of Michael Bloomberg and Rudy Giuliani. She had an undergraduate degree from Barnard and a master's degree from Princeton's Woodrow Wilson School. She also had another passion: music. She had studied clarinet at the Julliard School. In 2007 Anne was awarded a Fulbright Fellowship to study and work with Venezuela's National System of Youth and Children's music education. That program, called El Sistema, was founded in 1975 by Venezuelan musician and activist Jose Antonio Abreu. Its goal was to not only to expose young children living in the barrios of Venezuela to music education, but also to see music as an agent of social change.

When I hired Anne, she talked about her experience in Venezuela. Upon her return to the New York, she had started a small nonprofit organization to begin an El Sistema-like program here. She asked if it would be possible to bring that program to CUNY and house it in our unit with her leading it. I must admit that this was an unusual request, given the importance of the job I was hiring her for and knowing that she was asking permission to spend part of her normal work week on Harmony-related activities. Nonetheless, as I listened to her talk about El Sistema and Harmony, I was drawn to the idea of exposing low-income city kids of color to intense music education at schools that all too often had no music programs. The added bonus was that the music classes would be taught by CUNY graduate students in music. I let Anne know that she could bring Harmony to CUNY, but that her first priority was the chief operating officer position. Work on Harmony had to be on her own time.

For a few years, Anne tried to do both jobs, but it was clear that her passion and interest lay with Harmony, not the COO job. She needed to take care of Harmony, and I needed a full-time COO. I let Anne know that it would not be possible for her to continue in both roles; however, I would be willing to keep her on staff as the Harmony director if she could raise the funds to fully support the program, including her salary. I did agree to provide some funding for the program from our general funds. Anne accepted the arrangement, and Harmony had a full-time director.

The program at P.S. 152 opened in October 2008 with 44 second and third graders enrolled. All of the students received free five-day-a-week after-school music instruction, along with instruments (violin, cello, flute, trumpet, trombone, or percussion), music books, and supplies. The children were initially taught by undergraduate or graduate students and recent alumni of the Brooklyn College Conservatory, who were trained and given continuous professional development.

Under Anne's leadership, Harmony began to grow almost immediately. Anne's first challenge was to raise money. Fortunately, she was an effective fundraiser. While she was able to raise some public money, most of the dollars raised came from private foundations, corporations, and individual donors. Anne understood the importance of establishing a board of directors for the program and was fortunate that Roy Niederhoffer, a NYC-based financier and philanthropist, agreed to be the board chair. Roy was a musician himself, playing violin in the Park Avenue Chamber Symphony. He embraced the mission of Harmony. He not only supported the program with generous gifts, but also provided space for the staff at his own Manhattan office complex.

Over the next 12 years Harmony grew from that initial location at P.S. 152 to include 16 sites throughout the city. Most were in public schools, with a few at community-based organizations. By the 2021–22 year, the program enrolled close to 1,000 students, over 90% from minority backgrounds. The program was embraced by the Warner Music Company, as well as by the New York Philharmonic. Members of the Philharmonic provided master classes for the students a few times during the year, a wonderful experience for the students who had the opportunity to be taught by these accomplished musicians.

As part of the fundraising process, Anne organized annual galas. These were wonderful evenings, highlighted by the performances of the more advanced Harmony students. The galas honored some of the most prominent musicians in the world, who performed both individually and with the Harmony students at the event. Among the honorees were Joshua

Bell, Placido Domingo, Andre Previn, Paquito D'Rivera, Joyce DiDonato, and Anthony McGill. Bell, one of the world's premier violinists, became an active supporter of Harmony, as did McGill, principal clarinetist for the New York Philharmonic. McGill also became a member of the Harmony board. Wynton Marsalis hosted a fundraising event in Harlem where he played his trumpet alongside some of Harmony's most accomplished horn students, coaching them enthusiastically to "play out." Jamie Bernstein, daughter of Leonard Bernstein, co-directed a documentary film, *Crescendo! The Power of Music* about Harmony and a program in Philadelphia also inspired by El Sistema.[1]

The organizational structure for Harmony was complicated. Like all our SUD programs funded by outside grants, contracts, and donations, Harmony was administered by the CUNY Research Foundation. Harmony's staff were paid through the RF. At the same time, Harmony had its own board and independent status as an incorporated nonprofit organization that also could raise its own money. This was an unusual arrangement at CUNY, which raised questions from my fiscal staff as well as from RF about whether Harmony really should be a part of CUNY.

I guess I was able to sustain this arrangement not only because of my close relationship with many of the RF senior officials, but because our unit generated such a significant percentage of the grants and contract dollars managed by the RF. They trusted us, and over many years we had never misused money or received any critical audits conducted by state and city officials. It also was the case that Harmony was a relatively small program with an annual budget of not much more than $1 million.

In 2019, as I began to think about retirement, I began conversations with Anne about Harmony becoming fully independent of CUNY. As the only real advocate for the program in the Central Office, I worried that when I left, the program would have no support. I was convinced that Harmony could now stand on its own. It had become a mature organization with a committed and dedicated board. Anne was worried about losing the wide-ranging support of the RF, but she agreed that the program would be at risk when I left. CUNY had served as an incubator, but now the program could operate independently. Anne devised an exit strategy for Harmony, and in December 2019, it became completely independent of CUNY. Harmony is now a thriving nonprofit organization. Anne believes that the program is likely to grow and will serve close to 3000 students in the 2023–24 school year.

Throughout Harmony's time at CUNY, some of my staff pushed me to end the relationship. They thought I might be taking unnecessary risks in maintaining the program at CUNY while it also had independent nonprofit status. Some staff also felt it wasn't logical for Harmony to be part of our portfolio, given how independent it had become. Although they didn't accept my response, it was one that I really believed: In a city where the opportunity to learn to play an instrument was almost totally unavailable at most of the public schools serving poor kids, Harmony was an oasis. The hundreds of children enrolled in the program each year experienced the magic of playing music and the value it brought to their social and educational development. Harmony was a gift to its students.

Not all of the students became accomplished musicians, but many did. As we followed the students who started in Harmony in the second or third grade over the years to follow, we found that Harmony had changed their lives. Each year at the Harmony gala, former students, some aspiring musicians and some who have chosen other fields of study, speak about the contributions Harmony made to their lives. It brought them discipline, a sense of accomplishment, and enormous pride. It provided opportunity for them to perform and be acknowledged. It brought them joy. It was not easy to attend a program from 3–5 p.m. every school day, but the attendance at Harmony was always close to 90%. The students made lasting friends and played together in small ensembles and in orchestra. They saw new possibilities in life. Together and on their own, they made music.

I attended every Harmony gala, visited numerous program sites to observe the instruction, participated in organized events with members of the Philharmonic, watched recitals and concerts, and—always the best part—listened to the kids play. I wondered why the program had to struggle to raise money each year when it should have been funded by the Department of Education or the city and been a hundred times its size. Harmony is an example of the kind of program a great public university should help support, drawing on its resources and expertise, as it works to address the myriad problems and challenges confronting low-income children and families.

One final note about Harmony. With the announcement in February 2023 that Gustavo Dudamel would be leaving the Los Angeles Philharmonic to join the New York Philharmonic as its next music director, there was an extra excitement at Harmony. When Anne Fitzgibbon studied El Sistema while in Venezuela as part of her Fulbright year, she got to know Dudamel, who as a child in Venezuela had participated in El Sistema. Dudamel has actively supported music education for low-income children in Los Angeles. The Harmony staff hopes that Dudamel might give Harmony a role in that process in New York, and that more outside funders will come to recognize the value of supporting music education in the city.

Did I make the correct decisions in bringing both CAT and Harmony to CUNY? I believe I did. As with so many of our programs, CAT and Harmony further broadened the role of CUNY and its critical place in providing educational opportunities to New Yorkers. The beneficiaries of the programs have been the tens of thousands of public school children who experienced the joy of music and theater in their lives. CUNY also benefitted from the presence of CAT and Harmony. Harmony enabled many graduate students in music, largely at Brooklyn College, to become teachers in the program; that broadened the grad students' understanding of the value of music to young New Yorkers. It expanded the scope of their degree programs and provided some income. The work of CAT led to the establishment of a master's degree in applied theatre at the CUNY School of Professional Studies.

It also is true that both programs introduced CUNY to some prominent theater and music professionals, showing a side of CUNY that many of these people did not know existed. To have renowned artists like Lin-Manuel Miranda, Joshua Bell, and Wynton Marsalis, and organizations like the New York Philharmonic directly connected to CUNY not only benefitted the students in the programs but led to positive media attention and in general increased exposure for CUNY to the general public.

III. BUILDING AND SUSTAINING A WORKFORCE

From almost my first years in Continuing Education at New York City Community College, I was involved in workforce development. Over the course of my career, I oversaw dozens of training programs—entry programs, upgrading programs, and many collaborations with unions and city agencies to advance workers and increase their skills. I've observed many times how well-run programs can make a difference.

During those years, while running successful hands-on programs, I was also invited to join big-picture efforts—high level task forces and committees—to reimagine how the university, New York City, and New York State should address the broad question of workforce development. Thinking about workforce development at scale proved far more frustrating than running programs. Again and again, although well-intentioned and composed of members with experience and knowledge, these task forces and committees continued to recommend the same generic strategies. In the end, they could point to small successes but did not make a dent in meeting the challenges of low-wage work.

This section begins with the big picture and then offers two examples of programs targeted to specific areas of essential and often low-wage work-health and human services and early childhood education. Based on both research and practical experience, the programs illustrate what can happen when leaders are empowered to use their deep knowledge and creativity.

CHAPTER 17

Workforce Development

IN DECEMBER OF 2019, THE MEMBERS OF THE NYC WORKFORCE Development Board honored me for my 20 years of service. Under the Federal Workforce Innovation and Opportunity Act, signed into law in 1998, local boards must be established to oversee the dollars provided by the Act. Board members, appointed by the mayor, are generally leaders from business, unions, nonprofit organizations, education, and government. Originally appointed to the board by Mayor Giuliani in July of 2000, I was subsequently reappointed by Mayors Bloomberg and de Blasio.

At the short farewell ceremony honoring me, a number of my board colleagues gave tributes. In his remarks, Joe McDermott, executive director of the Consortium for Worker Education and a longtime colleague and friend, said, "John is severely underrated because he doesn't like notice. He seems to be always achieving more and in every program he does it better. So, while he's resigning from this board, he's not retiring, thank God."

I can't say that I agree with Joe's statement about not liking being noticed. (In fact, I do; I probably wouldn't be writing this book if I didn't.) But I appreciated his being one of the speakers. Given the many battles I had during my career with the CUNY faculty and staff union, the PSC, I was grateful for praise from one of the most important and influential union leaders in the city.

In response, I thanked my board colleagues and then reflected on my years of service: "I've always in my career tried to think about how we can shake up our institutions and make them better. And that's what I tried a little here on the board as well. My only advice to new board members is to try and figure out how to be active, how to push against the status quo, how to understand that there's far too many people who are working low-wage jobs in the city, and that inequality is rampant. What can we do as board members to say that is totally unacceptable? What can we do to support programs whose goal is to address these problems?"

Over most of my career I have tried to highlight the persistent problem of low-wage work for far too many New Yorkers. Working with others at CUNY and throughout the city, I've tried to solve it. I have given considerable thought to why, despite the fact that workforce development has been a city priority in every city administration during the past 40 years, as well as a priority of CUNY, that effort has continued to fall short.

It is not as if those of us working in adult and continuing education at CUNY have been unable to provide underemployed and low-skilled adults with educational and training opportunities leading to new jobs, promotions, and career advancement. We certainly have! Programs like the Early Childhood Professional Development Institute (PDI) and the John F. Kennedy, Jr. Institute for Worker Development have not only created opportunities for individuals, but they also have improved working conditions in the early childhood and developmental disability fields. I could point to many others. The CUNY adult and continuing education units enroll almost as many students as does the degree side of the university. By 1994–95, CUNY enrolled more than 148,000 continuing education students, almost all in non-credit programs. That number increased to a peak of almost 250,000 in 2013–2014, with LaGuardia Community College alone enrolling more than 60,000 students. Since then, the numbers have decreased some, but still reach over 225,000 students each year. In addition to CUNY, across New York City, nonprofits do an extensive and successful job of bringing people into the workforce and helping them advance. So, a great deal of good work is being done.

I also have been part of serious city and state-wide efforts to address the problem of low-wage workers and workforce development in general.

In 2005, Mayor Bloomberg created the Commission for Economic Opportunity to study the problem of poverty in New York City and propose solutions. The Commission led to the establishment of the Center for Economic Opportunity (CEO) in 2006, created not only to further study the problem, but also to fund innovative programs that would be evaluated carefully and expanded if successful. The Center, it was hoped, would create policies and start new programs that would "raise the employment and earnings of low-income parents, help parents balance their work and family obligations, and raise the educational attainment and skills of the next generation."[1] Among the Center's most successful funded efforts was CUNY's ASAP program. In addition, the CEO funded a number of other effective CUNY programs, including CUNY Prep and John Jay College's NYC Justice Corps.

In 2007, I was appointed as a member of Governor Patterson's Economic Security Cabinet. The goal of this effort was to "improve the lives of New York State's low-income individuals and families through enhanced collaboration and integration of the work done by multiple state agencies."[2] The cabinet had as one of its priorities to "maximize access to benefits that can significantly improve the economic security of lower wage earners." [3]

In 2011 Chancellor Goldstein created the CUNY Jobs Task Force. Chaired by Rick Schaffer, vice chancellor for legal affairs and general counsel, the task force issued its report "Jobs for New York's Future" in 2012. Task Force members included representatives from the private sector together with high level government officials. Two members of my team, Suri Duitch, my deputy at the time, and Shayne Spaulding, the university director of workforce development, were staff to the committee; Shayne was the report's main author. The task force examined industry and labor force trends in different sectors that were of "strategic importance to the University and New York City's economy." The chancellor also asked it to determine "How can CUNY and other institutions of higher education better prepare students for the labor market today and in the future." [4]

In 2014, Mayor de Blasio established the Jobs for New Yorkers Task

Force consisting of representatives from the private sector, organized labor, foundations, government, and education. I was appointed a member of the leadership team of the task force. After more than a year of work, the task force issued its report, "Career Pathways, One City Working Together." The report included a series of recommendations, concluding that the workforce system needed "to move away from a strategy of simple job placement to one that builds the skills that advance careers and increase earning potential for our city's working men and women." The report also highlighted the need to "engage employers and share information that will improve stability, working conditions, and opportunities for sustainable careers for the more than one million New Yorkers in low wage jobs." [5]

Certainly, the problem was defined. Moreover, each of these efforts was led and staffed by talented professionals who were committed to the goals of improving workforce opportunities for New Yorkers and reducing the level of poverty in the city. If some of these efforts appear redundant, it is because they were, and some of the participants, including me, served on more than one task force over the course of different administrations. During this ten-year period, many new workforce programs were established, some successful, others less so. Offices were restructured. New commissioners and deputy mayors entered government with the desire to reduce poverty. A significant amount of public and private money was made available. High school graduation rates increased by more than 20 percentage points, tens of thousands of youths and adults entered education and training programs leading to jobs and career opportunities, and CUNY increased its graduation rates at both its associate and baccalaureate level programs. But overall, the rate of poverty, while decreasing some, still left far too many New Yorkers, including a disturbing number of children, in poverty.[6]

During this time period, I attended what seemed like an endless series of meetings, forums, and conferences with workforce and government leaders on the topic of workforce and poverty. I would hear about the skills gap; the fact that employers could often not find qualified workers; that the new economy would not require a college degree, but rather technical and life skills; that certificate programs, stackable credentials, career pathways, and apprenticeships would be the answer; and that the new economy would not provide jobs for the unskilled.

But when I looked at the New York City labor market, I saw a different story. For one, it remained true that the single best way to get out of poverty for low-income New Yorkers was to obtain a college degree, particularly one at the bachelor's level. While a number of excellent community-based agencies and training programs enroll high school graduates from disadvantaged backgrounds into intensive certificate programs in areas such as information technology or business, and upon completion place graduates in good jobs, admission to successful programs like Per Scholas and Year Up is highly competitive and requires an applicant to have good basic skills. Only a small percentage of applicants are accepted.

At CUNY, a variety of non-credit certificate programs through our continuing education units, largely at our community and comprehensive colleges are offered, but many lead to relatively low wage jobs. Some colleges have created articulation agreements between these non-credit programs and their degree programs, but the numbers have remained small. As part of this articulation process, some campuses offer students who enroll in a degree program credit for prior learning for completing a certificate (SPS is a good example of this), but across the university these opportunities are limited.

One need only to look at specific NYC labor market data to understand why the city has had such difficulty providing career advancement opportunities for its residents. The bulk of the available jobs for New Yorkers lacking a college degree consists largely of low-wage jobs. In 2014, CUNY's Labor Market Information Service published a summary report on New York City's Economy. The report included a lengthy chart entitled Occupational Employment, Wages, and Projections and Educational Attainment, NYC, listing the number of jobs in a particular category and the projected change over the 10-year period from 2010 to 2020. The chart also included annual wage data from 2012 along with the level of education attained by members of the occupational categories. [7]

Unsurprisingly, the jobs that required bachelor's or advanced degrees paid far and away the highest salaries. But those categories that were the biggest in size and were projected to grow the most were largely the lowest paying. For instance, the two largest job categories included in the chart were personal care aides and home health aides. LMIS data projected that the demand for personal care aides would grow almost 49% over the ten-year period from 79,860 in 2010 to 118,900 in 2020. The demand for home health aides was projected to grow from 75,570 to 118, 900. The 2012 median wage for these jobs was approximately $21,000.

Other large job categories included childcare workers, maintenance and repair workers, janitors and cleaners, housekeepers and cleaners, receptionists and office clerks, laborers, cashiers, taxi and other licensed drivers, food prep workers, customer service representatives, and stock clerks. While none of these categories expected the type of growth projected for personal care and home health aides, each of them employed large numbers of people. They also were relatively low paid, with only one of these job categories, maintenance and repair works, having a median wage over $40,000; most of the other categories offered median wages of between $28,000 and $35,000.

Were there job categories that both paid well and employed large numbers of people? Yes, quite a few. Most of these, however, like teachers, lawyers, doctors, financial analysts and advisors, registered nurses, securities and financial services sales agents, and IT, computer, and web development professionals, required bachelor's or graduate degrees. And none of them were projected to add nearly as many future jobs as the personal and home health care aide categories.

Over my many years working in workforce development, it always seemed that if you looked at the 30 largest categories of jobs in the city, over half of them and most of the largest ones paid low wages, thus leaving many fully employed people in poverty or living just above the poverty rate. Yet these New Yorkers, largely people of color/members of minority groups were taking care of our children, the elderly, the disabled, and the neediest New Yorkers. Those low-income employees lived check to check and were often one health crisis, a loss of a job, a relationship break-up, or an arrest away from becoming homeless.

For the majority of working New Yorkers who fill the huge number of low wage jobs, there is a desperate need to increase the level of government and private sector support for workers—through expanded Medicaid, tax credits, childcare supplements, increased wages, college scholarships and financial aid. Such support should be at a level that ensures that full time workers, doing vitally important work, receive a living wage in this richest city in the world.

As we entered the 2020s, market trends had changed some with the boom in technology jobs, and so-called experts began to question the value of a college degree. Although there are certainly examples of success without a degree, for most people the data didn't support these views. Rather, I continue to believe strongly that a college degree is the best path to a decent chance to live a middle-class life. At the same time, however, I understand the responsibility of CUNY to provide education and training for those New Yorkers disinclined or unable to obtain a degree and the importance of developing career ladder opportunities for them.

Approaching retirement, although proud of the many accomplishments of our work at CUNY and in the city to address the issues of poverty and workforce development for so many New Yorkers, I found our failure to make more progress in the broader workforce area disappointing. It does appear that by 2023, strong advocacy from unions, and a tight job market have contributed to a significant increase in the hourly wage for New York City's lowest paid workers. At the same time, high inflation and the shortage of affordable housing make even these increases insufficient to move many workers and their families out of poverty. It is not enough to examine workforce issues in isolation. They are part of the larger economic and social picture and finally will be productively addressed at scale only in that larger context.

CHAPTER 18

Advancing Health and Human Service Workers

JFK Jr. and the Kennedy Institute

BILL EBENSTEIN ARRIVED AT THE CENTRAL OFFICE IN 1989 TO direct a new partnership between CUNY and Reaching Up, a nonprofit founded by John Kennedy Jr. Like other members of the large Kennedy family, John believed he had a responsibility to contribute meaningfully to public service or to address a social cause. In John's case, the cause was providing educational and career advancement opportunities to frontline workers in health and human services occupations, particularly those working in agencies serving children and adults with developmental disabilities. Frontline workers, also referred to as "direct care workers," had day to day responsibility for tending to the needs of the clients. They had extremely hard jobs that paid poorly, and those factors led to high staff turnover. John committed himself to reversing that. He approached CUNY to be his partner and provided initial funding through the family's Joseph Kennedy Foundation to establish what was called the Consortium for the Study of Disabilities.

John Kennedy Jr. was handsome, rich, and famous. When he came to meetings in our fourth-floor conference room, the word spread quickly that John Jr. was in the building. People came to the floor just to get a glimpse of a true celebrity. Bill Ebenstein had no patience for fawning over celebrities, and JFK Jr. seemed to recognize and appreciate that. The two very different men soon developed a relationship that was built on trust and common interest. Bill accepted John as a colleague, and not because of his status. John accepted Bill because he was a guy who knew what he was talking about.

Bill was stubborn in a good way. He disliked authority and being supervised, which at times led to intense discussions, even arguments, but he never let that interfere with his desire to bring change to the field. I admired Bill's tenacity. Bill spent 29 years at CUNY, being an integral part of the leadership team of our unit. He was known and widely respected outside CUNY. He developed and led an extraordinary number of programs, generating many dollars and becoming a major city and state leader in the area of workforce development in health care and human services.

An early component of Bill's work with John Kennedy was the establishment of the Kennedy Fellows program, which provided tuition assistance for direct-care workers to attend a CUNY college and earn a degree. Having a degree enabled them to qualify for supervisory or administrative positions and salary increments. The motto of the program was "Once a Kennedy Fellow, always a Kennedy Fellow." The workers selected as Kennedy Fellows became part of a vibrant community that was a strong advocate for improving the employment conditions of frontline workers in the field. To direct the program, Bill and I reached out to Lyda Clifton, who had just completed her work as the director of the SLIAG program, the university's effort to assist undocumented immigrants obtain permanent status.

Throughout the 1990s, Bill, Lyda, Bill's deputy Ashleigh Thompson, and the rest of his team worked together with John Kennedy and Jeffrey Sachs, the president of Reaching Up, to create many workforce-related programs. Each year approximately 1,000 direct care workers in jobs such as personal care attendants, nurse aids, home care workers, and childcare workers enrolled in credit and non-credit certificate programs throughout CUNY. These programs, including a 12-credit certificate in disability studies, a child and youth care worker training program, and a hospital and youth care worker training program, among others, led either to new career opportunities or enrollment in college degree programs.

Local 1199 SEIU United Healthcare Workers, a large and powerful union, was a partner in the development of a number of these programs. John Kennedy, Jeff Sachs, and Bill Ebenstein worked closely with Dennis Rivera, president of 1199, and Debbie King, the director of the union's Training and Upgrading Fund. A priority of the union was to provide its lowest-paid workers with opportunities for career advancement. The union looked to CUNY for assistance in creating new programs to accomplish this goal.

Bill, Jeff, and John became a close and at times what seemed like an inseparable team. They talked constantly, planned new programs, listened to frontline workers express their own opinions, and organized a series of events to celebrate student accomplishments. John Kennedy could not have been more committed to the goals of improving the working conditions of frontline workers and thus lowering the high rate of workers leaving the field. John brought compassion and humility to the partnership, while forcefully advocating for system-wide change. Unlike some philanthropists who believe their own ideas should carry more weight than those of experts in the field, John was eager to listen and learn from the people with experience, starting with the direct care workers. He had enormous respect for Bill, and also was committed to CUNY and its role in that process.

In July of 1999, John died tragically when a small plane he was piloting crashed. Those who had worked with John and admired him were overwhelmingly saddened. At the same time, Bill and Jeffrey remained strongly committed to continuing the work. In the year 2000 we established the John F. Kennedy Jr. Institute for Worker Education. It would be a CUNY-wide training, research and public policy entity. Housed in the Office of Academic Affairs, the institute was committed to providing education and career advancement for frontline workers. Bill was named executive director. The initial funding for the institute came from the Office of the Governor.

Over the next 10 years the institute generated millions of dollars in funding, including major grants from the New York State Department of Health, for its disability studies program and from the Social Security Administration for a youth transition research and demonstration project to improve educational and employment outcomes of Bronx youth with disabilities.

In 2009, at the 20th anniversary of the Kennedy Fellows Program, we celebrated the nearly 800 Kennedy Fellows who had been accepted into the program and the hundreds who had earned their college degrees and gone on to become social workers, teachers, nurses, and administrators in nonprofit and public agencies throughout New York. To honor the Fellows, John's sister, Caroline Kennedy, joined us and provided inspirational remarks.

As a result of Bill's outstanding work, he was named university dean for health and human services, while remaining executive director of the JFK Institute. Thus, following John Garvey, he became the second member of our SUD team to be named a university dean. A number of others followed over the years. As university dean, Bill broadened his portfolio. A particular interest was to increase the number of students enrolling and graduating from CUNY's nursing programs. While he already had overseen a grant from 1199 SEIU in 2002 to "gather and analyze information about enrollment patterns, academic patterns, academic achievement, demographics and graduation rates of 1199 members at CUNY schools,"[1] he was convinced that more was needed. The CUNY School of Professional Studies, of which I was the founding dean beginning in 2003, became the beneficiary of Bill's interest, creativity, and access to funding.

In 2012, Bill arranged for Marge Reilly and Maureen Wallace, two of CUNY's most senior nursing faculty, to be released from their campus responsibilities to become faculty fellows in his office. One of their major projects was to develop an online Bachelor of Science in Nursing degree program (BSN) at the CUNY School of Professional Studies. As the dean of SPS, I was delighted at the arrangement. Two years later, the program opened with Marge Reilly as its academic director. It quickly became the largest degree program at SPS, adding online master's nursing degree programs a few years later.

Bill also supported SPS in building three additional degree programs, including one of the first online degree programs in disability studies in the United States, a master's degree program in youth studies, and a bachelor's degree in health information management.

Bill was tireless. He had new ideas almost every day, along with a passion for his work and for creating opportunities for low-paid but vital workers. He envisioned myriad ways that the expertise within CUNY could be used to serve the needs of workers to improve their skills and advance themselves. And then he found the resources needed to make programs happen. Bill had some of the same characteristics as other dynamic and successful SUD leaders. Like many creative and committed people, his sharp focus meant he wasn't always easy, but his work changed the university and the city. When we disagreed, I tried to give him space and freedom, confident that the programs he created would be exemplary.

CHAPTER 19

The Early Childhood Professional Development Institute

WELL BEFORE OUR PHONE INTERVIEW ENDED, I REALIZED THAT Sherry Cleary was an exceptional candidate. I wanted to hire her. But I needed to convince her to leave her secure, tenured, wide-ranging faculty position in early childhood education at the University of Pittsburgh and come to CUNY for a far more tenuous, grant-funded role. She seemed a perfect choice to be the executive director of the Early Childhood Professional Development Institute (PDI), a small but important program established only two years earlier. Over the next few weeks, Sherry and I had several more conversations. Each time that we talked, I became more impressed. She was vibrant, creative, energetic, really smart, and had wonderful ideas about what she would do to build the program.

I was frank about the downside of the offer. I couldn't match the salary she was getting in Pittsburgh, and our position had little security. In fact, she would have to raise the money for the program, including funds for her own salary. On the other hand, I emphasized factors that I thought would intrigue her. In particular, I appealed to what I believed to be her entrepreneurial nature and her interest in leading an effort that could dramatically change the early childhood field and the conditions of the people who worked in it. I stressed that she would be joining our Senior University Dean unit, which by 2006 had been firmly established as the innovative arm of the university. There she would have the freedom to build something with genuine impact. She would be a senior member of a team that worked hard, supported one another, took risks, and could depend on my support to challenge the status quo. I also stressed how closely we worked with the New York City Department of Education and the many state and city agencies that oversaw early childhood education, as well as the private foundations that provided money for new programs and good ideas. Finally, I stressed our commitment to social justice and to addressing inequality.

Over the course of the search process, I felt that Sherry and I had developed a rapport, and I believed that the possibilities of the program intrigued her. But until I received her phone call accepting the job, I worried that she would turn it down. As positive as I felt about Sherry Cleary then, her impact on the early childhood field over the next 15 years far exceeded my expectations. She would become perhaps the most influential early childhood educator in New York State and a national figure. CUNY had hired a treasure.

The story of CUNY's participation in the development of the Professional Development Institute had begun in 2003 when members of a group called the Child Care and Early Education Fund approached me to consider bringing the newly established PDI to CUNY. The fund, comprising both private donors and public agency partners, had been created in 1999 to support "organizations engaged in bringing about systemic improvements in the quality and accessibility of childcare and early education." Its members included senior officials from the NYC Department of Education (DOE), the Human Resources Administration (HRA) and the Administration for Children's Services, as well as senior staff from more than 15 NYC-based private foundations and nonprofit agencies, including the United Way of NYC, the Robert Sterling Clark Foundation, the A. L. Mailman Family Foundation, and the New York Community Trust. A major goal of the fund was to establish an institute whose mission was "to ensure that all New York City early educators and child care providers have consistent access to and effectively utilize a comprehensive system of training and professional development that supports high quality services for the City's children and their families." [1]

CUNY wasn't the first choice to house the institute. Bank Street

College of Education had been involved in the early planning for the institute and was interested in hosting it. NYU had also expressed interest, while some members of the fund felt the institute should be housed at the ACS Satterwhite Academy. At some point however, a steering committee of the fund determined that the institute should be housed at a public institution of higher education. In New York City, that would be CUNY.[2]

Soon after, I began conversations with members of the fund's steering committee (including Patti Lieberman of the Mailman foundation, Laura Wolf from Robert Sterling Clark, Natasha Lifton from the United Way, Kay Hendon from HRA, and Ellie Ukolie from DOE) to bring the institute to CUNY. After a number of lengthy conversations, we agreed that PDI would become a program at the Office of Academic Affairs, that our SUD unit would administer and be responsible for the daily operation of the program, and that its executive director would be Barbara Coccodrilli Carlson. In our conversations, it was apparent that the fund members had come to CUNY because of the record our unit had established in implementing programs successfully.

In January of 2004, the Child Care and Early Education Fund awarded a one-year grant of $250,000 to CUNY to begin the project. Later commitments from members of the fund, including HRA and ACS, increased the program's first-year budget to approximately $600,000.

The program was housed on the seventh floor of our leased space at 101 West 31st Street in Manhattan, with Barbara Carlson and two others as the entire staff. We were starting this new significant initiative in the same year as the formal opening of the School of Professional Studies, the major expansion of work with the public schools, and all of our other existing projects, but our team once again welcomed the challenge.

Barbara, an experienced and excellent administrator, had worked in government and the nonprofit sector and held leadership positions in organizations serving young children and youth. Her initial task was to create a sound infrastructure for the institute that would not only establish it as an integral part of CUNY but also recognize the role of the many partner organizations and funders. As per our agreement with the funders group, that infrastructure would include an oversight committee made up of the Institute's public and private funders, along with an advisory committee consisting of early education providers, advocacy organizations, private institutions of higher education, and other training providers.[3]

Barbara and our partners understood that many challenges stood in the way of improving the quality of early childhood education. To address these obstacles, they needed to learn more about the actual workforce in the field. Joining with Cornell University's Early Childhood Program, the PDI began a study of the NYC early childhood workforce. This study "was designed to examine the characteristics of the workforce that have been linked to high quality early childhood education, including levels of education, program tenure, compensation, and participation in professional development."[4] The study was under way when, after two years as PDI Director, Barbara resigned. Although somewhat surprising to me and I believe to our other partners, her departure created the opportunity to hire Sherry Cleary, who became executive director in 2006.

Under Sherry's leadership, the next 16 years brought tremendous growth, visibility, and success to the PDI. Sherry exuded energy and enthusiasm. She had an incredible presence, was a wonderful public speaker, and knew how to build and establish relationships. Having worked in the field for many years, she had a vision for the PDI. Her reputation attracted new staff who wanted to work with her, as well as funders who trusted her to create important new programs. She could be forceful and tactful at the same time and was comfortable with managing conflict. She also had a great sense of humor. I never worried about Sherry's area and gave her enormous freedom to make decisions and take risks without having to check with me. I knew that if there were serious problems, she would let me know and ask for advice.

Almost immediately upon becoming the executive director, Sherry established herself as a prominent name in the early childhood field. Right away she focused on finishing the workforce study begun under her predecessor, including a set of recommendations that would lead to an action plan to change the system. When the study was completed in

2007, the PDI issued a policy brief that outlined its findings and recommendations. The report noted that:

- Stark differences in educational levels existed between community and school based early childhood educators. For example, nearly 90% of school-based teachers but only 43% of community-based teachers held master's degrees.
- Compensation varied significantly between school based and community-based educators, with community-based teachers paid an average salary of $36,000, while school-based teachers earned on average $27,000 more.
- Program directors did not reflect the diversity of their communities, and often lacked management and leadership skills.
- Professional development was greatly needed.
- Staff turnover and retention presented a major challenge.

These findings set a framework for much of PDI's future work, and Sherry immediately put in motion an array of programs and activities to address the challenges. She defined the three primary dimensions of PDI's work as "system building, public policy and communication, and innovation and implementation."

In interviewing Sherry for this book, when I asked her to highlight what she felt were the major accomplishments of PDI, she cited a number of programs that PDI developed. These were further detailed in a transition memo she sent to the CUNY executive vice chancellor for academic affairs and shared with me soon after announcing that she would be retiring from CUNY in July of 2022. These programs, the highlights edited here for conciseness, include invaluable tools to improve the field and essential services for the advancement of workers:

- Published the NYS Early Childhood Core Body of Knowledge (CBK) and the NYS Early Learning Guideline (ELG). The CBK is the competency-based book used across higher education for teacher education and as the framework for all state approved professional development. The ELG spans the first 8 years of life and includes a strong emphasis on family engagement, cultural competence, and gender and sexuality.

- Developed and administered Aspire, New York State's early childhood workforce database/registry. Aspire had 50,000 active users by 2022.
- Developed and administered QualitystarsNY, the state's quality rating and improvement system for all licensed and regulated early childhood programs, currently used by 900 programs in all 10 economic regions of the state, serving 55,000 children from birth to five years. Qualitystars has been funded to double its impact and serve more than 2,000 sites by the end of 2023.
- Created the NYC Early Childhood Research Network which has provided approximately $5 million to support 17 research studies and an Early Career Scholar Initiative to support diverse entry level research scientists.
- Through the New York Early Childhood Career Center and nine satellite centers statewide, provided career and higher education guidance to those interested in entering the field. Offered career fairs, panels, and job search workshops, individual advisement, and certification test prep. Awarded the Early Childhood Workforce Scholarship to be used at CUNY and SUNY colleges.
- Developed the 18-credit Children's Program Administrator Credential (CPAC), a graduate-level program offered by the CUNY School of Professional Studies for principals and directors of early childhood programs in schools and centers.
- Through the Informal Family Child Care Project offer professional development and coaching for unregulated family childcare providers in NYC.

These represent just a sample of the many programs that PDI has developed and administered since it began in 2006, growing from five staff members to 127 by 2022. The entire staff, including the director, is funded through the grants and contracts awarded to the PDI. They are employees of the CUNY Research Foundation. In fiscal year 2022 the PDI generated over $30 million in grants and contracts.

When Mayor de Blasio went about creating New York City's pioneering Universal Pre-K program, Sherry became one of a small group advising the mayor. She also was appointed by Governor David Patterson and re-appointed by Governor Andrew Cuomo as the co-chair of the 50-member New York State Early Childhood Advisory Council.

The influence and scope of services of the PDI speak to the importance of selecting visionary and innovative leaders. Sherry was that. The work of the PDI, however, was not Sherry's alone. Her gifted staff, who brought a similar energy and commitment to their jobs.

Even though the work of PDI was recognized all over the state and throughout the country, and Sherry became one of the state's most influential early childhood leaders, its accomplishments were less well known within CUNY. Sherry tried to establish working relationships with the many degree programs in early childhood education at CUNY, generally led by college deans of education. While she was able to establish good relationships with several deans, she had little influence in assisting the degree programs to modify their requirements, curriculum, or design. Even after Sherry was appointed as the CUNY university dean for early childhood education, most of her work remained with PDI and as a state and city policy influencer. She was never fully accepted by the deans and faculty of many of CUNY's teacher education programs.

Like many of the programs the SUD unit developed, other than space for staff, no tax levy dollars were used to support PDI. Its work, the recognition it brought to CUNY, its influence on early childhood policy—all were paid for by its grants and contracts. As with so many other efforts, the SUD unit used soft money to create innovative programming that changed a field and demonstrated how an urban university can and should respond to the needs of its city.

IV. INCREASING SUCCESS FOR CUNY STUDENTS

Many team members and I had long felt that CUNY's efforts toward improving retention and graduation rates for degree students were just not good enough and needed to be strengthened. Our earlier work with the CUNY Language Immersion Program (CLIP) and with the public schools showed positive impact on college access, but we believed we had more to contribute. Beginning with ASAP in 2006, the chancellor gave us important opportunities to help improve student success. As these major projects, directed at degree students and managed from Central, were rolled out, some campus administrators, as well as faculty representatives (the Faculty Senate and the PSC, the faculty union) began to push back.

CHAPTER 20

ASAP

Accomplishing What No One Thought Possible

IN THE LATE FALL OF 2006, CHANCELLOR GOLDSTEIN RETURNED from a lunch meeting with Mayor Bloomberg and asked to meet with Executive Vice Chancellor Selma Botman, Jay Hershenson, and me. In his usual understated way, the chancellor let us know that the lunch had been productive. He had received a commitment from the mayor to fund a new community college success program that would significantly raise graduation rates at CUNY's six community colleges. The funding would be $19.5 million for three years. Before we got too excited, the chancellor warned, the mayor had asked him what the program's three-year graduation rate would be. He had responded without missing a beat, "50%." At that point an initial silence in the room was followed by a combination of nervous laughter and disbelief. At the time, the three-year graduation rate at our community colleges was less than 15%, a figure consistent with other urban community colleges around the country. The chancellor asked us if 50% could be achieved. Although privately doubting that anything close to that could be accomplished, we said we would try.

College success and how to raise graduation rates at community colleges has long been a major topic of discussion in higher ed. But nowhere in the United States had there been a large-scale program that had raised graduation rates to such a significant degree.

A small group of CUNY faculty and Central Office staff began meeting to create the ambitious program. As was often the case when asked to develop new programs by the city or the chancellor, our time line was very short. We had less than a year to plan the program, publicize its existence, recruit students, and hire staff. We named the program Accelerated Study in Associate Programs, soon known as ASAP. A number of the planning committee members came from our SUD unit, including John Garvey, Eric Hofmann, Tracy Meade, and Leslee Oppenheim. David Crook, then dean of institutional research, joined us.

Given the short time frame, EVC Botman appointed Carol Kellerman, an experienced administrator with significant government and nonprofit executive experience, to be the program's interim director. Kellerman had assisted other organizations, including PENCIL (Public Education Needs Civic Involvement), where she served as interim president.

Although no community college program anywhere in the United States had results that came close to ASAP's goal of a 50% three-year graduation rate, there was extensive literature focused on college success. The planning team studied programs that had demonstrated meaningful results and decided that CUNY needed a comprehensive approach that would address the most common obstacles to college completion. We needed to make completing college a top priority for students and those who worked with them. After meeting for a few months, the planning team agreed on integral parts of the ASAP structure, attempting to sustain momentum toward the degree by addressing financial, academic, and logistical obstacles to degree completion:

Facilitating Degree Completion

- ASAP students would attend full time, taking a minimum of 12 credits per semester and be grouped in cohorts.
- A limited number of majors would be available.
- Participants would initially receive block schedules, enabling them to take all their classes in morning, afternoon, evening, or weekend sessions.
- ASAP students would be encouraged to enroll in summer and winter session courses.

Financial Support

- Any gap between financial aid and tuition would be waived.
- All participants would receive free NYC Transit Metrocards.
- Textbooks would be free.

Advisement and Academic Support

- Advising would be enhanced, with a much lower student-adviser ratio than typical. Advising would also be intrusive in that students would be required to attend regular advisement meetings, including a weekly seminar.
- ASAP students would have access to program-dedicated tutors.
- Participants would have access to career services, job referral, and placement.

Continuous Program Assessment

- ASAP itself would be evaluated rigorously from its outset.

Almost from the beginning, ASAP was criticized throughout CUNY. A number of CUNY community college presidents wondered why we needed a new program administered by the Central Office. They pushed the chancellor to give the dollars earmarked for ASAP directly to the campuses. They insisted that the reason for their low graduation rates was the lack of adequate fiscal resources; with this infusion of money, they argued, they would be able to significantly raise graduation rates. They also contended that to establish a new and separate program on campus would be divisive and unfair to all of the non-ASAP students who wouldn't be receiving extra services.

The chancellor responded forcefully to the criticism, indicating that we needed a pilot program with a different structure. It was critical, he insisted, for the presidents to publicly support the program. He expected them to manage criticism from their faculty and staff. By 2006, the chancellor had consolidated his power. While he was open to criticism and welcomed opposing viewpoints, once he made a major decision, the presidents were expected to go along. The presidents understood Goldstein's power. Going forward, the criticism of ASAP from the presidents almost totally disappeared, at least publicly.

Campus faculty and staff also voiced criticism of the program, expressing particular concern about the requirement that students must attend full time. They argued that the full-time requirement was a sign that the people creating the program did not understand who CUNY students were or the many obstacles they faced in attending college. Didn't we know that many community college students had to work to support themselves and their families, that others were receiving public assistance, and that most were poorly prepared academically for college level work? Far too many students, the naysayers reasoned, couldn't possibly attend full time.

We had answers to the criticism, based on our own extensive experience in administering programs for disadvantaged populations, on CUNY data, and also on the research we had done in the beginning stages of developing the ASAP program. We responded by asking two basic questions: Did the opponents know the graduation rates at their own colleges? Did they know what percent of first-time freshmen at CUNY's community colleges started full time? Few of the critical faculty and staff had any idea of the graduation rates at their own colleges; this data was rarely shared or discussed on campus. As for requiring full-time attendance, we pointed out that 87% of first-time freshmen at the community colleges enrolled full time, and it wasn't until the second semester and beyond that far too many of them either dropped out of school or became part-time students. The critics refused to believe the figures, even though they were straight from the CUNY Office of Institutional Research, based on campus data. The data also showed that students who didn't maintain full-time status for at least a substantial portion of their enrollment rarely graduated, or else took many years to do so.

Other criticisms of our model related to limiting the choice of majors available for ASAP, making the advising so intrusive, and placing the ASAP students in cohorts. Like the presidents, the faculty and staff criticized the special status and benefits that ASAP students would receive. They accused the ASAP planners of having a paternalistic attitude toward students, treating them as though they were still in high school and couldn't make their own decisions.

In fact, we did want to limit the number of decisions the most unprepared students entering CUNY had to manage. We believed that the advising was supportive, not intrusive. As for the special status of ASAP students, we agreed that was true: they would be treated differently. But if we could demonstrate that the pilot program led to a significant increase in graduation rates, we could then argue for additional funding that would provide extra benefits for other CUNY students as well. We needed to try something. We needed to start somewhere.

Ultimately, we went forward with the original plan. We made certain that the program would be evaluated carefully from its outset, and that the success of the program would be based on an honest look at the results. The criticism of the ASAP model did not disappear, but the chancellor and city officials gave ASAP their full support.

We began working with the campuses to set up their respective ASAP offices, each headed by an ASAP campus director. We also provided the campuses with their budget allocations for the program and asked them to begin hiring the campus ASAP staff. Finally, we began to publicize the program widely throughout the NYC Department of Education, community-based organizations, and the admissions offices at the community colleges. We hoped to recruit more than 1,000 students for the upcoming fall 2007 semester.

ASAP began enrolling students in the late spring of 2007. Each of the six ASAP colleges offered a summer orientation program to welcome students to campus, introduce them to faculty and staff, and provide a good understanding of the elements of the program. Students attending the orientation seemed excited to be part of a new program. As the opening of the fall semester approached, our initial enrollment targets were in sight. While we were hardly relaxed, we believed that the program would open on time, and that the model could be successful.

In September 2007, ASAP officially began with an enrollment of 1,132 students, slightly above our target. All six CUNY community colleges had ASAP programs. With a graduation goal of 50%, a figure that seemed almost impossible to meet, we made a decision that would increase our chances of hitting that goal. All students accepted into the first cohort were fully skills-proficient and did not have any remedial needs. Yes, for this first cohort, we cherry-picked students more likely to succeed. But even for incoming first-year students who were skills proficient, and therefore needed no remediation, our goal of a 50% graduation rate was still double their normal rate. We were comfortable with the decision.

An important milestone for the program was the hiring of a new ASAP Director. Carol Kellerman had made it clear that she would help us start the program but would then move on. A second interim director stayed only a short time. By late 2008, I turned to one of my own SUD staff, Donna Linderman, to lead the program. Donna had worked in our K–16 unit for the previous six years in leadership positions and had been increasingly recognized as one of our future stars. Hiring Donna to lead ASAP was one of my best decisions. ASAP was perhaps our most high-profile program, and Donna provided strong leadership as it continued to expand, while also representing the program compellingly to external audiences. She was an exceptional administrator, both tenacious and creative. She was an excellent writer, who also understood budget, data, and the need for evaluation. As ASAP's permanent director, Donna administered the program with skill and care.

The results for the first cohort of ASAP were extraordinary. In 2010, three years after they enrolled, this first-year cohort of ASAP students achieved a graduation rate of 55%. A comparison group, also consisting of non-remedial students, had a graduation rate of only 24%, which was typical in the pre-ASAP past. Even more surprising was that this first ASAP cohort had a two-year graduation rate of 32.9%, almost three times the comparison group rate of 11.4%. Although a two-year rate was not one of our goals, it was an amazing accomplishment. ASAP's Success was celebrated at a special recognition ceremony hosted by Mayor Bloomberg and Chancellor Goldstein for ASAP students, faculty, and staff in June 2010.

These results were the catalyst for a major expansion of the ASAP program. In October of 2011, Chancellor Goldstein announced that over the next three years the program would grow, enrolling more than 4,000 students by the fall of 2014. That expansion would be made possible by new state funding together with private funds from the Leona M. and Harry B. Helmsley Charitable Trust, the Jewish Foundation for the Education of Women, the Robin Hood Foundation, the Stella and Charles Guttman Foundation, and the Gilbert Family Trust. In the fall of 2014, ASAP enrolled 4,352 students.

Understanding the importance of evaluating ASAP as it grew, in 2010 CUNY entered an agreement with MDRC, a highly regarded research and evaluation organization. MDRC designed a random assignment study to evaluate ASAP, relying on funds from the Robin Hood Foundation and the Helmsley Charitable Trust.

In the summer of 2013, a few months before the mayoral election, Matthew Goldstein retired as CUNY's chancellor. This was momentous for the university. Matthew and CUNY Board Chair Benno Schmidt had reversed the university's course. The formerly "adrift "institution was now financially more stable and academically sounder and more respected. CUNY was, nevertheless, still subject to political forces and the sudden reversals they could bring. Goldstein's departure was also momentous for me, of course. I had depended upon his admiration for our programs and his steadfast support. Bill Kelly, the President of the CUNY Graduate Center, became interim CUNY chancellor. I knew Bill well and had confidence in his leadership.

ASAP had more than fulfilled the chancellor's promise to Mayor Bloomberg. But as the Bloomberg administration approached the end of its third and final term in the fall of 2013, we worried that the strong support would wane under a new mayor. ASAP was Mayor Bloomberg's program, and new mayors often prefer to spend money on their own initiatives rather than those of their predecessors. We felt we would be fortunate simply to maintain the funding level from the city.

Having gone through a number of mayoral transitions during my time at CUNY Central, I had observed up close how the university tried to position itself to impress new mayors with the importance of fiscal support for CUNY. That process included putting together a kind of laundry list of programs—some new, others already in place—that deserved funding and were consistent with the new mayor's agenda. Putting together that list was an inclusive process that involved most members of the chancellor's cabinet. As an integral part of that process, I made sure that ASAP expansion was included on the list. Given its early success, I tried to remain hopeful that even as a Bloomberg program, it would be considered for some new funding.

The new mayor, Bill de Blasio, was well known to CUNY leaders. Prior to taking office in January 2014, he had served as the city's public advocate and as a member of the City Council from 2002–2009. He believed in the importance of CUNY to the city and in the value of public higher education. The university leadership was hopeful that he would respond favorably to some of our requests for funding.

Once we submitted the list of funding requests to City Hall, I returned to my daily work. I had been through this process before. It usually took a long time to hear back from the city. When we did eventually hear, we would then enter a protracted period of negotiations about which programs would be funded and the timeframe for money to be received.

Not many weeks later, however, I was surprised to be called to the chancellor's office to discuss the funding request to the new mayor. That meeting included only Interim Chancellor Bill Kelly, Vice Chancellor Jay Hershenson, and Executive Vice Chancellors Allan Dobrin and Lexa Logue.

Bill and I had become good colleagues. As I entered the room, I looked at his face and could tell that something important was about to be announced. Bill quickly got to the business at hand. He said that of all the program requests CUNY had made, the city was interested in funding only one: ASAP. He then delivered the bombshell: The program would receive an additional $77 million to expand from 4,000 students to 25,000 students. The chancellor also indicated that, assuming that the expansion was successful, the dollars would be added to CUNY's operating budget. I was ecstatic. I understood the challenges ahead, but the idea of scaling up a relatively small pilot program was amazing. If our outcomes remained the same, tens of thousands of CUNY students would graduate sooner and at far larger numbers.

I always wondered who had made the decision at City Hall to expand ASAP. In July of 2022, I had an opportunity to ask former mayor Bill de Blasio directly, one neighbor to another. Although we did not know one another, we both were long-time residents of Park Slope. I had just parked my car after returning from a morning tennis game. The city was in the midst of a horrible heat wave, with the morning temperature already close to 90 and the humidity really high. I was dripping sweat, having foolishly played 90 minutes of singles in the heat. As I slowly walked up 6th Avenue approaching 10th street, the former mayor was walking toward me from the opposite direction. Despite my disheveled look, I said, "Good morning, Mr. Mayor." He paused, and I thanked him for the decision he had made at the beginning of his first term to support the huge expansion of ASAP. I told him I had wondered for years how that decision had come about. Did he remember? Why had he decided not to fund any of CUNY's list of proposed programs except ASAP? How had he settled on $77 million and 25,000 students?

The mayor immediately became engaged, telling me that he of course had known about ASAP and its incredible success. He explained that while his own top funding priority had been more money for the Department of Education, two of his top deputies (First Deputy Mayor Tony Shorris and Dean Fuleihan, the director of the Mayor's Office of Management and Budget), were strong supporters of CUNY. Knowing about the success of ASAP, they argued for the expansion. De Blasio then shook my sweaty hand and thanked me for the success of the program. I finally knew how and why ASAP had received this incredible allocation of dollars.

Not surprisingly, that 2014 decision of de Blasio's had not been universally applauded at CUNY. Soon after the announcement of the ASAP expansion, Interim Chancellor Bill Kelly called a meeting with the community college presidents to get their reaction. As the president of the Graduate Center, the chancellor knew his colleagues well. He also understood the presidents' belief that the chancellor and Central Office had too much authority and power, a feeling he shared in some measure.

The meeting did not go well. The presidents were unhappy that no other programs were funded and that the city had added no money to the community college budgets. True, ASAP money would be coming to their campuses, but it was dollars they could not control. They also complained that ASAP got all of the attention outside of the university while other successful community college programs were overlooked. They were unhappy that ASAP was administered from the Central Office and was situated in the SUD office. They claimed Donna Linderman and I made decisions arbitrarily and had far too much power. They felt that ASAP, now seven years old, should be run by the colleges with little or no interference from our team. A few of the presidents were pretty strident about their criticism.

The chancellor tried to respond calmly to the complaints, emphasizing ASAP's amazing results and the impact on students. When he saw that his comments did not change the tone of the conversation, he decided to simply end the meeting. He met with me afterward and expressed exasperation at the tone of the meeting and what he felt were many unfair criticisms of the program. The expansion would move forward as planned, he assured me, and with his full support.

With new funding dramatically increasing the size of the program, the ASAP Central Office team and our campus partners opened new programs at New York City College of Technology, Medgar Evers College, and the College of Staten Island in their associate degree programs. At CUNY, those three colleges, which offer both associate and baccalaureate degrees, are known as comprehensive colleges.

New campus staff were hired, including a large number of advising staff. The Central Office ASAP team also took on significant program-wide responsibilities to support the expansion, including citywide outreach and marketing, a robust data management system to document student contact and outcomes, training and professional development for all staff, and a year-long collaborative process with college ASAP staff to refine the advisement model. It was apparent from our student surveys that lower advisor to student ratios and more individual attention given to students were exceedingly popular with ASAP students. Campuses also came to realize that as the ASAP population grew, the caseloads of the regular campus advisors decreased, making them more readily available to non-ASAP students.

From a student population of 4,352 enrolled in ASAP in the 2014–15 academic year, the program grew to 8,016 in 2015–16, 15,473 students in 2016–17 and to 25,477 in 2018–19 We reached our target in four years. By the fall 2018 semester ASAP was enrolling approximately 32% of all full-time students in CUNY's associate degree programs and 24% of our overall enrollment, including part-time students. By the end of the fall 2022 semester, ASAP had served more than 88,000 students since its outset. We also were proud of the fact that after the first year of the program, we enrolled students who had one or two remedial needs, and those students also met our graduation target.

One concern expressed about ASAP was its cost. In 2007, when ASAP began, the program cost almost $6,000 per student. But as the program grew, the cost per student decreased. By 2019–20, the cost had decreased to $3,440 per student. Counterbalancing the cost, however, there were also substantial benefits. According to a 2013 cost-benefit study led by Dr. Henry Levin of the Center for Benefit-Cost Studies in Education at Columbia University's Teachers College, public money spent on ASAP "had large financial returns for both the taxpayer and the ASAP student. For every dollar invested in ASAP by the taxpayer, $3.50 are returned per associate degree in increased tax revenues and social service savings, and for each dollar invested in ASAP students, $12.20 are returned through increased earnings." Dr. Levin and his team concluded that "the total net benefit for 1,000 enrolled ASAP students is $46.5 million higher than for 1,000 comparison group students who do not enroll in the program."[1]

The MDRC study results, published in 2015, were equally positive. The random assignment study concluded that "ASAP's effects are the largest MDRC has found in any of its evaluation of community college reforms." More specifically, the MDRC study found that over the first three years of the program, "47% of ASAP students with developmental needs and 56% of fully skills-proficient ASAP students have graduated vs. 19% of non-ASAP students with developmental needs and 28% of fully skills-proficient non-ASAP students."[2] The study also showed that "students from underrepresented groups appear to show more benefit from ASAP than other students." Perhaps most importantly, the study found that ASAP students graduated at more than double the rates of non-ASAP students. The program continued to assess graduation rates; an internal CUNY evaluation found that across the first 11 cohorts of ASAP students, the three-year graduation rate was 52%, more than double the 24.6% for a matched comparison group.

As the results became public, ASAP attracted the attention of other states and community colleges across the country. The essence of ASAP was captured in an article written by Ann Hulbert in the January/February2014 issue of *The Atlantic*, six years after ASAP had enrolled its first student cohort. She wrote:

> The secret of ASAP's success lies outside the classroom. The program enlists extra tutors and caps some classes at 25 students, but otherwise doesn't touch pedagogy. Instead, it aims to counter the community college culture of early exits and erratic stops and starts. ASAP is designed to instill, and make it possible to fulfill, the expectation that college will be a continuous, full-time commitment, just as it is for traditional four-year students on leafy campuses.

Hulbert went on to conclude: "The implicit philosophy behind the program is simple: students, especially the least prepared ones, don't just need to learn math or science; they need to learn how to navigate academic and institutional challenges more broadly, and how to plot a course—daily, weekly, monthly—toward long-term success."[3]

Articles on ASAP appeared in *Inside Higher Ed* (March 19, 2019), and in other higher education publications. Senior education officials in the Obama administration reached out to learn more about the program. Donna Linderman began to be invited to speak at national conferences and forums and was asked to meet with state government and community college officials across the country to discuss how ASAP could be replicated. Community colleges in five states (California, New York, West Virginia, Tennessee, and Ohio) began replication projects. By 2021, ASAP was being replicated at 14 colleges in seven states. In 2020 ASAP won the Innovations in American Government Award from the Ash Center for Democratic Governance and Innovation at Harvard University's John F. Kennedy School of Government.

ASAP, perhaps the most successful community college initiative in the United States, continues to achieve exceptional results. Unlike most higher education programs that start as small pilots, it has grown to an unprecedented scale. It also changed the prevailing view of what was possible for community college graduation rates. ASAP became fully accepted as one of the jewels of the CUNY system, still administered out of the Central Office but continuing to work closely with each of its campus partners.

At CUNY the ASAP model led to one more experimental program. The CUNY Accelerate, Complete, and Engage (ACE) program modeled after ASAP, was designed to improve the four-year baccalaureate graduation rates at CUNY's senior colleges. With the support of the Robin Hood Foundation, the Mayor's Office of Economic Opportunity, and the Jewish Foundation for the Education of Women, ACE was launched in 2015 at CUNY's John Jay College of Criminal Justice. By 2019, the four-year graduation rate for the program's first cohort was 17 percentage points higher than the comparison group (59% to 42%). Since then, similar programs have been started at Lehman College, the College of Staten Island, New York City College of Technology, York College, Queens College, and City College, bringing enrollment in ACE to more than 2,800 students. We have learned that adapting many of the same elements that lead to success for community college students has the potential to significantly increase the four-year graduation rates at CUNY's senior colleges.

There is much to learn from the success of ASAP. Foremost, perhaps, is that senior leaders need to admit it when there is a problem. In this case, low graduation rates had long been considered inevitable and therefore not needing to be addressed, or at least not in an urgent way. Having acknowledged the problem, leaders need to address it with new thinking and bold action. For big problems, simply tinkering with programs is not enough.

- Leaders need to communicate to the university/college community why there is a need to make changes. This should include sharing data to assist in making the case that change is necessary.
- Get Board of Trustee support as one of your first priorities.
- Try to secure new funding for the project from either public or private sources. To achieve this, become familiar with the agendas of potential funders and show them how your project fits their priorities and will reward their investment. Securing new funding will also demonstrate internally that you will not be using regular operating funds and thereby decreasing an already underfunded campus.
- While it is important to offer faculty and staff an opportunity to participate in the planning process that will lead to change, it is even more important to avoid stalling; keep moving forward despite the predictable opposition from those who resist change.
- Find among your institution's faculty, administrators and staff those who believe that the change is necessary. Empower them to join with others in building new models. In selecting those to lead the process, make sure you include the best thinkers, together with those who also know how to implement.
- Set high but achievable outcome measures and measure the results with serious research from the outset of the project. Use results to show where changes to the program are needed, as well as to demonstrate success.
- Be prepared to respond publicly to unfair criticism and to protect and defend faculty and staff who are attacked.
- Focus on keeping student success at the center of all discussions about the need for a new program. For example, for ASAP, those of us leading the initiative continually pointed out the horrifyingly low CUNY community college graduation rates, particularly for students of color, as the main reason new thinking was imperative.

ASAP, which began in 2007, continues to receive national recognition. In the spring of 2023, the PBS "NewsHour" featured one of the ASAP replication colleges, Cincinnati State Technical and Community College. The three-year graduation rates for students in the program, called C-State Accelerate, almost doubled. Noting that the success of ASAP is not new, the segment included clips from a 2016 PBS "NewsHour" story on ASAP. The reporter for the recent segment wondered why more colleges are not replicating ASAP.[4]

In addition, *Inside Higher Ed* highlighted ASAP in a 2023 article entitled "Scaling the Secret Sauce for Completion Rates," by Sarah Weissman. The article discusses the success of the replication efforts, now at 14 colleges in seven states. Weissman reports that "some ASAP proponents have called for Congress to consider funding these programs nationally."[5]

In September 2023, John King, chancellor of the State University of New York system, announced that SUNY will replicate ASAP and ACE at 25 campuses across the state. A *New York Times* article about King's announcement quotes Donna Linderman, now senior vice chancellor for student success at SUNY: "Students feel that someone has their back, that there's this comprehensive set of resources around them that are very thoughtfully put together. There's always someone there who is thinking about what could be a challenge for you."[6]

Finally, in a welcome bit of irony, the July 2023 edition of the *Clarion*, the CUNY Professional Staff Congress newspaper, quotes members of the PSC on the value of ASAP and the need to maintain its present level of city funding. The headline reads, "Protecting a Vital Resource for Students."[7] I was genuinely pleased to learn of the union's strong support for ASAP, but the article also recalled for me the early years of the program, when some of these same faculty members so strenuously opposed it.

CHAPTER 21

Building CUNY's First New Community College in 40 Years

> The individual in charge of this, the same individual who is running the new community college, is on a roll. He's highly regarded by the administration at 80th street. He brings in a lot of money, and after 25 years of knowing him I'm perfectly willing to say in the public record he has less respect for academic integrity than anybody I know in that office. Anything that sells and brings in a buck is fine. (Comment about me by Sandi E. Cooper, at the February 2, 2010 Faculty Senate Plenary session. Cooper, a professor of history at the CUNY College of Staten Island, was the former chair of the Faculty Senate, having served in that position from 1994–1998).

IN THE FALL OF 2007, I MET WITH CHANCELLOR GOLDSTEIN TO let him know about a plan to submit a proposal to the Robin Hood Foundation requesting funds to pilot what we were calling the CUNY Community Academy. We envisioned the pilot as a project at a community college that would reimagine the first year of study. I had spoken to Deborah McCoy, a program officer at Robin Hood who supported our work, and was confident that the Foundation would fund the pilot. As I began to explain the scope of the project, the chancellor interrupted, saying, "I am not really interested in this kind of pilot program." Before I could begin to argue with him, he went on to say that rather than a pilot project, he was interested in creating a new community college and that I should let the foundation know of his ambition. He wanted the plan for the new college to be bold, imaginative, and different. He wondered out loud whether a community college structured differently might address the persistent challenges of improving graduation rates. He said that it would be the first new CUNY college to open in almost 40 years. He asked me to lead this effort and put together a team to begin the planning process.

Once again, the chancellor had shocked and surprised me. After all, just a month or so earlier, we had begun the first student cohort of our ASAP program, which seemed to have the same goal of increasing community college graduation rates. Why now a new community college? Thinking about the magnitude of such a project, I worried whether our unit had the bandwidth to take it on. I also realized that the idea of a new college would certainly face fierce internal criticism, perhaps even greater than the opposition to CUNY SPS and ASAP. At the same time, the chancellor's idea was visionary and courageous. This new college wouldn't duplicate ASAP, but rather would constitute a second and different experiment. Unlike ASAP, which was non-instructional, the new community college would reimagine the students' academic experience. I assured Chancellor Goldstein that I would be pleased to lead the project and thanked him for the opportunity.

Creating a college is a huge undertaking, involving not only building all of the structures and systems required, but also securing approvals from trustees, the New York State Education Department, and Middle States, the accrediting body. Beyond all that, creating this college would go far beyond following a template if it was to meet the chancellor's charge to "reimagine" community college while at the same time meeting the requirements for approval.

The first challenge was to select a project leader and put together a planning team. Executive Vice Chancellor Selma Botman, John Garvey, and I agreed to ask Tracy Meade to head the project. Tracy oversaw our work with the New York City Public Schools as the university director for collaborative programs. She combined all of the characteristics that we felt were needed to lead a project of this importance and magnitude. She was tough and tenacious, unafraid of conflict, and firmly committed to providing new opportunities for students. Prior to coming to CUNY, she had been a faculty member at a Midwestern community college. As the director of collaborative programs, Tracy administered many of our high school-to-college transition programs and had overseen the successful restructuring and expansion of College Now. The low community college graduation rates, particularly for students of color, deeply distressed her. She believed that only by challenging the status quo could we increase graduation rates. She had a sound knowledge of teaching and learning, was an exceptional writer, and was one of the best idea persons in our unit. Tracy was familiar with many of the national figures doing the most interesting community college work and would not be shy in reaching out to them for advice and assistance. Finally, Tracy was dedicated to achieving social justice and willing to address inequity, the kind of person who would reach out to someone being harassed or threatened in the subway or a city street.

Tracy readily accepted our offer to lead the project. She understood its importance and was confident that she had the skill, focus, and leadership qualities to build a different kind of college. She also liked challenges, making her perfect for this role. As it happened, the three-year planning process would face many challenges and obstacles and would prove to be even more complicated than we originally imagined. We were fortunate to have Tracy in charge.

In February 2008, Executive Vice Chancellor Selma Botman sent an email to all CUNY college presidents announcing that CUNY would be "developing a blueprint" to establish a new community college. The email also announced that the chancellor had asked me to oversee the planning phase of the project, which would be led by Tracy Meade, and that in the near future we would create a planning team of interested CUNY faculty and staff. The email further stated that "we expect to have a fully developed community college model for review by the chancellor by June 1, 2008." Vice Chancellor Botman concluded: "This is a wonderful and rare opportunity to build a new model for associate degree study from the ground up. As we move ahead, we will welcome and solicit your input."[1]

This was hardly the first time that we were given a project deadline date that seemed almost impossible to meet, but a five-month time frame for such an ambitious undertaking was perhaps the greatest challenge my colleagues and I had ever faced. The work needed to start immediately and be non-stop.

Selecting members of the planning team was the next step. Seeking members with diverse backgrounds and experience, we included a number of staff from our unit together with representatives from other units in the Central Office, CUNY campuses, and the New York City Department of Education, as well as two outside consultants who were former senior officials at CUNY. A steering committee was established to oversee the planning process. Tracy and I were part of that group, along with two CUNY community college presidents, a campus provost, and virtually all of the CUNY vice chancellors.

The work of the planning team, though exhaustive and inclusive, began by "seeking to answer a simple question: In light of what we know today about community college education, what would we do differently if given the opportunity to create a new institution?" Team members took the question to faculty, staff, and administrators across the system's community colleges. The responses were candid, identifying daily challenges and offering suggestions to improve the effectiveness of community colleges and increase the number of graduating students. In total, meetings were held with 75 CUNY faculty, staff, and administrators along with a similar number of outside experts throughout the United States. Having so many faculty members involved in the planning process was gratifying. It countered the intense criticism we received from many faculty governance and union leaders, and other faculty. It was much more difficult for them to complain that the planning process was not inclusive or interested in faculty input.

In addition to the many meetings that the planning committee members held, Executive Vice Chancellor Botman invited the entire university community to respond to a survey on the idea of creating a new community college at CUNY. Of the 156 respondents to the survey, 55% were CUNY faculty.

At Tracy's suggestion, we created an advisory board of prominent educators from across the country. Almost everyone we asked to join this committee said yes. Throughout the planning process, they offered advice, criticism, and encouragement. Among the 11 members of the advisory board were Randy Bass, Georgetown University; Norton Grubb, Graduate School of Education, University of California Berkeley; Tom Bailey, founder and director of the Community College Research Center at Teachers College, Columbia University; Nancy Hoffman, Jobs for the Future; Bob Hughes, New Visions for Public Schools; Marcia Lyles, deputy chancellor for teaching and learning at the NYC Department of Education; Melissa Roderick, co-director at the Consortium on Chicago School Research; and Ronald Williams, vice president of the College Board and former president of Prince George's Community College. Having an advisory board with such noted educators not only provided us with ongoing feedback, but also gave us a degree of credibility to counter the criticism we received.

Almost from the beginning, supported with funds from the Bill and Melinda Gates Foundation, a team of documentarians—Alexandra "Sandy" Weinbaum, Camille Rodriguez, and Nan Bauer-Maglin—worked to create a record of the development of the New Community College. Their report, "Rethinking Community College for the 21st Century," recounts the process, analyzes the model, and outlines issues for consideration.[2]

Six months later, in July 2008, we delivered to the chancellor a comprehensive concept paper simply titled "A New Community College."[3] The paper was not an implementation document. Instead, it outlined the most prominent features of the new college. It was written almost entirely by Tracy, who tried to incorporate much of what we had learned over the past months in our many meetings and conversations. I recall giving the chancellor the document at the end of the work week, hoping for a quick and positive response, with a go-ahead to move forward. His response was quicker than I had imagined. He called over the weekend, a day after he received the concept paper. He loved it, finding it innovative, bold, and beautifully written. He seemed exhilarated. We talked about the next phase of the development process, during which we would share the document with the university community. That process would start in September, the start of the Fall 2008 semester.

The concept paper described key features of the new college. All of these elements would be organized around the theme of "creating and sustaining a thriving New York City":

- A mandatory pre-college component would include an interview as part of the application process to ensure that students had a good understanding of expectations and college requirements; assistance for students to complete their financial aid forms (Federal FAFSA and NYS TAP applications); and a summer college bridge program to introduce students to the college.
- For at least the first year, full-time enrollment would be required.
- A common first-year core curriculum would eliminate traditional remediation, replacing it with a City Seminar, a Math Topics and Quantitative Reasoning Course, and a Professional Studies Course. These courses would all require intensive reading, writing, and math, with extensive hours provided.
- The number of majors would be limited to six or seven to start.
- A Center for College Effectiveness would provide data and assist college staff and faculty in assessing their work.
- An Office of Partnerships would develop internships and other hands-on opportunities to connect students and faculty academic work to the life of the city.
- Academic affairs and student services would be closely linked to create an integrated network of student support.
- The initial class would number approximately 1,000 students.
- Learning communities would be established, with all first-year students assigned to a house.

In phase two of the project, we shared the concept paper throughout the university while creating teams to participate in actually building the college. To fill the teams, the university sent out a notice to the CUNY community asking for faculty and staff to participate. Three hundred faculty and staff responded. We selected 119 of them to join 11 working committees to address college admissions, governance, hiring of staff and faculty, library and technology, selection and building of majors, student services, the first-year experience, facilities and budget, and other topics. We also needed to begin developing the extensive documents required to bring the proposal to the CUNY Board of Trustees, the body responsible for approving the new college, and to the New York State Education Department, requesting that the college receive accreditation.

We were overjoyed at the positive response from so many faculty and staff throughout CUNY who wished to be part of the development process. At the same time, we began to receive significant criticism from leaders of the Faculty Senate and the Professional Staff Congress, the faculty and staff union.

Tracy and I held public forums at each of the six CUNY community colleges to review the concept paper, answer questions, and listen to comments. Forums were open to all faculty and staff. They were generally well attended, ranging from around 50 people at Hostos Community College to more than 200 at the Borough of Manhattan Community College. In total we spoke to more than 500 people, the majority being faculty.

I began each forum by providing a brief summary of the project and then moving to answer questions and listen to comments. The forums were largely civil, although attendees at the BMCC forum expressed a lot of hostility toward Tracy and me. They questioned our lack of faculty credentials to lead such a project and criticized what they regarded as our failure to understand the concept of shared governance and the importance of the faculty role. A number of faculty also contended that we didn't comprehend the many obstacles that community college students face, and that so many students were poor and of color. Some critics accused us of trying to corporatize the university and create programs that were totally vocational. Almost all the forums drew questions about whether a new college would negatively affect their own college budgets and whether we would have tenure-track faculty. Would we require full-time study? What would eliminating remedial classes mean? We were accused of recreating high school for students by having a mandatory set of courses/curriculum for all first-year students and by mandating counseling sessions. One or two participants asked whether it was ethical to enroll students in an untried experiment.

In answering the questions and responding to the personal attacks, I tried to remain calm and respectful. I had learned over many years that when criticism becomes loud and hostile, whether in small or large meetings, it is better to lower your voice while still responding forcefully to false accusations. At the BMCC forum I tried mightily to follow my own advice, but at times I felt a need to show some emotion in my responses.

At every forum, as I had when I presented ASAP, I asked whether the participants had read the concept paper. Some had, but most indicated they had not. I urged them to do so. I also asked whether they knew the graduation rates at their college. At every campus, almost none of the faculty and staff in attendance knew the rates, nor had they been engaged in conversation about how to increase them. I pointed out the overall three-year graduation rate for CUNY associate degree students was a little over 11% at the time. Even the six-year rate for the entering class of fall 2002 was only 24.6%. Those figures were provided by the CUNY Office of Institutional Research. There was always some surprise. More often the response was that Tracy and I did not understand that so many of CUNY's community college students were both economically and educationally disadvantaged, and that was the major reason for students not graduating. I had to wonder if some faculty thought we were attacking their competence and effectiveness.

To the questions about faculty status, I replied that there would be tenure-track faculty at the college and that searches for the first group of faculty would start soon. The question of governance was more difficult. A working committee was addressing governance, I explained. While I promised that the new college's governance structure wouldn't violate university rules and policies, it might be different from the traditional structure at the other community colleges.

Regarding mandatory full-time enrollment, I pointed out that 87%

of CUNY Community College students start full time, but then many move to part-time status in later years for a variety of reasons, ranging from course availability to time constraints and personal issues. I also indicated that there were six other CUNY community colleges that enrolled part-time students, and that students could choose to go to one of them if they needed to attend part-time. I emphasized, that the longer it takes for students to graduate, the less chance there is that they will get to the finish line.

In response to the more personal attacks and the accusations that I was going to corporatize the university or didn't understand the CUNY student population, I said that if they knew anything about my background and my 35 years at CUNY, they would be aware that those accusations were unfair and untrue. I thought it was important to push back on false accusations and assumptions. I needed to defend myself swiftly without being defensive or offensive, and then move on.

Actually, I enjoyed most of the campus forums and tried to duck under the criticism. In some ways it was good preparation for the far more intense criticism to come from the PSC and Faculty Senate leaders as the planning for the college continued. In February of 2009, PSC President Barbara Bowen sent a letter to Chancellor Goldstein outlining her long list of concerns regarding the concept paper. She also objected to the "University's failure to include the University-wide PSC leadership in the discussions that led to its development."[4] The chancellor responded immediately, promising that as the planning process moved forward, if "some aspects of the developing plan impact the terms and conditions of employment of our faculty and staff, we will work closely with the PSC to discuss those matters, and if it seems advisable, to set up a committee for that purpose." [5]

In October 2009, Bowen sent a letter to all Professional Staff Congress members. The letter began: "I am writing to update you on what could turn out to be one of the most important issues before us this year: CUNY's fast-moving plan for a new, vocationally oriented community college." She went on to voice approval of the idea of re-imagining community college education and building a new college, but then indicated that this project was "An Opportunity Lost." She stated that "with its limited, largely vocational curriculum and mechanical focus on graduation rates, it risks being a contraction, rather than an expansion, of CUNY's educational vision. It also raises troubling issues about faculty autonomy, shared governance, and adherence to the union contract." She listed five specific criticisms:

1. There is no commitment to tenured faculty or academic departments.
2. The college offers largely vocational education.
3. The college is driven by graduation rates, which is a flawed and inadequate way to measure student success.
4. The college, as currently conceived, violates several contractual protections.
5. The college could obscure the need for increased funding for the existing CUNY community colleges.[6]

Soon after the chancellor received Bowen's letter, I reviewed it with him. He asked me to draft a strong response. In early November, my response to Bowen was sent to the entire CUNY community through eNEWS, the regular newsletter sent out by the Central Office. This was one more time that Chancellor Goldstein had protected me and shown a willingness not only to ignore criticism, but to respond strongly if he believed the criticism was inaccurate and unfair.

I began my response by stating that I was "writing to correct several significant inaccuracies in an October 22, 2009 letter President Barbara Bowen sent to Professional Staff Congress members on the subject of CUNY's proposal for a new community college." I then challenged each of her five specific criticisms. Regarding tenured faculty, I pointed out that at every forum and public meeting I had indicated that the new college would hire tenure track faculty. As for offering largely vocational education I stressed the conscious decision to open the college with a limited number of majors and that majors such as business, IT, urban studies, liberal arts, human services, and environmental sciences are hardly thought of as vocational, and in fact similar majors exist throughout CUNY. I also indicated that the chancellor and I had both promised that the new college would comply with the existing collective bargaining agreement, and that the new college would not have an impact on the budgets of the other CUNY community colleges. Finally, I didn't shy away from the importance of having graduation rates as a key performance measure, while adding that a "comprehensive array of performance measures and data are being planned for the new college." I concluded by once again speaking to the inclusive nature of the planning process and asking for the cooperation of the PSC leadership as the project moved forward.[7]

In addition to the criticism from the PSC, the CUNY Faculty Senate raised concerns. That was hardly surprising, since a few years earlier the leaders of the Senate had been strong critics of the School of Professional Studies. Some of them had been harsh critics of my leadership. The fact that I was asked to lead the team building the new community college did not sit well with many of the former leaders of the Senate. That last point was brought home to me from a tennis player friend, Don Hume, who was a faculty member and Faculty Senate delegate at CUNY's Kingsborough Community College. One day, on the way to the courts, Don let me know that the previous day he had attended a University Faculty Senate delegate meeting where a major topic of conversation was the new community college and my role. He laughed as he described the harsh words expressed about me as "extreme" and even "venomous." He pointedly kidded me, saying, "This monster is not the John I know." Almost 15 years later, we still play tennis. Don is now a department chair at Kingsborough, and every once in a while, he brings up the hostility aimed at me. We laugh together.

Despite the criticism, throughout the planning process we met many times with Faculty Senate leadership. Those meetings were generally civil although there was always some degree of criticism and personal attack. We involved Senate leaders directly in the planning process, and the chair of the Faculty Senate and two other UFS leaders joined the project's steering committee.

In contrast to the sharp criticism by the Faculty Senate and PSC leadership, we were receiving recognition and praise both from inside and outside of CUNY for trying to build a new, innovative community college. Perhaps the most glowing response to the concept paper came from Gail Mellow, president of LaGuardia Community College, one of CUNY's largest and most diverse institutions. Gail was one of CUNY's more prominent presidents. She had a national reputation and was a strong advocate for community colleges and their students. She was often invited to speak at national forums on community college education. Gail had been a reluctant supporter of ASAP and quietly critical when ASAP was first proposed, so I wasn't sure how she would react to the idea of a new community college. We had asked her and Regina Peruggi, the president of Kingsborough Community College, to be members of the project's steering committee. They agreed. Both Regina and Gail participated actively in committee meetings, sharing valuable insight into how community colleges function and the challenges they face.

A week after the concept paper was released, I received a letter from Gail that began: "The concept paper for the New Community College is nothing short of brilliant. You have succeeded in proposing something that is profoundly revolutionary, and as such, holds great promise for success. If enacted, this groundbreaking initiative would propel CUNY to become the national epicenter for educational innovation in community colleges. The concept paper is an extraordinary piece of work, sure to be heralded by the best minds in the business when you bring it to a more public audience." The letter ended, "In general, this is CUNY at its best—forward thinking, urban-centered, visionary, and radical in the sense of challenging fundamental structures." [8]

The concept paper also received praise, as well as many helpful suggestions, from most members of the outside advisory committee. The fact that so many CUNY faculty had volunteered to join the various committees planning the college was also reassuring.

Major higher ed publications began to give attention to the project. In 2009, *Inside Higher Ed* published two articles on the college, one in February entitled "Shaking Up the Community College Concept" and one in December called "The Great Community College Experiment."[9]

The Chronicle of Higher Education had an article in its April 18, 2010 issue, "City U. of New York Plans a Grand Experiment: A New College."[10] The articles, which included quotes from me, the chancellor, Tracy Meade, Gail Mellow and other educational leaders, were complimentary, stressing the innovative nature of the college. The *Chronicle* article ended with the following paragraph: "New York, of course, is a city of big ideas—and big risks. Mr. Goldstein's bet is that the new college will pay off big. He could be right. But even he can't take all the uncertainty out of that gamble."

Those of us planning the college understood the risks. We did a lot of worrying, which at times resulted in heated discussions, often between Tracy and me. We also understood that there still was much work to do and tried not to let disagreements get in the way of moving forward.

We had hoped to open the college in the summer of 2011. Given the huge volume of work that was ahead and the need to get State Education Department accreditation, we moved the formal opening of the college to the summer of 2012. We called it simply the New Community College (NCC).

In 2009–2010, we were fortunate to receive planning grants from the Bill and Melinda Gates Foundation and the Carnegie Corporation. In addition, Mayor Bloomberg's Gateway to the Middle Class plan specifically endorsed CUNY's effort to build a new model for community college education. These grants and the mayor's support enabled us to hire new planning team members and begin a formal process to recruit and hire the first college faculty and staff. We also began a search for a college president.

A broad outreach campaign resulted in almost 1,100 applications for the first eight faculty positions. These positions were to be full-time, tenure-track lines, demonstrating to the PSC and Faculty Senate leaders that what we said was true. Search committees were quickly established; interviews for the positions began in May of 2010 and continued throughout the summer. By the fall, eight faculty had been forwarded for hiring.

The actual hiring of faculty was complicated since at the time of the hiring, there was no official New Community College. Nor would there be until the Board of Trustees, the State Education Department, and governor approved its founding. In the meantime, we had to figure out what institution the new faculty would be affiliated with. Lexa Logue, by then the executive vice chancellor for academic affairs, provided a solution. The new faculty would be initially appointed to positions at three of our existing community colleges (Kingsborough, LaGuardia, and BMCC), where they would teach one course and be released from further teaching and other campus responsibilities to work on "planning NCC curriculum and participating in other aspects of institution-building." [11]

That process for bringing the new faculty on board required the support of the three campus presidents and provosts, as well as the approval of the respective college departments. We were pleasantly surprised when these appointments moved forward quickly with the support of the campus department chairs and campus governance. By the end of the fall 2010 semester, the eight faculty members had begun work. A number of important staff positions were also filled, including the college registrar, admissions director, chief information officer, financial aid officer, and head of facilities.

Later in in 2010, Scott Evenbeck was appointed as the college's founding president. He had previously served as the founding dean of University College at Indiana University-Purdue University, Indianapolis (IUPUI) where he also was a professor of psychology. He had a national reputation as a creative educator and had been directly involved in designing and implementing an innovative first-year experience at IUPUI.

During 2010 the majors available to students when the college opened were determined. The initial plan had been to start with 12 majors. Given the lengthy process required to create majors and the amount of time spent on designing the first-year curriculum, the planners instead decided to start with six majors. There was simply not enough time to build more. But limiting the number of majors was also deliberate. From our review of the literature and consultation with national experts, we had come to believe that one factor hindering student success at community colleges was that at time of enrollment they were asked to select a major from a dizzying number of choices. That often led to poor decisions and the need to change majors at a later point, resulting in a loss of credits. The majors initially selected for the NCC were associate degrees in business administration, health information technology, human services, information technology, liberal arts and sciences, and urban studies.

With the opening of the college firmly set for the summer of 2012, the pace of the work increased. It seemed that every month a new milestone was reached. Perhaps most importantly, in February of 2011, the CUNY Board of Trustees voted to approve opening a new community college. Later in the year, an application for accreditation was submitted to the State Education Department. Stuart Cochran, who had worked in the SUD office before being reassigned to be Tracy's deputy, took the lead in drafting the application to the State Education Department. In September of 2011, the governor approved the founding of the college.

Through 2011, new faculty and staff were hired, including a provost and vice president for academic affairs, a group of peer mentors, student success advocates, college counselors, IT professionals, and other support staff. And the college got a home. It initially would be located in leased space on 40th Street in Manhattan, across from Bryant Park. This was a wonderful location, but the site had a maximum capacity of around 1,000 students. As the college grew, it would need a larger and more permanent space.

As 2012 began, we heightened outreach and prospective students began to apply. Like all CUNY community colleges, the NCC would be an open enrollment institution, but it had a provision to interview all students. The purpose of the mandatory interview was to ensure that the students fully understood the nature of the new college and its expectations. Interviewing was time consuming, but also exciting; it meant actually talking to real students. What had been four years in the making was really going to happen.

Meanwhile, there was an inevitable and significant shift in ownership of the project. As faculty came aboard and began to work together, issues of governance and faculty prerogative surfaced. Tracy and I had been immersed in the project for years. We had developed the concept paper and had been responsible for hiring staff. We hoped that the new faculty and staff would accept the new school model and our role in the development process. We soon recognized, however, that a few of the faculty had different views of the roles and prerogative of the Central Office planners. This proved hard for us to accept and led to a major disappointment at one of the planning meetings. We were talking with faculty about governance issues when one of the faculty, later joined by others, asked Tracy and me to leave the meeting. They said that it was inappropriate for us to be part of this conversation; the faculty had to talk among themselves.

Tracy and I reluctantly left the meeting, winding up at a nearby coffee shop in downtown Manhattan. Both of us were upset. Tracy was not only angry, but quite emotional. She couldn't accept that the faculty didn't understand that we had worked incredibly hard and under enormous pressure to help design the college, and that for it to succeed the barriers between faculty and administrators had to be broken down. She also worried that the group would not be true to the model. I was upset, too, but realized that most of our work was done. With a president now appointed and faculty and staff on board, we were no longer in charge. We had to begin letting go.

This one incident didn't stand in the way of moving toward the college's opening, but it was disappointing. We returned that day to a later meeting in the building, trying not to let our dismay show. While upset, Tracy and I committed ourselves to the remaining tasks at hand.

Moving away from the project was not easy. It was, however, a lesson learned. Once you are no longer in charge of a project or even indirectly involved, you have little or no say on how it is operated. That was made even clearer to me later in my career as I left my position at the Central Office and approached retirement. I could only watch as new leaders determined the future of my unit and the direction it would take.

The New Community College opened its doors in August 2012, welcoming a class of more than 300 students. By then, Scott Evenbeck had been president for a year and a half, additional faculty and staff had been hired, the majors were selected and designed, the facility renovated, and other components of the college built. Tracy Meade left the

Central Office to become a dean at the New Community College, as did Stuart Cochran, who later became dean of strategic planning and institutional effectiveness.

To mark the opening of the college, its next-door neighbor, the New York Public Library, hosted a triumphant celebration for students and the hundreds of people who had been part of the planning process. There was joy all around, with remarks from Chancellor Goldstein, New York Public Library President Tony Marx, city and state officials, and President Evenbeck. I arrived early to the event. On the way to the Library, as I walked up 40th Street past the building now housing the college, I took note of the beautiful two-story mural that filled the entire window, announcing to the thousands of passers-by that CUNY was opening a new college. What an achievement that was. At the same time, it was another signal that my role of leading the team building the college was over.

A few days later the *New York Post* published an op-ed piece by Chancellor Goldstein titled "CUNY's Newest 'First', Reshaping Community College." He wrote: "What's new—and most notable—isn't just its campus overlooking Bryant Park, or merely the fact that it's the first new community college in the city in more than four decades. Nor is it necessarily its president, Scott Evenbeck, its faculty or its classrooms. Rather, what makes this development uniquely significant is its novel approach to community college education." The chancellor went on to say that "it is not enough to talk about access to college: it is the attainment of a college degree that will most help students. Fostering student success requires more than an open door to a community college: What's been needed is a wholesale reimagining of community college education. Which is why CUNY's New Community College was created specifically to help students graduate—and to equip them with the skills and credentials that they will need to flourish in the marketplace."[12]

The college has continued to fulfill expectations.

- At its December 11, 2012 meeting, the New York State Board of Regents awarded the New Community College accreditation for five years.

- On April 29, 2013, in honor of a $15 million gift to the New Community College by the Stella and Charles Guttman Foundation, the CUNY Board of Trustees renamed the college, the Stella and Charles Guttman Community College.[13]
- On August 27, 2014, Guttman Community College held its first formal graduation, awarding associate degrees to more than 80 students. In his message to the graduating class, President Evenbeck said, "When we opened CUNY's newest community college in over 40 years in 2012, we set out to graduate approximately 35% of our first cohort within three years. Today, approximately 25% of our inaugural class is graduating in just two years, an outstanding achievement and a testament to your hard work and dedication." At the graduation President Evenbeck presented me with the college's presidential medal.
- "Guttman's three-year graduation rate is "more than twice the national average and has been 40% or higher since the first graduating class in 2014." Additionally, "Guttman sends a higher percentage of its graduates to senior colleges than the other CUNY community colleges. 86% of Guttman alumni go on to baccalaureate programs, with most transferring to CUNY senior colleges."
- In 2016 Guttman received the best in New York State designation from Edsmart.org. In 2018, Guttman was ranked the top community college in New York State by BestColleges.com, and in 2020 Guttman was ranked as the best community college in the nation by Niche.com.[14]

Guttman's enrollment peaked at a little over 1,000 students in 2019, the capacity for its 40th Street location. While the original enrollment goal set by the planning team was 5,000 students, CUNY has not yet been successful in locating a larger space for the college.

The design and creation of a new community college was a major initiative, and no decision was more important than picking the right person to lead it. I was fortunate that Tracy Meade was available and willing to accept that role. The wrong choice here could have doomed the project from the outset.

The strong resistance to the project from the leadership of the University Faculty Senate and PSC was disappointing. I have given a lot of thought to the question of why these two bodies opposed this project so vociferously as well as many of the other initiatives that I led, including CUNY Start, CLIP, ASAP, and SPS. Some of it could be attributed to concerns that I was not a traditional academic with the proper credentials. I also represented management, and there is an inherent tension between faculty and the administration at most universities. In addition, while many CUNY faculty participated in the planning and development of Guttman and our other large projects, all of these efforts were mandated and administered by the Central Office and thus were viewed as being "top down." Certainly, and as I have mentioned, change is not easy to accept when it is based on the view that the present way of doing things has not been successful. No one likes to be criticized. Furthermore, change appears threatening to those who are invested in or benefit from the status quo—and truly believe they have been doing a good job in difficult circumstances.

While I did understand the reasons behind many of these concerns, only rarely did I hear anything about students in the criticisms we received. How could it be that a three-year graduation rate at CUNY of barely above 11% could be accepted and almost never discussed? Even on those occasions when it was discussed, why was none of the responsibility directed internally? Why was the default to blame the K–12 system or the social conditions and disadvantages of the CUNY students, or the students themselves? Why was there not more reflection?

Nobody had all the answers, but so many were not even acknowledging the questions. New approaches to this work were sorely needed.

CHAPTER 22

CUNY Start

Creating an Alternative to Remediation

IN THE SMALL CONFERENCE ROOM, A CLASS OF PERHAPS 15 ADULT students clustered around a conference room table on the seventh floor of one of our SUD (Senior University Dean) satellite office spaces on the corner of 31st Street and Sixth Avenue in Manhattan. They were participating in a pilot program for students who had recently obtained their high school equivalency diplomas (GEDs) after completing one of our preparation classes. The space was somewhat dreary and far from ideal. Nonetheless, the students were enthusiastically and actively engaged in the work.

Having earned their equivalency diplomas, these students were eligible to enroll in any of CUNY's community colleges. But they had opted to take this evening course instead. They hoped that by deferring their matriculation for one semester, they could avoid non-credit remedial courses and start their college experience fully prepared for credit-bearing courses. This tiny pilot would grow in a few years into CUNY Start, a program offered to several thousand students at eight CUNY colleges. Further, it became a key element of the eventual end of traditional remedial instruction at CUNY.

CUNY Start was one more program that began because Leslee Oppenheim, together with a few of her staff, had identified a problem they wanted to address. In 1995, they had created the CUNY Language Immersion Program or CLIP, also an intensive pre-college program but for a different population of students: English language learners. Now, in 2008, when they reviewed the data on graduates of the CUNY High School Equivalency Prep program, they found that a large number of those graduates were not successful when they transitioned to CUNY degree programs. Almost all of them failed to pass at least one of the three CUNY assessment tests (reading, writing and math), and as a result were placed in remedial classes. There they typically languished, spending semesters struggling to pass these non-credit programs, using up financial aid, and far too often leaving college with very few credits accumulated.

Not unique to CUNY, this was a national problem for students entering college with GEDs. Nor was the problem unique to holders of the GED. Students with regular high school diplomas—a far larger segment than GED holders—were also struggling in college, especially at community colleges, and being placed in non-credit remedial courses that turned out to be a dead end. Unlike the students in CLIP, who were immigrants needing to learn English, most remedial students were not immigrants. They were either native speakers of English or bilingual, having learned English as children.

The failure of remediation at CUNY, whether for GED holders or high school graduates, was a topic of discussion throughout our unit for many years. Leslee, John Garvey, Tracy Meade, Derrick Griffith, and others had carefully examined the data for students who participated in remediation and were struck by their lack of success in passing remedial classes. Remedial courses were meant to help but in effect became a barrier to taking credit classes and ultimately graduating. This was particularly the case for students who failed all three assessment or skills tests. We believed that the problem lay not with the faculty teaching the courses, nor with the students, but rather with the remedial model that, despite good intentions, was not set up for them to succeed.

Some people did blame the students, however, dismissing them as unprepared and not suited to higher education. Some blamed the NYC Department of Education for granting diplomas to such poorly prepared students and then sending them to us. Although they had high school diplomas, students who placed in the lowest level of remedial English courses had great difficulty reading college-level books or writing a short essay; in the lower-level math courses, they struggled with elementary algebra and sometimes with basic arithmetic. A much larger number of students entering college placed in the upper levels of remedial English and math, but the pass rates for those courses were perhaps 50% for English and much less for math.

While some faculty and academic leaders were willing to examine the structure of traditional remediation at CUNY and initiate modest changes, their experiments did not attain success at the scale that was necessary. This was due in part to the belief on many campuses that it was essential to support local approaches to instruction even when they did not lead to good results for students. This point of view opposed any consideration of a university-wide common approach. Moreover, for many years, neither the university nor the campuses had engaged in serious examination of the results of remedial programs.

The new program Leslee and her team proposed was built around a curriculum developed by math and reading/writing instructional experts from the CUNY adult literacy program. Leading the development of the math curriculum was Steve Hinds, a gifted math educator. The development of the reading/writing curriculum was led by Gail Cooper, an equally talented literacy educator.

Students serving as pilot participants agreed to delay enrolling in a CUNY college in order to attend what we at first called the College Transition Initiative (CTI). The course was designed to enable them to pass their skills tests and bypass remedial courses when they began CUNY as matriculated students. Unlike many programs in place across the university, this one did not focus on prepping for the test. It was an experience that taught the students a different approach to literacy and to math. The early results of the small program seemed promising. The program began in the spring semester of 2008 and enrolled a second cohort of students in the fall 2008 semester. While we didn't conduct a formal evaluation of the program, we followed the progress of the students carefully. Attendance was excellent, as was retention. Most of the students who began completed the semester, and the skills tests results also were good, with a significant number of the students either testing out of remediation or passing one or two of the skills tests.

Near the end of the fall 2008 semester, I approached Lexa Logue, the new executive vice chancellor for academic affairs (Selma Botman had left CUNY earlier in the year to become president of the University of Southern Maine) to suggest that we create a campus-based pilot program based on the College Transition Initiative. Lexa was an experienced and focused higher ed administrator who had the full confidence of Chancellor Goldstein, for whom she had worked when he was president of Baruch College. I met Lexa when she was working in the Office of Academic Affairs for a short period of time before she was appointed to the EVC position, but we were not close colleagues. I knew, however, that she was a serious researcher and scholar who believed that it was crucial to base academic decisions on data, research, and assessment of program outcomes.

At this point we lacked hard data about the success of the CTI other than some limited outcome data. I feared that Lexa, given her background, would not approve our going forward with a new pilot program. I should have understood that Lexa also believed strongly that CUNY needed to modify how it conducted remediation. She recognized immediately that CTI could be an initial step in that process.

With Lexa's approval, Leslee, Steve, Gail, and other members of Leslee's team began to develop a far more comprehensive program. It would start in the Fall 2009 semester and would be called the CUNY Start College Transition Initiative (later changed to CUNY Start). The program would begin at two community colleges, LaGuardia and Kingsborough. As in our small pilot, students would temporarily defer the start of their degree program to participate in CUNY Start. The students eligible for the program would be those whose CUNY Assessment Tests indicated the need for significant remediation.

CUNY Start incorporated several elements from the CUNY Language Immersion Program (CLIP) for English language learners, which by 2009 had over 10 years of success. In addition, other components distinguished it from the typical campus remedial programs:

- Like CLIP, CUNY Start would be intensive. Students would receive 25 hours of instruction per week if they needed assistance in both reading/writing and math and 12 hours of instruction if they went part time and enrolled in either math or reading/writing.
- Also, like CLIP, it would be low cost. Students would pay $75 for a full semester of instruction. Public assistance recipients would go for free. All books and supplies would be provided to students cost free.
- Reading and writing would be integrated in a single course, as in CLIP. This differed from many campus remedial programs, which offered separate reading and writing courses.
- By the second year of the program, new teachers would spend a semester observing and jointly teaching with a lead teacher before they were given their own class. All instructors would receive ongoing professional development.
- The math and reading/writing curricula would be uniform across classes and campuses.
- A program-wide evaluation component would be implemented from the start.

Initial enrollment for the program was deliberately small, with a total of 141 students enrolled during its first year at Kingsborough and LaGuardia. By the second year (2010–11), programs were added at Borough of Manhattan and Hostos Community Colleges, bringing the total enrollment to 403. When Bronx and Queensborough Community Colleges began programs in the third year, total program enrollment grew to 1,172. During the following five years programs were added at Guttman Community College, Medgar Evers College, the College of Staten Island, and New York City College of Technology.

The expansion of CUNY Start was not without controversy. As the program grew and more students volunteered to enroll and defer regular admission, campus administrators and admissions officers expressed concern that the program would decrease first-time freshman enrollment, bringing about a negative budget impact on the colleges. While that concern was understandable, we pointed out that if CUNY Start succeeded, any initial enrollment decrease during the first semester would be offset by entering students who required less or even no formal remediation once they matriculated. This would save their financial aid dollars, provide a quicker path to taking credit classes, and hopefully lead to higher rates of retention and graduation.

There also was concern, especially on the part of the union, that an expansion of CUNY Start would lead to fewer remedial classes being offered through the college departments; therefore, adjunct faculty teaching the lowest-level remedial classes could lose their positions. Again, there was some truth to that, but there were also strong counter arguments. Most importantly, under the existing remedial structure, students entering CUNY needing to take all three remedial courses almost never made it to graduation. Over half of those students would leave CUNY with very few credits accumulated. We didn't want to simply write off those students, assuming that they could not succeed in college. Instead, by offering a new model for those students who needed the most help, we hoped to create their best chance for success.

The leadership of the union and faculty governance raised a second concern strongly: Who would be doing the teaching? What would their workload be? What benefits would they receive? This was a real issue, as those of us developing the program agreed. Like the CUNY Language Immersion Program (CLIP), faculty in CUNY Start had the status of continuing education teachers (CETs): they were paid hourly for 30 hours a week over five days, of which 25 hours would be in the classroom. Most instructors taught two classes of math or two classes of reading/writing, with a maximum class size of 25 students. When CUNY Start began, even those teachers were considered hourly employees.

Finally, in 2017, when the collective bargaining agreement was settled at last, it included a separate category for CUNY Start faculty that included full-time status for teachers. They would get an annual salary with salary step increases as well as contractual increases, sick leave, and pension benefits. Salaries were quite a bit below those of full-time faculty, but the agreement provided full-time, permanent status for CUNY Start and CLIP teachers. The number of teaching hours remained the same.

I looked at this settlement as a partial victory. I would have preferred that salaries be set higher but recognized that achieving full-time status was a good thing, which would make it easier for the program to attract and retain teachers and staff. I also understood that I lacked the power or influence to do better. It was a small victory, but still a victory. Adjuncts teaching ESL or remedial reading and math at CUNY were rarely if ever able to achieve anything close to a full-time salary, whereas CLIP or CUNY Start full-time teachers would have an annual salary with benefits.

Watching the union and CUNY management negotiate during this long process was eye-opening. I was not surprised when at times each side was rigid and difficult, but there were also moments of cooperation and respect. If not for the lengthy overall contract negotiation for the entire CUNY system, we likely would have reached an earlier agreement on our small slice of union negotiations on CLIP and CUNY Start. During this process there was far less acrimony than there had been a few years earlier around the CUNY School of Professional Studies, Guttman Community College, and the ASAP program. For one thing, this time we had more data to demonstrate both the negative effects of remediation and the success of well-designed and implemented interventions.

The CUNY data provided by the Office of Institutional Research had grown much more robust and available, but we had also taken an important step toward the evaluation of our programs by starting our own SUD unit, Research, Evaluation, and Program Support (REPS). Tracey Meade had envisioned a coordinated program evaluation shop that would both help make decisions and demonstrate results for every SUD program. We hired Drew Allen, a talented young researcher, to lead this effort, which grew to have a staff of 30, drawing on a percentage of every grant award. REPs proved to be tremendously valuable in developing programs, preparing proposals, and demonstrating effectiveness.

A formal evaluation was a key component of CUNY Start from its outset. In 2013, under Drew Allen's leadership, REPS issued a report:

"CUNY Start: Analysis of Student Outcomes." Among its findings were the following:

- Of students needing remediation in reading, 57.3% of CS students achieved proficiency compared to 33.1 per cent of comparison group students. In writing, 61.9% of CS students achieved proficiency, compared to 26.1 % of comparison group students, and in math, 53% of CS students achieved proficiency compared to 10.2% of comparison group students.
- Of students needing remediation in all three skill areas, 20.6% of CS students achieved proficiency in all areas, compared to 1.2% of comparison group students. Of all students with two remedial needs, 34.1% of CS students achieved proficiency in those two areas compared to 7.1% of comparison group students.
- In their first semester as matriculated students at CUNY, CS students attempted an average of 9.7 credits and earned an average of 7.5 credits with a GPA of 2.45. Comparison students attempted an average of 5.0 credits and earned an average of 3.3 credits with a 2.08 GPA.[1]

These early results were promising, but we needed more data to fully assess the quality and success of the program. Fortunately, we were approached by MDRC, the leading research and evaluation organization that had evaluated ASAP. They asked us to support their application for a United States Department of Education Institute of Education Sciences (IES) grant to evaluate the program. A three-year grant was awarded in 2015, and as part of the randomized controlled study, students were followed through the winter of 2019. The study determined that CUNY Start substantially increased college readiness, slightly increased credit accumulation, and modestly increased graduation rates.[2]

By the time I left the Central Office in 2020, CUNY Start was established as a permanent program at nine CUNY colleges. We added a Math Start program for students who wanted to increase their math proficiency before starting credit classes. The Math Start program was offered in 8–10 week cycles and provided 14–20 hours of instruction per week. Together CUNY Start and Math Start enrolled more than 3,200 students in fiscal year 2022, employed 175 staff, and became an integral part of the overall restructuring of remediation at CUNY. The program's director in the Central Office was Mia Simon, who had assumed many leadership roles in SUD during her 20 years at CUNY. The CUNY Start program had come a long way since its start around a conference room table.

Because the State provides aid for community colleges on an FTE (Full time Equivalency) basis for what is defined as non-credit remedial programs, both CUNY Start and CLIP not only paid for themselves but generated more revenue than they spent. I continued to have conversations with the senior budget office officials to point this out and to ask for even greater fiscal support for the program. While my persistent reminders did help convince the university that full-time status for teachers and staff was affordable, they did not lead to any major increase in overall funding.

CHAPTER 23

Opportunity for Dreamers

IN THE SPRING OF 2014, AFTER A NATIONAL SEARCH, JAMES B. Milliken became the new CUNY chancellor. The appointment surprised and disappointed me. I had assumed that Bill Kelly, who had been appointed interim chancellor in the summer of 2013, would get the permanent position. I was rooting for him. Bill was a close colleague and friend who had supported me, the many Central Office programs I supervised, and the CUNY School of Professional Studies (SPS), where I was by then serving as founding dean while retaining my Central Office responsibilities. Frankly, I also did not look forward to having to prove myself once again to a new leader. And I was certainly not looking forward to the inevitable transition when a new chancellor began. This would be the sixth chancellor since I began working in the Central Office in 1986.

J.B., as he liked to be called, began on June 1, 2014. Soon after, he set up individual meetings with his cabinet members. During my 30-minute meeting, I tried to describe my portfolio, which included my dual role at CUNY Central and at SPS, while indicating how our team had been responsible for designing and implementing some of CUNY's most successful programs. The meeting was pleasant. But as I thought about it afterward, I wondered whether I had really engaged him. Perhaps I had talked too much about our accomplishments.

As a follow-up to the meeting, I invited the chancellor to attend the Peter Jennings Scholarship event. With the help of Jay Hershenson, the chancellor agreed to attend. Named after the ABC News anchor who had died in 2005, the annual ceremony honored 8–10 students who had attended the CUNY adult literacy program, earned their high school equivalency diplomas, and were matriculating at a CUNY college in the fall. The awardees received college scholarships.

After speaking at one of the earlier events, Peter Jennings had adopted the program, attending and speaking every year until he died. He always made a point of letting the audience know that he had never received a high school diploma. In giving out the awards, he spoke poignantly to each of the awardees, reviewing their very personal and heartwarming stories. Most of the scholarship winners were immigrants. Because of its importance to Jennings, his widow, Kaycee Freed Jennings, helped establish the scholarship program and assumed Peter's former speaking role at the annual ceremony with sensitivity and emotion.

The new chancellor stayed for the entire event. In his short remarks, he made a point of stating that CUNY is about providing educational opportunity for students from GED to Ph.D. After the event, he sought me out to let me know how moved he was by the stories, and that he appreciated how well the event was organized. I let him know this was one more of Leslee Oppenheim's many achievements.

I don't know whether his attendance at the Peter Jennings event influenced Chancellor Milliken's decision, but a few weeks later he emailed Jay and me to let us know that he had been approached by Donald Graham, the former publisher and chair of the board of the *Washington Post,* to discuss a new organization that Graham had founded. Called The Dream.US, it provided college scholarship opportunities for undocumented immigrants whose status was DACA (Deferred Action for Childhood Arrivals) or TPS (Temporary Protected Status). Undocumented students were ineligible to receive federal financial aid, including grants and loans. Graham had noted that although many CUNY students had DACA or TPS status, very few were currently receiving scholarships from The Dream.US. He wanted to give CUNY the opportunity to become more formally involved in the program and increase those numbers.

The chancellor asked me to reach out as soon as possible to Candy

Marshall, the president of The Dream.Us, to learn more about the program. He let me know that this was a priority for him. To engage and impress someone of the stature of Don Graham so early in his administration would be a major win for the chancellor. Indeed, it was a win-win since the chancellor strongly supported providing opportunity to Dreamers.

I was delighted that the chancellor asked me to take the lead in this project. It was an early sign that he understood the skill and depth of our team. In our initial conversation, Candy Marshall explained that while The Dream.US was relatively small, Don Graham was committed to raising significant funding for scholarships and expanding outreach to many more colleges and universities—especially CUNY, given the size of the undocumented and DACA population in New York City. At the time, she said that CUNY students had been awarded only about 30 scholarships, far fewer than Miami-Dade College.

As always in starting new projects, I needed to select a staff member to direct it. Once again, I tapped Rachel Stephenson, who had been doing a terrific job in designing and administering the CUNY Service Corps. With the proper support, Rachel could broaden her portfolio by accepting this role as well. She got along well with outside partners, believed strongly in widening services for undocumented students, and understood the importance of moving quickly.

The Dream.US awarded scholarships of up to $25,000 to cover tuition, fees, books, supplies, and transportation for students enrolled in two-year or four-year degree programs. In the fall of 2013, CUNY Institutional Research had calculated that the university enrolled almost 6,700 undocumented students, although a smaller number had applied for or received DACA or TPS approval. Based on those numbers, we set an application target of 800 students. To qualify for the scholarship, students had to be first-time college students, be eligible for in-state tuition, and have a high school GPA of 2.5 or greater. They also had to demonstrate significant unmet financial need. In addition to first-time first-year students (including those who had earned no more than 12 college credits), the aid was also available to students who had earned an associate degree and were seeking to complete their bachelor's degree at a participating college.

In early September, we hosted an orientation meeting for all CUNY campuses to explain the program and to encourage them to participate. Nineteen campuses signed on, despite being required to take on significant responsibility without additional staff: recruit students, designate a dedicated student advisor, compile and report persistence and completion data, assign a program liaison to supervise the program, and participate in university-wide meetings. The deadline for the national competition was tight. For CUNY students to be eligible to receive awards for the upcoming spring semester, their applications had to meet The Dream. US October 12 deadline, just over a month away.

In organizing the CUNY-wide effort, Rachel Stephenson and her team worked together with the campus liaisons and staff to make sure that eligible students not only received information about the program but were encouraged to apply. Our team hosted training sessions for campus staff, preparing them to help applicants. In turn, campus staff held group information sessions for eligible applicants and assisted students with their applications to ensure that they were completed accurately.

Despite the short time frame, 678 CUNY students submitted applications. In December, we celebrated the announcement that 242 CUNY students had been awarded scholarships, and 227 of them had accepted the awards. By the second year of CUNY's participation in the program, our students received 350 scholarships, half of the overall total of 700 scholarships awarded by The Dream.US. This was a figure far beyond anything we could have predicted.

Overjoyed with the result, Chancellor Milliken publicized it widely, within and outside of CUNY. Like previous chancellors, he came to recognize our unit's ability to build successful programs under extreme pressure and within short time frames.

We also were praised and thanked by Don Graham, Candy Marshall, and Gaby Pacheco, a Dreamer herself, who was the director of immigrant rights for The Dream.US. They often invited us to private events that

Don Graham hosted to publicize the program and solicit new donors. Don's commitment to building the organization was unwavering. When Donald Trump was elected president and attempted to abolish DACA (an action later rejected by the courts), Graham responded by accelerating the expansion of the scholarship program.

Over the next few years, we monitored the performance of the CUNY Dreamers who had received scholarships. Of the first few cohorts, over 85% of the students graduated, and many of the community college students went on to transfer to baccalaureate programs. They also had high GPAs. We held annual events to celebrate student success and created an alumni network of graduates with whom the staff maintained contact and invited to later celebrations.

A little over a year after CUNY began participating, Don Graham and The Dream.Us team hosted an event to thank CUNY and recognize the Dreamers. In his opening remarks, he surprised the audience by announcing that he would be donating an additional $15 million to support The Dream.US. Another speaker at the event was Bill Ackman, founder and CEO of Pershing Square Capital Management, a hedge fund. Ackman spoke about his own family's immigrant experience and the importance of immigrants to the United States and to American life. He ended his short remarks by announcing that he would match Don Graham's gift with his own $15 million donation. The students reacted with a standing ovation. Joining in the applause, I once again recognized the need to approach people who had vast amounts of money to build the kinds of programs that could provide opportunity for our students. I celebrated the $30 million announced that evening. But I struggled, too, wishing that government support could be available to these talented, committed students. Because of the students' immigration status, they cannot be supported with city or state funds. That means that programs like The Dream.US can survive only with outside philanthropic help.

The Dream.US continued to expand throughout my remaining time at CUNY.[1] As the program brought in new partner colleges whose students competed with our CUNY students for scholarships, the number of scholarships awarded to CUNY students stabilized at around 200 per year. For the student recipients, these scholarships made it possible to complete college. Meanwhile, Dreamers remained in limbo, as the fight over immigration policy in Washington continued. As I write this, Dreamers still await action from Congress to enable them to obtain permanent status and a path to citizenship.

V. LOOKING AHEAD

The rising momentum and generally good budgets of the Goldstein years gave way after his retirement to a period of some instability, with numerous changes in the chancellor's office and a much tougher funding situation. The latter, due in part to a low point in recurring budget cycles, resulted also from a stance toward CUNY in Albany that could almost be described as punitive. At the same time, although the programs developed and administered by my unit continued to thrive, support for the unit itself as an innovative and independent program shop—what David Kirp had described as a "skunkworks"—began to wane.[1]

CHAPTER 24

The Inspector General Raises Questions, CUNY Presidents Hire Lawyers, and I Begin to Think about Leaving the Central Office

AS ALWAYS, I WOKE UP EARLY AND TURNED ON MY BLACKBERRY TO check for messages. This was probably not a great way to start the day, but it was a habit I couldn't change. On this particular morning in late October 2014, there was a message from Chancellor Milliken, who had been in his position for almost five months. His message was short and to the point: "I'd like you to give some thought to what you think would be most important for CUNY to accomplish in the next few years, how to deliver on its essential mission. You might provide me with some bullets that we could later discuss."[1] After re-reading the email more than once, I concluded that this was an opportunity requiring a quick response.

Later that day I brought together Tracy Meade, Suri Duitch, Donna Linderman, Sherry Cleary, and Cass Conrad, all members of my senior team, to discuss how best to respond. Suri volunteered to draft an initial response, and overnight she produced a high-quality draft for our review. After spending a day editing and revising the document with our team, I sent it to the chancellor. We defined four areas that we thought the university should examine:

- Increase graduation rates, which would encompass several major efforts: continuing to strengthen our relationship with the public schools to ensure that more students entering CUNY would be prepared to do college level work; expanding ASAP at the community colleges and introducing a similar program at the senior colleges; and restructuring or even eliminating remediation.
- Reach out and enroll a larger percentage of the 800,000 New Yorkers who had earned some college credits but no degree. Many of these former students had attended CUNY colleges but left college without a degree.
- Revamp and better support the career services offices on our campuses and work to establish closer relationships with the city's business community.
- Upgrade technology, modifying our present systems and expanding the capacity to offer online courses and degree programs.

A day after we sent the email, the chancellor responded. Like his initial request and most other notes from him, it was concise: "This is excellent, John, as I knew it would be. Thank you. I will be back to you to discuss some of this, but for now it's just right. Thanks."

Although I didn't know where this would lead, I was pleased that he had liked what we proposed. A few days later I was speaking with Julia Wrigley, interim executive vice chancellor for academic affairs, who had attended the chancellor's senior staff meeting earlier that day. (Although I was a member of the chancellor's cabinet, his inner circle was the senior staff: Julia, Rick Schaffer, Jay Hershenson, and Allan Dobrin). The chancellor had led off the meeting by announcing that one of his major priorities would be to focus on increasing graduation rates. Whether or not our document had anything to do with this, it was a good thing.

Before long, however, my initial optimism faded. It was becoming clear that the chancellor would not be successful in bringing significant change to CUNY. While J.B. was smart and decent, and he had any number of good ideas, he had very little authority to institute change on his own. J.B. also was an outsider, having come to New York from Nebraska without the ingrown personal relationships and political connections needed to operate within the city and state. In Andrew Cuomo, J.B. was confronted by a governor who wanted to control the public higher ed agenda, but who never seemed to appreciate CUNY. To make matters worse, Benno Schmidt had stepped down as the board chair. Schmidt had been a strong supporter of Chancellor Goldstein. As a former president of Yale, he understood higher ed and the need for a chancellor/president to have a meaningful degree of autonomy. Schmidt also had become a strong supporter of CUNY. In June 2016, to replace him as board chair, the governor appointed William "Billy" Thompson. A prominent public figure in the state who had been the two-term city comptroller, Thompson had run for mayor against Mike Bloomberg in 2009. That race was far closer than anyone expected, with Thompson losing by only 5 percentage points.

It was clear that Governor Cuomo's appointment of Thompson was intended to gain a further degree of control over CUNY and limit the independence of the chancellor. Soon after Thompson's appointment, CUNY became embroiled in an apparent scandal prompting a major investigation of the university by the state inspector general. Whether deliberately or not, the scandal served the purpose of enhancing the board chair's power, while forcing the chancellor to focus much of his time and energy on resolving it.

In the *New York Times* of July 14, 2016, David Chen reported that City College President Lisa Coico was being investigated by federal authorities as "part of a federal inquiry into her finances and the use of federal research grants."[2] In early October 2016, President Coico resigned. A month later, on November 15, Chen had another *Times* story titled "Lapses by CUNY Officials Made System Ripe for Abuse, Report Says." That article drew from a preliminary report just released by the New York State inspector general. According to Chen's piece, the preliminary report had been prepared at the request of CUNY's board chair, William Thompson, as a result of the resignation of the City College president.

In the article, Chancellor Milliken is quoted: "I take the findings and recommendations of the inspector general very seriously, and will work with Chairperson Thompson, the Board of Trustees, and the inspector general immediately to address the recommendations. CUNY must have in place the policies and practices that reflect and ensure the highest levels of integrity, accountability, and transparency."[3]

What was most striking about the report was that it went well beyond the City College situation. It accused the entire university of mismanagement. The report specifically criticized CUNY presidents for giving out money "with no meaningful accountability." In Chair Thompson's request to the IG, he asked for an investigation of "all of the college foundations, alumni associations, or other affiliated entities."

In the following months, the IG investigation took center stage at CUNY. All presidents and deans of professional schools were informed that they would likely be deposed by the IG's office about their spending, with an emphasis on examining the use of funds from their development foundations as well as the earnings account funds generated from grants. The university also received a federal subpoena from the U.S. attorney for the Eastern District requesting documents and information related to "presidential discretionary funds."[4]

Soon after the *Times* article, two of the most effective and powerful people in the Central Office left. Rick Schaffer, the university general counsel, retired, and Jay Hershenson, senior vice chancellor for university relations and secretary to the board, moved to a new position at Queens College. It was obvious to everyone that they had been pushed out. Also leaving were several other senior administrators who had been members of Chancellor Goldstein's team. Both Rick and Jay were strong supporters of our unit's work and had always been helpful when I needed advice. I was sorry to see them leave their positions.

To replace Jay, Chair Thompson brought in Gayle Horowitz as the new secretary to the board. She also was named senior advisor to the chancellor. Given that Allan Dobrin, executive vice chancellor and chief operating officer, had left his position in the summer of 2016, Chancellor Milliken had lost three of his top four senior administrators within a short period. Only Vita Rabinowitz, executive vice chancellor for academic affairs, remained. Gayle, who had been city deputy comptroller when Thompson was comptroller and had worked for him in other capacities, assumed enormous power. She had a direct line to both the chancellor and board chair. Gayle, both smart and tough, seemed to share the belief that CUNY was not well managed and needed a course correction. She had a sharp tongue, often treated staff brusquely, and made decisions quickly and decisively. I mostly stayed away from her, but over time we established a collegial relationship.

When I mentioned to my brother, Bill, then a sitting judge in Bronx Supreme Court and a former criminal defense lawyer, that there was a chance that I would be deposed as part of the investigation and might have to testify under oath, he erupted. "You are not going without a lawyer," he shouted. He underscored vociferously that those conducting the deposition "don't wish you well." Bill referred me to Seth Rosenberg, an attorney he knew and respected, who would prepare me and represent me in the event I was called to testify. By then all of the presidents and professional school deans had been advised to retain lawyers. Later, the university got a board resolution passed assuring the presidents that they would be reimbursed for lawyer expenses up to $25,000 if there were no negative findings.

While I liked Seth, who reassured me that I had nothing to worry about, I hated the few meetings I had with him. I disliked having to answer questions about many aspects of my work life, including how my salary was paid through the Research Foundation and my use of discretionary funds. The prospect of testifying caused me sleepless nights. I thought to myself, how would these investigators understand the importance of using earnings account and grant funds to begin new programs and support my entire operation? I was angry that the CUNY board was not at all publicly defending the presidents, which suggested that we were guilty of something before any charges were filed. To me, the IG preliminary report was both premature and unfair.

Ultimately, around eight or nine of the 24 presidents were required to testify. I was not one of them. Those who did testify found it a miserable experience. Over the next year or two, we all waited for the IG to issue a report, for Lisa Coico or other presidents to be charged with some crime, or for more newspaper articles. None of that happened. Nothing happened. No report was ever issued, and Lisa Coico was never charged with any wrongdoing, although she lost her job, and her reputation was damaged. The investigators went away. The whole affair proved to be nothing but a distraction, taking up a huge amount of time, costing the university lots of fees for lots of lawyers, stressing out the supposed targets of the investigation, and ultimately making CUNY appear corrupt. It led many administrators to become even more risk averse, worrying that doing something that bent the formal rules even a bit could lead to being investigated—even when bending the accepted practices was often the only way to get new things done.

The damage to the university and to the chancellor was severe. By the winter of 2018, the chancellor announced that he would be leaving. He understood that his authority, scant to begin with, had been diminished. He no longer had the support of the board chair and other key board members, and the job certainly was no longer fun. He also had a major health scare, announcing publicly that he had cancer, though he expected to make a full recovery. J.B. was a good person, who embraced the mission of CUNY and was deeply committed to students. He was somewhat aloof and didn't make decisions quickly, but my guess is that he recognized early on that he would not be permitted to be an independent chancellor, which of course severely undercut his ability to function in a positive and creative way. It is interesting to note that not long after he left CUNY, he was named chancellor of the University of Texas system, one of the most prestigious higher ed positions in the country at a salary far above what he was earning at CUNY.

I shared the chancellor's view that the Central Office was no longer fun. On the outside, my unit continued to thrive, with many of our programs expanding and being recognized. My SUD unit was still being approached by the city to help solve problems, having recently signed several agreements: with the Department of Correction to begin an education program at Rikers Island aimed at lowering the level of violence in the facility; with the Department of Immigrant Affairs to build a program providing legal services to largely undocumented immigrants; and with the Department of Homeless Services to start a program for Homeless Veterans. But we also were beginning to feel more isolated. The atmosphere in the Central Office had deteriorated. Overall, morale was down, the governor's budget did not treat CUNY very well, and the operating side of the house had become far more powerful than the Office of Academic Affairs.

For the first time, I began to talk with close colleagues about leaving the Central Office, either by going to CUNY SPS as the full time dean or simply retiring. I also shared with Jerry Markowitz, who was recording my oral history, that I was pretty sure that the Senior University Dean unit would not survive my leaving. The support that our work had received from a strong chancellor, Matthew Goldstein, had not survived the changes in leadership and the reduced authority of a new chancellor. That became a constant thought as the next two chancellors and executive vice chancellors arrived.

To replace J.B., in June 2018, the board turned to Vita Rabinowitz to be the interim chancellor as a search for a permanent chancellor began. Vita, the executive vice chancellor for academic affairs, was a safe and strategic choice by the board. She was a wonderful person, well liked, funny, and engaging. Vita was committed to the CUNY mission and to student success. An established scholar, she was also a team player who had spent a career at Hunter College as a faculty member, dean, and provost, before coming to the Central Office. Perhaps foremost from the board's perspective, Vita was viewed as someone who would not make waves. The power of the Central Office would remain on the operating side of the house and with the board chair. Understanding that she lacked the authority to make significant major decisions without first checking with Gayle or Marc Shaw, Vita tried to avoid conflict, and often was told what to do. It also was apparent that few major decisions could be made without first checking with the governor's people in Albany.

Nevertheless, it is greatly to Vita's credit that she succeeded in moving CUNY toward critically important student-focused goals, especially regarding transfer and remediation. As chancellor, she dismantled

CUNY's cumbersome and ineffective structure of remediation, something almost no one could have imagined only a few years earlier. Of course, substantial numbers of students still arrived not fully prepared for college work. Drawing on ample evidence and emerging national trends, CUNY would now handle these students in a different way. Those needing the most preparation were directed to CLIP for English language instruction or to CUNY Start for reading, writing, and math—both intensive programs developed by my SUD unit. Instead of years of non-credit courses, students could progress to credit-bearing courses after a summer or a semester and without using any financial aid. Students who could manage first year courses if they had extra support—a much larger segment of entering students—were now placed directly into those credit courses and given the support to help them succeed.

During the year Vita served as interim chancellor, I continued to be part of her cabinet. She certainly appreciated the SUD unit's talent and long history of success, but she was too preoccupied with the many duties of her office to devote any significant time to thinking about how best to work with us. Vita worked incredibly hard, but everyone understood that she was in an interim position, and the appointment of a permanent chancellor was what mattered the most to the future of the university.

Through the year-long search, it appeared that the board struggled to find the right candidate. I had no insight into the process, though we heard rumors that in addition to outside candidates, two CUNY presidents, Gail Mellow from LaGuardia Community College and Felix "Felo" Matos Rodriquez, from Queens College, were under consideration. After considerable delay, Matos Rodriguez was appointed as the chancellor, effective May 2019.

I knew Felo well going back to his days as president of Hostos Community College and later as president of Queens College. He was a good colleague and friend. I felt it was important and significant that for the first time CUNY had a person of color as its chancellor. Felo was a seasoned administrator with an impeccable academic pedigree that included degrees from Yale and Columbia. From our many previous conversations, I understood that we had different perspectives on the role of the

Central Office and its relationship to the campuses, as well as on the role of the college presidents. I had headed large university-wide initiatives and believed that their success was dependent on the unified perspective and coordinated management of these efforts. On the other hand, as a college president, Felo had chafed at what he regarded as Central's intrusions on his autonomy. Still, I hoped that he would have the authority to be an independent chancellor who could make major decisions on his own without having to get the approval of the governor and his staff. I also worried about whether Board Chair Thompson would support the new chancellor as he established his agenda, especially a request to the governor for additional state fiscal support.

Soon after the chancellor started, Angie Kamath, whom I had hired as the university dean for continuing education and workforce development, and I met with the chancellor to discuss his interest in strengthening student career preparation. We had a good conversation, but at the end of the meeting he expressed the view that any new initiatives can't be "top down," but rather must bubble up from the campus level. I agreed that the presidents needed more autonomy and that the Central Office provided too many mandates, often in an arrogant manner, but I also believed that there was a need for a strong Central Office. I assumed that Felo was directing these thoughts squarely at me and the work of our unit. By then the office of the Senior University Dean—my office—had a staff of more than 300 people. While SUD was a unit within the Office of Academic Affairs, we had a degree of independence far greater than almost any other department in the Central Office.

One of the new chancellor's first decisions was to appoint two new executive vice chancellors, one for academic affairs, and the other for the operating side of the house. For the academic affairs position, he selected Jose Luis Cruz, the sitting president of Lehman College and one of CUNY's most effective presidents. For the other position, EVC for administration and finance and chief operating officer, he named Hector Batista, a former head of the Brooklyn Chamber of Commerce, who also had held a number of senior-level positions in government as well as the nonprofit and private sectors. Batista's close relationship with Board

Chair Thompson, coupled with his lack of higher education experience, led to speculation about whether his appointment was the chancellor's alone or done under the pressure of the board chair.

I knew Vice Chancellor Cruz well from his days at Lehman College and thought highly of him. While he was reserved almost to the point of appearing shy at times, he was a good communicator who wrote extremely well and had a quiet, confident presence. It was clear that he understood how power and authority worked.

I was pleased that the chancellor continued to have me as a member of his cabinet. But he indicated that it was up to me whether I wanted to retain both roles: senior university dean in the Central Office and founding dean of the CUNY School of Professional Studies, particularly because of the growth of SPS. By then I was beginning to spend far more time at SPS, understanding that my Central Office role and the role of the SUD unit had changed and been diminished within the university since the departure of Matthew Goldstein. The senior members of my SUD team had been appointed to the newly established cabinet of the EVC for academic affairs, and I had been invited to be part of that cabinet as well. But it was becoming apparent that both the chancellor and vice chancellor had already decided to eliminate the SUD unit once I left the Central Office. Its role would be consolidated under the overall Office of Academic Affairs. At this point, I was no longer interacting with either the chancellor or vice chancellor on a regular basis. Unlike in previous administrations, I was rarely called upon to give advice or be part of major decision-making conversations. This did not trouble me as much as it might have. I no longer felt the same sense of urgency or possibility as when Matthew Goldstein and Louise Mirrer were in charge and Benno Schmidt chaired the board. Felo and his team were certainly competent, but I no longer saw the active agenda or big ideas that had so engaged me.

In January of 2020, I let the chancellor know that I wanted to leave the Central Office in early April. I hoped to remain at CUNY as the full-time dean of the CUNY School of Professional Studies until my retirement. Felo was gracious in accepting my timeframe for departing SUD. He assured me that he supported my staying at SPS until I retired.

PART 3

The CUNY School of Professional Studies

Transitions and a Capstone

The CUNY School of Professional Studies (CUNY SPS) officially opened in 2003. For the next 17 years, I held two distinct CUNY positions and titles—Founding Dean of CUNY SPS and Senior University Dean for Academic Affairs. There was a good deal of synergy between my two positions, but being responsible simultaneously for leading both a huge Central Office unit and a new CUNY institution was administratively complex. It also was not easy to explain my role either inside CUNY or beyond. Many a time I listened to people introducing me at events, meetings, or social occasions where they either identified me by one of my titles or presented a description of my role that no one could have understood. I could never blame anyone for failing to adequately describe what I did. It sometimes wasn't easy for me, either.

When I thought about where to place the story of SPS in this book, I had a dilemma. Its development as a school took place at the same time as I also was leading the SUD office and overseeing some of CUNY's most significant projects, including ASAP, Guttman Community College, and CUNY Start. Trying to fit the development of SPS into the chapters that highlighted the many SUD programs would be confusing at best. Also, by the time I retired in 2021, SPS had become much more than just a small, niche professional school. While it didn't have college in its official name, SPS functioned as one, offering an array of degree programs at the bachelor's and master's level, and many credit certificate programs. In addition, its large, grant supported area had grown to provide non-credit programs to tens of thousands of adult students annually. SPS deserved its own section in the book.

CHAPTER 25

The CUNY School of Professional Studies

Establishing a New School for Adult Students

I STOOD AT THE PODIUM ON THE STAGE OF ALICE TULLY HALL, one of Lincoln Center's venerable performance venues, preparing to give welcome remarks to the 2009 graduating class of the CUNY School of Professional Studies. Looking out at the audience, I got chills. The 1,100-seat auditorium was filled to capacity. Upfront were the 275 graduates, dressed in their celebratory caps and gowns. They looked glorious. Behind them sat members of their families, friends, and partners. On the stage, members of the SPS faculty and staff were joined by CUNY Chancellor Matthew Goldstein and Selma Botman, president of the University of Southern Maine and our keynote speaker for the evening. From 2004–2008, she had been CUNY's executive vice chancellor for academic affairs.

I concluded my remarks with the words of Samantha Brahms, a graduating student, who wrote in the commencement program: "I hope that when we go out into the world, we find joy in whatever we do. That we wake up in the morning and do not dread going to work. That we feel we accomplish something, small or large. That we pursue our dreams no matter where they lead us. May we have enough confidence in ourselves to be the successes that everyone here today knows we can be."

Walking back to my seat, I was moved by the energy in the room and the happiness of our graduates. My thoughts, however, brought me back to the late fall of 2002. I was on an Amtrak train with then Executive Vice Chancellor Louise Mirrer. We were returning to New York from Baltimore after a conference on adult learners sponsored by Johns Hopkins University. It was on that train ride that Louise first introduced me to the idea of creating a new school for adults at CUNY.

THE BEGINNING

The conference in Baltimore had been an eye opener. Much of the conversation at the well-attended gathering was about how to enroll more adult students and how to serve them through new approaches that better met their needs. CUNY certainly attracted adult students, but how well did we meet their needs? Little thought had been given to that question. At CUNY, adult students usually entered traditional degree programs, which had been designed for first-time freshmen enrolling directly from high school. These programs often simply did not work for many of these students because those who designed and administered the programs had not considered the maturity of adult students, or their need for flexibility in requirements and scheduling.

A logical alternative would be continuing ed, which already served many thousands of adult learners successfully. The problem was how to offer degrees designed for adult students through continuing ed. At CUNY colleges, a huge divide separated the credit side of the house from the non-credit side, which was run largely through adult and continuing education units. Although continuing ed units at universities all over the country ran degree programs for adults, CUNY did not—despite attempts over the years to enable continuing ed to pilot adult-focused credit certificate and degree programs. Campus culture and governance procedures reserved the right to build new credit programs solely to the traditional, tenure-track faculty. If CUNY faculty were not themselves interested in creating a program tailored to adult learners, it would not happen at all because they would not permit anyone else to do it.

Louise saw the need to build a new school that would serve only adults. She envisaged an innovative school that could respond to the needs of employers, unions, and nonprofit organizations. It would offer graduate as well as undergraduate level degree programs. In addition, courses would be developed for working professionals seeking career advancement and professional development, as well as for adults seeking training for entry-level jobs. A grant-funded component would provide training to city workers, similar to programs developed through my Senior University Dean unit at the Central Office.

Within a few days of returning to New York, Louise and I met with Chancellor Matthew Goldstein to discuss the idea of a new school. Louise had already spoken to Matthew about the idea and knew he was supportive. As the three of us talked, it was obvious that this project would be a go. As was often the case with new projects, the chancellor didn't go into the details, but simply outlined broadly what he was looking for. Near the end of the meeting, he did make one very definite statement. He would appoint me as the school's founding dean, but at the same time, he wanted me to keep my position in the Central Office as the senior university dean for academic affairs. Holding dual jobs would present a major challenge, but I said yes, confident that I would have the full backing of Matthew and Louise throughout the development process. And I had in place a great senior team to support me at SUD. Without them, I would not have been able to contemplate taking on another full-time position. The chancellor indicated that he would announce the project publicly around the new year, and that the school would be called the CUNY School of Professional Studies.

Meanwhile, as the fall continued, I began to put together a small team to start the planning process. I called on Brian Peterson to take a leave from his position directing three large grant-funded programs in our Central Office unit to be the project's lead person. In addition, Shirley Miller, who had spent many years at LaGuardia Community College in a senior position in continuing ed but was now working in our unit, joined the planning team. A few months later I added Suri Duitch, who had just finished writing the university's master plan and was someone with whom I had worked closely when she held a senior position in city government.

As the planning began, we barely had a concept. We had no staff or faculty. No space. And no dollars allocated. I understood little of what it meant to create a new accredited CUNY school and the many, many components that were entailed. I also failed to predict the level of hostility and opposition to the proposal of a new school from the PSC and the University Faculty Senate.

With the planning process just under way, in March 2003 Randi Weingarten, president of the United Federation of Teachers (NYC's public school teacher's union), approached CUNY with a request. She asked for assistance in developing a new credit certificate program to prepare the city's elementary school teachers to teach the balanced literacy curriculum then being introduced. This was an important request from one of the city's largest and most powerful unions. Louise Mirrer, with the support of the chancellor, decided to have the fledgling CUNY School of Professional Studies, then barely an idea, develop the program. Louise believed that SPS would have the flexibility to complete the development in time for a fall 2003 opening. While this kind of certificate program was exactly what Louise had in mind when she envisioned creating SPS, we had a major problem: there was no SPS as yet. Somehow, we would have to get the school approved by both CUNY's trustees and the State Education Department by June in order to meet the UFT request for a fall start. We also needed experts to design the course of study and select and train the instructors.

Enter Rick Schaffer, CUNY's general counsel and vice chancellor for legal affairs. Rick was a relative newcomer to CUNY, having arrived in 2000. But he had quickly earned the confidence of the chancellor and other Central Office senior officials. Confident but not arrogant, Rick brought to the job a degree of flexibility that was unusual in top lawyers in large, bureaucratic organizations. I had served on the search committee that recommended Rick to the chancellor, and from the outset I enjoyed working with him and found him approachable.

Rick was aware that as originally conceived, the CUNY Graduate School and University Center was intended to house both a graduate school for university-wide doctoral programs, and a university center for other university-wide programs. At the time, the university center role was limited to the CUNY Baccalaureate program (CUNY BA), but Rick and Louise proposed a formal structural change enabling the University Center to include a newly created School of Professional Studies in addition to the CUNY BA Program.[1] By proposing that SPS be housed initially in the University Center, Rick was able to quickly develop a governance plan that could be approved almost immediately by the CUNY trustees and the state. It was a creative solution, neatly bypassing the multi-year process that would have been necessary to establish SPS as an independent CUNY institution.

The plan Rick proposed was both simple and consistent with the goal that SPS would become a different kind of CUNY institution, one that would be nimble and able to build programs quickly. The dean of SPS would be appointed by the president of the Graduate School and University Center in consultation with the chancellor. The new dean would report to the president or the president's designee. The actual governing committee would consist of 12 members, including the president of the Graduate School or the president's designee, the executive vice chancellor for academic affairs, the dean of SPS, and nine faculty members. Three faculty members would be appointed by the University Faculty Senate, three by the chancellor, and three by the president of the Graduate School and University Center. The governing committee would advise the dean of SPS on the administration, coordination, and development of its programs and curricula. The nine faculty members of the governing committee would be responsible for recommending the awarding of certificates and degrees to the CUNY Board of Trustees.

To help allay the concerns and gain the support of the University Faculty Senate, the governing plan included language stating that SPS "will offer no degree program that is identical or substantially overlapping with respect to both degree of award and program title to a program currently offered by another CUNY college." The plan also stipulated that for each new program the school would establish a separate curriculum committee that drew on faculty from across the university, one-third appointed by the UFS.[2]

A few weeks before the June 23 meeting at which the trustees would vote on the governing plan of SPS, the chancellor wrote to UFS chair Susan O'Malley, who wanted assurances that SPS would be limited to non-degree curricula. Matthew could not give those assurances. He declared, "As I have said many times, we do not anticipate at this time offering any degree programs through the School of Professional Studies. But we must not hamstring a School that has been created with the specific purpose of opening up new opportunities for the University. Should the School ever wish to offer a degree program, there would be of course full consultation with faculty, including the Faculty Senate. And a rigorous process of review, which the University and the State always require, would ensure that the degree was as valued as any other at CUNY."[3]

The leadership of the University Faculty Senate and the faculty union, the PSC, were not pleased with the governing structure Rick Schaffer had developed. They voiced concern both that the power delegated to the dean seemed excessive and also that SPS would be staffed almost entirely by part-time faculty. Nevertheless, opposition to the creation of the school was somewhat muted. Perhaps that was because the very first program to be approved by SPS would be the credit certificate program requested by the UFT. It would be hard for the Senate and the CUNY Professional Staff Congress to oppose a program so important to Randi Weingarten and the teacher's union.

Still, It was not surprising when, only a week after the Board of Trustees approved the resolution creating SPS, the chancellor received a letter from Brian McLaughlin, President of the New York City Central Labor Council, claiming that the school was not endorsed by the "home Union." This lack of endorsement, he warned, "will be a deterrent to other unions seeking to work with the School." He went on to say that "the PSC's concern that the contractual obligation for evaluating and supporting part-time faculty cannot be met by the School of Professional Studies in its present form is especially serious. Further, the PSC reminds me that CUNY by-laws and practice require full-time faculty to plan and oversee curriculum especially curriculum that leads to a degree. It would be uncomfortable if not impossible for other unions to embrace the new school if it is in violation of the collective bargaining agreement." [4]

While relieved that the letter arrived after rather than before the vote to approve SPS, we recognized it as a sign that the Faculty Senate and the PSC would continue to oppose SPS and its governance structure. At the time, we did not foresee how intense that opposition would be, particularly when SPS proposed to develop online degrees three years later.

Because SPS was to be part of the University Center, we simply notified the State Education Department and Middle States of the changes to the governing structure of the University Center as approved by the CUNY trustees. SPS was an official school. We were ready to move on to creating our first program, the 12-credit certificate in literacy leadership in cooperation with the UFT.

Our first task was to identify a director for the literacy program. Fortunately, Charles Malone, a full-time faculty member from the literacy concentration of City College's graduate program in education, agreed to come on board. Working with him to develop the program were University Dean for Teacher Education Nick Michelli and several teachers from the UFT's Teacher Center. We quickly hired our first adjunct faculty, all of whom were UFT teachers, many with experience as CUNY adjuncts.

The first course began in the summer, enrolling 213 students. The tuition paid by the UFT for these students was approximately $213,000. We celebrated the first revenue generated by SPS. In the fall semester of 2003, we offered all four certificate courses. City College had agreed to accept the 12 credits for transfer if the students later enrolled in its master's program in literacy acquisition and development. During the 2003–04 academic year the literacy certificate enrolled 577 students. The UFT was pleased with the program, and in 2005, we added a second certificate program in cooperation with the UFT in math leadership.

It was greatly affirming to have a successful first program. We had demonstrated that we could act nimbly, and develop a needed, high quality program with an important outside partner in just a few months. The program was true to our mission to respond to the needs of the city and serve adult workers.

Over the next three years SPS created 12 certificate programs, two on the undergraduate level and 10 for graduate study. Some were developed with outside partners, and others independently by SPS, to meet some specific educational need. The school built nine undergraduate and 16 graduate courses. Graduate-level courses were developed in cooperation with two of New York's most prestigious institutions, the American Museum of Natural History and the Lincoln Center Institute for the Arts in Education. The eight American Museum of Natural History courses were taught jointly by CUNY faculty and prominent museum scientists. Brooklyn College faculty reviewed these courses and accepted them for credit in the college's graduate programs in science education. During the next two years (2004–06) 309 students took these credit bearing courses.[5]

During this period, SPS developed several groundbreaking academic initiatives: a graduate certificate program in immigration law in partnership with CUNY's Citizenship Now Initiative; a graduate certificate in disability studies in partnership with the John F. Kennedy Jr. Institute for Worker Education; a credit course entitled The Nature of New York: Its Natural History and Environment developed under a grant given to SPS by Theodore Kheel's Institute to Nurture New York's Nature;[6] and graduate level certificates in theater, developed in partnership with the Paul A. Kaplan Center for Educational Drama and the Creative Arts Team. These certificates enabled students to enter new fields, advance in their current fields, or meet requirements for additional education.

Among the non-credit programs developed, the largest was the Public Authorities Governance program. That program, designed by SPS at the request of the New York State Commission on Public Authority Reform, offered a full day of mandated training for all members of the many Public Authorities established in the state. The goal was to help the appointees learn about the responsibilities of being a member of an authority and to avoid potential conflicts of interest. To develop the curriculum for the program, SPS worked with full-time faculty from Baruch College and City College who would also teach a component of the day's training.

Despite the concerns expressed so forcefully by the PSC and the UFS regarding the academic quality SPS programs would have, in fact, full-time CUNY faculty and other experts were largely responsible for the curriculum and often the instruction in these programs. CUNY graduate programs accepted SPS courses for transfer credit. We worked well with CUNY faculty; it was with faculty leadership where the tension arose. To faculty governance, we were "the administration." To the union, we were "management." It was hard to break out of these caricatures. To a degree, this was inevitable. We were opening up new territory where negotiation was needed and to be expected. But the flat-out opposition and personal attack surprised us.

In this three-year period, enrollment at SPS increased significantly, as did the school's revenue. By FY2006 we had enrolled more than 1,500 adult students and had added many new staff and adjunct faculty. The school began to be recognized inside the university, as well as by local and state government. It was viewed as a CUNY unit that could respond quickly to education and training needs. While our growth pleased me, I wasn't satisfied. It wasn't fast enough. I struggled with the restrictions on SPS, particularly the one that indicated, at least to start, we would not develop degree programs. That restriction, however, was about to change. The change would lead to a transformed SPS, bringing us considerable acclaim, but also conflict, criticism, and harsh, ongoing battles with the PSC and Faculty Senate. CUNY and SPS were about to enter the world of online education.

SPS BECOMES CUNY'S ONLINE INSTITUTION

In the early fall of 2005, Selma Botman, who had succeeded Louise Mirrer as CUNY's executive vice chancellor for academic affairs, approached me to ask if SPS would develop the first online degree program at CUNY.

Selma had already floated the idea to several other CUNY colleges, but none expressed interest. Although some CUNY colleges offered online courses, none had full degrees online.

CUNY was already late to online education. Selma was well aware that online programs were springing up all over the country, including large programs at other public institutions like Penn State, the University of Maryland, the University of Illinois, and Selma's former home, the University of Massachusetts. CUNY was sitting on the sidelines of a race to build new online programs and to compete for students, largely adults, who were unable to attend in-person classes because of life circumstances. Selma pointed out that "over 40,000 students had left the University in good academic standing but without a degree since 1999." [7] In addition, hundreds of thousands of other New Yorkers had some college, but no degree. There was a demand, and Selma was eager to meet it.

When I interviewed Selma for this book, she pointed out that in her short time at CUNY she had noticed that our unit at the Central Office almost always responded quickly and effectively to requests to develop new programs. She could see that SPS was beginning to serve a similar role at the campus level. Selma's long career had demonstrated to her, as mine had to me, that change did not come easily to higher ed. To succeed in her goal of bringing online degrees to CUNY, SPS was the logical choice, given its short history and its mission to be innovative and responsive to new and worthwhile opportunities. Sitting at a table with a dozen or so CUNY faculty and SPS staff discussing building an online degree, she recalled, was her "most pleasant moment at CUNY."

Selma's invitation was an exciting opportunity for SPS. That I knew nothing about the online world and was almost phobic about technology myself was not an insurmountable obstacle. Our team had moved into other new areas knowing little about them. We were confident that we could find the talent to create the degree, believing that there were CUNY faculty who would want to become part of that process. We were committed to planning the degree in time for it to open for the fall 2006 semester, one year away.

One of my first decisions was to select George Otte to oversee the development of the program. George was an associate professor of English at Baruch College and the Graduate School. He was also the university director of instructional technology. George had been an active member of the CUNY Steering Committee on Academic Resources and Education (SCORE), which the year before had prepared a feasibility report on developing online degrees at CUNY. Through SCORE, George had worked with many CUNY colleagues who believed in the value of online education. As we'd hoped and expected many of them readily accepted George's invitation to join his faculty development team.

At the same time, SPS staff, under the supervision of Brian Peterson, began to build the infrastructure necessary to support the program: finances, marketing, admissions procedures, library access, student services, and a range of technology support. By the end of 2005, a letter of intent, at that time the first major step in getting a CUNY degree approved, was circulated to all CUNY campuses for review. For the next eight months, a coordinating committee made up of George, faculty, staff, and me met every week to provide updates, review problem areas, and plan next steps.

At least three levels of tension across the university complicated the process of developing an online degree and fueled opposition. One level concerned the mechanics of online course and degree development, raising questions about intellectual property and compensation. Who "owns" the online course? Should course developers receive a flat one-time fee for their work, or are they entitled to some compensation—analogous to a royalty—each time a course is run? Once a course is being offered as part of the curriculum, it must be dynamic and responsive to new knowledge or changes in perspective. Who should be responsible for review and revision? Such questions are knotty but can be resolved, as indeed they have been at many institutions.

A second level of tension—one that continues to this day—concerned the idea of online education itself. As we already knew and as was confirmed when George Otte recruited enthusiastic faculty members for his development team, many CUNY faculty members were eager to use online tools and develop courses and degrees. They were comfortable with technology, which they saw as a way to strengthen and enliven their teaching. Often, they were frustrated by lack of interest or outright resistance at their home campuses. That resistance to online instruction came from faculty who ranged from skeptical to fiercely opposed. Some found it at best a pale substitute for face-to-face classroom teaching. That they may have had no experience with high-quality online instruction, or harbored deep misconceptions, did not lessen their disapproval or resolve skepticism. And, of course, it is true that online instruction—like face-to-face classroom teaching—can vary greatly in quality. Oversight is essential, but at the same time oversight can appear to threaten the faculty's sense of academic freedom.

A third level of tension directly involved SPS itself and whether it should be permitted to offer online degrees. The opponents of SPS represented a range of views about online education, some being ardent practitioners and others dismissive. Their opposition to the SPS degree stemmed from concerns about faculty prerogatives and governance. These tended to be faculty members whose experience in governance or as leaders made them more alert to such issues than were many of their faculty colleagues.

Signs of opposition to SPS developing an online degree began appearing in early September, almost immediately after the public announcement of the university's intention. Selma was invited to the September 27th Plenary Session of the University Faculty Senate (UFS) by UFS Chair Susan O'Malley to discuss the program and answer questions. George, Brian, and I accompanied Selma to the meeting. While the faculty were respectful to Selma, the comments from the faculty were uniformly critical of SPS developing the degree, wondering why Selma had not asked one of CUNY's colleges to develop the degree. Other questions related to the governing structure of SPS, how many students would want to enroll in the program, and the fact that SPS lacked full-time faculty. Selma did a good job of responding to the questions, but it was clear that the UFS would not support the program.

A week later, on October 6, 2005, the *New York Sun*, a daily newspaper in the city at the time, published a story by Jacob Gershman, entitled "CUNY Plans Online Push to Entice Students to Return." The article provided a good summary of CUNY's intention to build an online liberal arts degree that would enroll adult students who had begun college but had to stop before earning their degree. The article quoted Selma Botman: "This is the next phase of CUNY's mission to serve people in New York City." Selma added that "the targeted applicant would be someone who wants to earn a baccalaureate degree but cannot make it to a campus, even if they live or work nearby." The article also reported that Susan O'Malley, chair of the University Faculty Senate (UFS), said that the professors at CUNY she has talked to "have strong concerns about whether an online program would meet the university's academic standards, and about the level of control the faculty would have over the curriculum."[8]

Sandi Cooper, the former chair of the Faculty Senate, who in that capacity had strongly opposed almost every program I developed, was up to form when it came to the online degree. In a long email to the UFS Listserv on December 11, 2005, Cooper referred to Selma's arrival at the September UFS plenary session with "an entourage of people from the newish School of Professional Studies." Her email included a laundry list of complaints about the online degree. She wrote that what she called SOPS (the School of Professional Studies) was "set up with the explicit promise that it was ABSOLUTELY NOT supposed to offer undergraduate degrees." She went on to say that the "UFS opposition to OLBA is based on a determination that no degree issued by CUNY reflect low standards and merely serve as a consumer commodity. This is not a power trip. It is a moral obligation. We stand for standards."

Cooper's assertion that SPS was set up with the promise to not offer undergraduate degrees was not true. In fact, Chancellor Goldstein, as noted earlier in this chapter, had written to Susan O'Malley two years previously stating that while SPS at the time had no intention to offer a degree program, he wouldn't "hamstring" the school in the future; if it wished to offer a degree program, there would be consultation with the faculty, including the UFS.

The UFS leadership encouraged CUNY faculty and staff to criticize and oppose the letter of intent that had been widely distributed throughout the university. We received many letters and emails opposing going forward with the program. We tried to respond to all of them, providing information about the program and attempting to correct inaccuracies. We pointed out that the degree was being constructed by many CUNY faculty who believed in online education and its value to adult students. On the other hand, we were pleased to receive communication from CUNY faculty who approved of the program as well as encouragement from faculty at institutions around the country that were already offering online degrees.

The faculty working on the degree named it Communication and Culture, aware that Chancellor Goldstein had promised not to begin a degree identical or substantially overlapping an existing program at another CUNY college. Although other communication programs existed throughout CUNY, George Otte and the faculty who named and created the degree were confident that it did not contradict the chancellor's promise.

The Governing Committee of SPS approved the program proposal 10–1 in January of 2006, with only Susan O'Malley voting no. Of the remaining two committee members appointed by the Faculty Senate, one voted yes, while the second member did not vote. The proposal went to the Central Office for review before being forwarded to the Board of Trustees for consideration at its February 27, 2006 meeting. A month earlier, on January 31, 2006, the UFS passed a resolution by a vote of 66 to 2 opposing the letter of intent.

Despite the opposition, at its February meeting the trustees approved the proposal for the SPS online degree. The next and last step would be approval by the State Education Department. The Faculty Senate made one final effort to prevent the program from going forward, with Susan O'Malley writing to SED Assistant Commissioner Joe Frey on March 15, 2006, voicing the many concerns about the program, along with the hope that the commissioner would reject the proposal.[9] Commissioner Frey responded to the letter on April 3, writing back to O'Malley that after considering all of the material submitted, "the Department has determined that the proposed programs meet the registration standards set forth in Part 52 of the Commissioner's Regulations."[10]

The online program was officially launched on April 24, 2006, with a website, a public announcement from Chancellor Goldstein, and a broad marketing effort that included sending direct mail to former CUNY students who had left the university in good academic standing. We received more than 2,000 responses to the initial marketing effort, and 411 applications. In late August, 239 students began the program, 80% of them former CUNY students. We had been right in thinking that there was a group of former students who would come back if we could create the conditions that made it possible.[11]

We entered the Fall 2006 semester with exhilaration, considering this a new day for SPS and for what we hoped would be the thousands of future adult students who would be able to earn a degree once thought impossible.

BUILDING NEW DEGREES

The first year of the online program went well. The technology worked. The faculty were fully engaged and excited about being part of something new. And the students seemed to be enjoying their experience and grateful to be able to resume their education. For the most part, they were pleased with their instructors. One common theme heard from students was how hard they had to work. That first year, we did lose students who just were not able to manage both school and the rest of their lives. Although we could not address all of the life issues that impeded students' progress, we learned how to provide better counseling and support services. We also learned how to ensure that course expectations were clear from the beginning and assignments were carefully spaced and structured. Because so many students attended part time, we also lost students for financial reasons. The minimal government financial aid available to part-time students was inadequate to meet their needs. As years went on and the school grew, we began to raise funds for scholarships and financial aid, although it was never enough.

We soon began to think about developing our next online degree, a BS in business. As with our first degree, we identified a small group of faculty to build the program, wrote a letter of intent, and waited for the response. Compared to the reaction to communication and culture, the response to the business degree was tame. A group of business faculty and their provost from Baruch College expressed some criticism, but after George Otte answered their questions, Baruch's president and provost supported the program. Many of the other CUNY colleges offering in-person business degrees also supported the proposal.

The Faculty Senate did oppose the degree. At the June meeting of the trustee Committee on Academic Policy, Program and Research (CAPPR), the senate's representative voted against the program; however, their criticism of the proposal was less strident. The Board of Trustees approved the proposal at its June meeting.

As for the PSC, although the union didn't raise specific criticism to this degree, its leaders filed a formal grievance over the course development agreement established to pay faculty for developing online courses for SPS degrees. That agreement, developed by Rick Schaffer with the assistance of George Otte, provided a one-time payment of $3,000–$5,000 to faculty members, along with a process that paid them for a period of time for teaching the course. Ultimately, ownership of the course went to SPS. The union's formal grievance was decided in favor of the university by the Public Employment Relations Board, and the agreement with minor modifications still stands.

The business degree began with a class of 150 students, and by the spring 2008 semester, SPS had an enrollment of 570 students in its two online programs.

The time-consuming, multi-step process of building a new degree at CUNY, which required approvals at the college, university, and New York State levels, far too often took multiple years. Before SPS was established, it rarely happened in a single year. This lengthy time frame limited CUNY's ability to respond quickly to a changing world. While CUNY faculty and staff generally blamed the slowness of getting review and approval from State Ed for the length of time it took to develop a degree, I believed that CUNY and the individual colleges were also at fault. Far too often, the college proposing the degree had little sense of urgency, and the process just dragged on. Things would stall from May to September while the faculty were on vacation. Or the college would not provide faculty with enough support to prepare proposals in a way that met the detailed requirements. SPS was committed to breaking that paradigm, and that was one of the school's major achievements.

From 2007 to 2021 when I retired, SPS established 25 new baccalaureate and master's-level degrees, in addition to the existing degrees in business and communication and culture. In a number of key areas, the development process was assisted by outside financial and faculty support provided largely through the Central Office. We were more than fortunate that Bill Ebenstein, the founding director of the JFK Jr. Institute for Worker Education and the Consortium for the Study of Disabilities in my SUD unit, had become the university dean for health and human services. He had a vision to help SPS establish new degrees in three areas. First, Bill believed it was essential to build an online Bachelor of Science in Nursing degree (a BSN). The BSN was becoming the degree of choice for many New York hospitals and health clinics that hired CUNY nursing graduates. Registered nurses with associate degrees were no longer receiving automatic job offers, as had previously been the case. Bill correctly predicted that before long there would be some kind of mandate from the state requiring nurses to have bachelor's degrees. To prepare for that, Bill assigned two of CUNY's most prominent nursing faculty, Marge Reilly and Maureen Wallace, who were working as nursing fellows in his office, to help build a new online bachelor's degree in nursing at SPS. The resulting BSN program at SPS opened in 2014 and quickly became the largest undergraduate program at SPS. Bill's prediction of a state mandate also came to pass when in 2017 Governor Cuomo signed a bill requiring that nurses in New York State obtain their bachelor's degrees in nursing within 10 years of licensure.

Secondly, Bill believed that the university needed specific degrees in the area of disability studies, at the master's, bachelor's, and certificate levels, to provide career advancement opportunity for workers who started as direct-care workers and were stuck in relatively low-paying jobs. Again, Bill provided dollars that enabled us to hire a leader in the field, Mariette Bates, to lead the development of degrees in disability studies. These programs, while small in comparison to the nursing programs, were some of the first programs in this field in the entire country.

Several years later, Bill's third priority was realized. He provided support for SPS to create a new master's program in youth studies. Under the exceptional leadership of Sarah Zeller-Berkman, that program also added a bachelor's program in 2021.

Among the broad range of other degrees created were master's degrees in applied theatre; data science; business management and leadership; research administration and compliance; psychology; museum studies, done in partnership with the New-York Historical Society; and bachelor's programs in liberal studies, health services administration, health information management, psychology, sociology, information systems, and human relations. All but three of the degree programs were fully online, the only exceptions being in-person degrees in applied theatre, human relations, and youth studies.

Not surprisingly, as we built new degrees, our enrollment increased and revenue grew. From the spring of 2007 when we opened the business degree until the fall of 2020, when Covid was raging, SPS never had a semester when enrollment and revenue did not grow in comparison to the previous year. By 2020 and the beginning of Covid, the SPS degree programs enrolled more than 4,200 students, a figure close to the enrollment at a few of the more established CUNY colleges.

Developing so many degrees proved taxing to the staff and faculty. At times there was pushback to how hard I was driving them to meet timetables. I had many conversations about whether it was fair or realistic to believe that we could develop and begin a new degree in 12–18 months. I listened to the criticism and at times modified my thinking. I did worry about burning out staff, but I often was stubborn about extending deadlines because we had to work within the trustee calendar for submissions. A proposal that did not meet the early November deadline for the December board meeting or the April deadline for the June board meeting would lose a year or more before implementation. I also facilitated the process through the relationships I had developed with Ekaterina Sukhanova, who oversaw review of proposals at the CUNY Central Office, and with State Ed officials to get them to expedite the approval for SPS programs up for review.

WE GET OUR OWN SPACE

By 2010, burdened by the lack of a permanent home and tired of having to rent space for both classrooms and offices, I raised this issue with the chancellor, Executive Vice Chancellor Allan Dobrin, and Iris Weinshall, vice chancellor for facilities planning, construction and management. They readily agreed that SPS deserved space, and before too long Iris had identified a Midtown office building that would become our new home. Our move in 2013 was an important moment in the history of the school, providing five block-long, freshly renovated floors on West 31st Street between Sixth and Seventh Avenues, down the block from Penn Station, and surrounded by subway stations.

Besides ample classroom space, the move gained us a large and beautiful conference room, a good number of private offices, and our own lobby entrance. A full floor of leased space in a building a few doors down the block became home for most of our academic directors and their staff.

Iris was one of my favorite CUNY colleagues and during her seven years in the position, we became good friends. She had come to CUNY after holding senior level state and city government positions. She was tough, smart, and irreverent. Conversations with Iris were filled with colorful language, and it was hard not to laugh around her. She also was really competent. Iris always responded quickly when I needed advice on how to negotiate some aspect of the Central Office. I was very sorry when she left CUNY in 2014 to become the chief operating officer at the New York Public Library.

NATIONAL RANKINGS AND RECOGNITION

By 2014, with its new degrees and its enrollment growing, SPS was attracting more notice within the CUNY system and beyond. While most students lived in metropolitan New York, we were starting to enroll students from around the country and a few international students as well. Within CUNY, more and more employees, whether "tax levy" (those paid through CUNY's budget) or Research Foundation (paid through grants), took advantage of tuition benefits to enroll in the quality online programs offered by SPS, both at the bachelor's and master's level. Often, when I visited other CUNY colleges or attended university-wide meetings, colleagues would approach me to let me know that they were SPS students or graduates, and how much they enjoyed and respected the school. They also told me that as a result of their degree, they had received promotions. This feedback always felt great.

At this point in our history, we decided to enter the competition to receive a school ranking. *US News* was the gold standard of the ranking business, and although I had always been suspicious of how these rankings were determined, *US News* was now ranking online programs. Getting a relatively high ranking could be invaluable to the reputation of SPS and to our marketing efforts. Providing the information required by *US News* was an onerous task, demanding many hours of preparation. Our office of institutional research, though small, stepped up to meet the challenge, and we applied to be included in the 2016 rankings.

We anxiously awaited the publication of the online rankings at the beginning of January 2016. I recall picking up the phone to hear an exuberant Andrea Fagon, our head of marketing, letting me know that SPS was ranked 27th of the more than 215 colleges and universities offering online courses throughout the United States. We were thrilled with such a high ranking. We publicized it widely on our web site and in our marketing materials. CUNY did as well.

Over the next five years our rankings rose, highlighted by a ranking of #8 in the country in 2021—out of 357 ranked schools—and #10 in 2022 out of 358 schools. Other online programs in the top 15 included

Arizona State, Ohio State, North Carolina State, Penn State World Campus, UMass Amherst, Washington State, and the University of Georgia. To be in the company of these large and historic state universities was an honor for SPS and a recognition of how far the school had come since beginning its first online program in 2006.

In addition, our psychology bachelor's program was ranked second in the country in 2022 and our business program #30. The B.A. in sociology received the *U.S. News* #5 ranking for online programs, and *Fortune Education's* 2023 list of best online master's in data science put the SPS program at #16. *US News* also recognized SPS under the category of best programs for veterans, # 5 in the country out of 101 schools ranked in 2022. We were on the national map.

CHAPTER 26

SPS Grows

Opportunities and Obstacles

WHILE WE CELEBRATED THE ENROLLMENT GROWTH, CREATION OF many new degrees, and high national rankings for the School of Professional Studies and our online programs, the growth of SPS was not entirely smooth. We continued to face criticism from CUNY union and faculty leaders, as well as encountering other major challenges. At the same time, we built upon our success by expanding our foundation board, and our non-credit, largely grant supported unit, PEWL, flourished.

MY GREATEST DISAPPOINTMENT

The contentious May 25, 2017 meeting was coming to an end. It had been called by University Provost Vita Rabinowitz, whose email invitation stated, "I just learned of concerns about a proposal for an online MA in American History developed by the CUNY School of Professional Studies (SPS) in partnership with the Gilder Lehrman Institute of American History. I write to invite you to an information session, hosted by me, that will allow these concerns to be aired and also allow the proponents of the proposed degree to address them forthrightly."[1] The governing council of SPS had just approved the proposed degree on May 19 by a vote of 19–1. I hoped the CUNY Board of Trustees would approve the proposal at its June meeting.

Approximately a year earlier, James Basker, president of the Gilder

Lehrman Institute of American History, had approached me. He asked me to consider partnering with Gilder Lehrman on the development of an online master's program in American history that would provide the opportunity for high school and middle school history and social studies teachers from all over the United States to enroll in a quality, low-cost master's program.

The Gilder Lehrman Institute (GLI), founded by Richard Gilder and Lewis Lehrman in 1994, is a nonprofit organization devoted to improving history education nationally. Since its founding, GLI has developed programs for schools, teachers, and students in all 50 states. By 2017 that was a network comprising more than 90,000 teachers and 13,000 high schools and middle schools (In 2023, GLI reports that number as having grown to 31,000 schools). Each year the Institute offered support and resources to tens of thousands of teachers. It had become perhaps the nation's leading organization providing professional development opportunities in American history to K–12 teachers.

The program Basker proposed would be offered entirely online with all courses taught by CUNY SPS faculty. As a special enhancement, each course would include "video introductions produced with leading scholars filmed on location at historic sites." These scholars "will be recruited by GLI from the Institute's large network that includes winners of the GL book prizes, professors who have taught in GL Summer Seminars, members of the GL Advisory Board and other eminent historians." [2]

To us at SPS, the idea of providing a quality history degree to teachers, with a special goal of reaching teachers serving disadvantaged rural and urban communities in some of the poorest states in the country, was hugely appealing. This would be a nationwide program with only a tiny percentage of its students coming from the New York City area.

Based on my own experience, I should have realized that there would be pushback against the program. But I didn't anticipate how hostile and strident the criticism would be. That criticism came initially and most vocally from the history department chairs and professors from CUNY colleges with existing master's programs. Among their many concerns, several unfounded or based on incorrect information, the chairs noted:

1. The program lacks academic rigor and is highly unlikely to meet even the minimal threshold for serious study at the graduate level, and as it is designed to serve teachers, will do a terrible disservice both to the MA students it will enroll and to their K–12 students throughout New York State.
2. The program subcontracts instruction of CUNY students to another institution, staffed by non-CUNY faculty, and the academic content of the program amounts to video instruction provided by the GL Institute, not by CUNY faculty, and that this undermines the principle of faculty control over curricular development and instruction at CUNY.
3. The program will undermine existing graduate programs in History within CUNY that provide topflight instruction to rigorous standards to CUNY students.
4. There had been inadequate consultation with the faculty who administer existing MA in History programs at CUNY. [3]

Soon after the initial reaction from the History Discipline Council, history faculty from throughout the university wrote to Vita strongly opposing the program. Their letters criticized the credentials of those who developed the program and were expected to teach. The history faculty's letters also warned that the program represented a dangerous trend toward privatization. One claimed that the use of "esteemed historians" would "undermine the authority and academic freedom of the instructor." Another lamented the use of outside Gilder Lehrman faculty to assist in the development of the curriculum. A few faculty just criticized online programs in general.

The University Faculty Senate and the Professional Staff Congress also weighed in and publicly opposed the program. The UFS passed a resolution demanding that "CUNY, the Board of Trustees and the School of

Professional Studies suspend any progress or action on this proposal until proper consultation with all of CUNY's History graduate programs and with the Academic Affairs committee have taken place."

Barbara Bowen, the president of the PSC, wrote to Vita Rabinowitz repeating many of the faculty's arguments against the degree. She added her fear that the program, which included a possible lower tuition for existing high school teachers "could put at risk the jobs of faculty, especially part-time faculty, represented by the PSC." Bowen urged that the program be withdrawn from board consideration until there could be a "thorough, faculty-based review of the academic quality of the proposed program . . . and "its impact on other History MA programs throughout CUNY." [4]

Amid all of this criticism, distinguished CUNY history professors who had long involvement with Gilder Lehrman spoke up to support the program. Andrew Robertson, professor of history at Lehman College and the acting executive officer of the Ph.D. Program in History at the Graduate Center, wrote to Jim Basker that he would attend Vita's meeting to "defend Gilder Lehrman's reputation and the promise this holds for prospective MA students and for CUNY. This SPS-proposed program will not compete with existing CUNY campus MA programs. My colleagues are seriously misinformed about the implication of this proposal. This reaction is, unfortunately, clear evidence that even fine scholars can succumb to Internet exaggeration." [5] Carol Berkin, Presidential Professor at Baruch College and a faculty member at the CUNY Graduate Center, also supported the program, and said she would attend.

The meeting with Vita, held in one of the large conference rooms at the Central Office, was well attended, with 50 or more people present. From the very beginning, the meeting went badly. The faculty who spoke up were hostile and accusatory. George Otte, Carol Berkin, Andy Robertson, and our Gilder Lehrman colleagues joined me in trying to answer questions respectfully. We tried to correct what we believed were misconceptions and inaccuracies. We pointed out that the videos by the esteemed Gilder Lehrman faculty were actually resources for the courses, and that each course would be taught by CUNY/SPS faculty. We emphasized how fortunate the students would be to see videos by some of the most prominent historians in the United States.

We also stressed that in no way would the program have a negative impact on the enrollment at the existing CUNY history master's programs. We repeated any number of times during the meeting that this was a national program, focused on enrolling and providing educational opportunities for high school teachers throughout the country; virtually none of those students was likely to attend one of CUNY's in-person history master's programs. I couldn't help but point out that the existing history programs had serious enrollment issues. The enrollment for the six CUNY college programs had declined from 246 students in 2012 to 164 students in 2016, along with a decrease in program graduates from 67 to 49. Rather than cost jobs as the union had indicated, I reasoned, we would be adding many adjunct and possibly a few full-time faculty positions as a result of the program if our own enrollment projections were anywhere close to accurate.

During the meeting Vita tried to walk a fine line between supporting the program and SPS while being respectful to the questions and criticism. I had enormous respect for Vita and recognized that, as the university's chief academic officer, she was in a difficult position to face such vehement opposition from some of CUNY's leading historians and faculty leaders. I did believe, however, despite my affection and friendship with Vita, that under Matt Goldstein and Louise Mirrer's leadership, we wouldn't have had such a meeting. Instead, we would have answered the criticism in writing and moved forward with getting the program approved. This was a quality program, in partnership with a distinguished organization. It had enormous potential to provide opportunity to thousands of needy teachers throughout the country. The meeting was a very public fanning the flame of what could have been a much smaller fire.

At the conclusion of the meeting, I spoke briefly with Carol Berkin, who expressed her rage at the tone of the meeting and frustration at the level of resistance to change from her fellow historians. She declared that it was this kind of resistance to change that had led her to decide to retire in 2012. That evening, I wrote to Vita, saying, "I found much of the meeting disheartening, with many of the faculty accusations a direct attack on what we have worked so hard to create at SPS." [6] From the SPS point of view, all of us who had built the program were angry and sad. Vita responded to my email right away, letting George Otte and me know that she still supported the program and "didn't want to lose GL no matter what." She did feel, however, that the proposal would need some modifications and perhaps a more independent review.

A week later, after consulting with the chancellor, Vita sent a message to the faculty and administrators who attended the meeting thanking them for a frank conversation and informing them that she had decided to "postpone the planned June presentation of this proposal to the Board of Trustees." She added:

> We have seen nationally recognized success with graduate as well as undergraduate online degrees at CUNY SPS, and the partnership with the Gilder Lehrman Institute for American History presents a great opportunity to extend that success—and access—to a special audience of K–12 teachers. It is our plan to move forward with a version of the proposal in the fall, informed by your input, to realize this opportunity.

Vita went on to say, "CUNY SPS followed every current rule and procedure in bringing the proposal forward," although also stating that perhaps we needed a different consultation process for new online degrees.[7]

The Gilder Lehrman Institute's Jim Basker had been unable to attend the meeting, but we spoke soon after. Jim shared my anger. As a Barnard professor, he was familiar with faculty governance issues and resistance to change. He did say, however, that never in his long career had he ever seen the rigidity, hysteria and insults expressed by the CUNY faculty and certain administrators. How could it be that they were opposing a program that would be providing access to MA degrees and courses to teachers desperate for this kind of opportunity? How was it possible that they could be against a program that would also produce jobs for young historians, bring recognition to CUNY, serve thousands of worthy students over the next five years, and bring needed revenue to the university? Jim and I agreed that this was more about preserving turf and maintaining control over rapidly diminishing programs. It reflected a visceral opposition both to online education and to SPS.

A few days after this conversation, I called Jim and said it was time to throw in the towel. Despite all of the good work to date, I just didn't feel that SPS could afford to spend any more time or energy on getting the program passed. Response from Vita and the chancellor had been measured and cautious in pulling the item from the June trustee agenda and agreeing to a more consultative review process. But the delay meant that we likely would never get to the finish line. Jim agreed with me, expressing gratitude for all SPS had done to get us to this point. He would find another partner for the degree. He also said that while he would continue to work with individual CUNY faculty, there would be no attempts to partner with CUNY in future degree-building efforts. At this point, all I could do was thank Jim him for reaching out to us.

Later that day, I called Vita to let her know of our decision. Although she expressed disappointment, I felt that our decision to pull the plug was perhaps a relief for her. This was one less headache for the chancellor to address. Gilder Lehrman moved on, and Gettysburg College in Pennsylvania ended up partnering with Gilder Lehrman to offer the degree.

The failure to move this history degree and a potentially fruitful partnership forward was painful. And it was hard to accept. This was a worthy program. To this day, more strongly than ever, I believe that the criticism was built on untruths, misperceptions, and falsehoods. The opposition leaders gained nothing for their own programs while foreclosing on a potentially exciting and beneficial new program that could have helped many others and CUNY at large.

THE MURPHY INSTITUTE: HOW POWER AND POLITICS AFFECT DECISION MAKING

At its June 26, 2017 board meeting, CUNY trustees approved the establishment of the CUNY School of Labor and Urban Studies as part of the Graduate School and University Center. The board's action was the culmination of a multi-year effort by organized labor to convince CUNY to establish a separate school of labor that would directly serve union members.

SPS was an integral part of that story, which had begun three decades earlier in 1984 when the Worker Education Program (WEP), dedicated to providing educational opportunities to union members, opened at Queens College.[8] Gregory Mantsios was appointed to direct the program. Over the next 20 years, WEP provided a host of services to union members and other adult students, including counseling, tutoring, and financial assistance, and the opportunity to enroll in credit and non-credit classes. Financially, the program was mostly supported from the Central Office, which paid rent for a leased facility on West 43rd Street in Manhattan and provided funds to support staff and faculty. The program also received allocations from both the state and the city, along with the labor community. Dollars spent by Queens College were offset by tuition revenue and a tuition waiver process.

During that 20-year period, I was aware of the program's existence in my role of overseeing adult and continuing education at CUNY. But I didn't work with it directly. I was totally unaware of a 20-year history of conflict and disagreement between the Queens College administration and the program. That conflict seemed to worsen after James Muyskens became president of Queens College in 2002. In 2004, Vice Chancellor Jay Hershenson asked me to join him in a meeting with President Muyskens and other members of his senior team to look for a way to resolve the conflict. By then I had gotten to know President Muyskens and considered him a thoughtful and reasonable person. It was pretty clear from the meeting, however, that the situation was unlikely to be solved without totally restructuring the program and perhaps having it reside at another CUNY institution. Further proof of the tension came in an email that Greg Mantsios sent to Jay Hershenson with a copy to me on August 25, 2004. The first point in the email stated, "I can't overstate the level of anger and frustration that everyone is feeling towards Queens College. We are dealing with a 20-year history of problems—this really seems to be the last straw. Everyone definitely wants out."[9]

In August of 2004, at the request of the chancellor, Jay had asked Vice Chancellor Michael Zavalle to produce a white paper on the Worker Education Program and its relationship to the college. The paper was comprehensive and analytical. It made a series of recommendations but concluded: "As a last resort, if the University, Queens and WEP find the recommendations in this white paper to be an unacceptable basis upon which to negotiate an agreement, the feasibility of separating WEP from Queens and attaching it to another University entity, such as the School of Professional Studies, could be considered."[10] By the time the paper was released, the situation had gotten even worse. Chancellor Goldstein was receiving enormous pressure from major union leaders, all strong allies of CUNY and also supporters of Greg Mantsios, to sever the relationship with Queens College and give WEP a new home.

To resolve the problem, the chancellor decided that the program would move to SPS and be renamed the Joseph S. Murphy Institute for Worker Education and Labor Studies. The late Joe Murphy, a former CUNY chancellor and Queens College president, had been a strong labor advocate. By giving the program the status of an institute, it would have the capacity to run university-wide programs and partner with other CUNY colleges. CUNY also would provide additional financial resources.

This solution appeared to please both Greg Mantsios and union leaders. Arthur Cheliotes, president of Local 1180 of the Communications Workers of America and the chair of the program's labor advisory board, wrote a letter to Chancellor Goldstein: "I want to take this opportunity to thank you for supporting our efforts to expand educational opportunities for the City's union members. A University-wide home for Worker

Education and the Labor Resource Center creates a historic partnership between the academy and organized labor, and a way for us to realize together, the potential for the city and its workforce." [11] To celebrate the new partnership, the university hosted an event attended by most of the major union leaders in the city, together with the chancellor and most members of his cabinet. In his remarks, the chancellor thanked me for my willingness to be part of this arrangement, and I too spoke.

While bringing the Murphy Institute to SPS would enhance our status, I could see from the start that the partnership would not be simple. Greg Mantsios would not be easy to supervise. He was used to getting his way, had strong opinions, and rarely compromised. If he didn't get his way with me, Greg would go to union leaders, particularly Arthur Cheliotes, who often contacted the chancellor to complain. I was not looking forward to those kinds of headaches.

The SPS staff worked hard to support the staff of the Murphy Institute and to integrate Murphy's administrative functions into the existing structure of SPS. That included the offices of admission services, the registrar, the budget office, the bursar, and information technology. SPS would also provide guidance and support to Murphy as it built new degree and certificate programs.

Greg Mantsios reported directly to me, and I tried to attend Murphy meetings and events and get to know the members of the labor advisory board. I met regularly with Arthur Cheliotes and Greg, and each semester the chancellor and I attended a meeting of the advisory board.

Murphy had an exceptional faculty. Several held full-time appointments at the Graduate School, as well as their part-time consortial appointments at Murphy. They included Stanley Aronowitz, Steve Brier, Josh Freeman, Frances Fox Piven, Mimi Abramovitz, and John Mollenkopf. These were some of the most prominent professors at CUNY and in their respective fields, and they were people I greatly admired and respected. As Murphy created new degrees in labor and urban studies at the graduate level and an undergraduate degree in urban and labor studies, it was able to hire its own full-time faculty, and they too were impressive. I got to know all of the faculty, attended many of their meetings, and interacted with them as they joined SPS governance and ad hoc committees.

As Murphy transitioned to SPS, I was struck by several factors. Foremost was that Murphy's budget was far larger than I had imagined. So was its staff. Over the previous 30 years, Greg Mantsios and his union partners had successfully persuaded the university, state, and city to provide significant and permanent funding to what was in fact a small unit. Even after building its first degree programs and adding a few certificate programs while at SPS, Murphy enrolled just above 350 students. Although Murphy also included in its own headcount an additional 800 or so students who were part of programs it helped administer at other CUNY campuses, neither the university nor the partner colleges formally considered these students to be Murphy students. Indeed, Murphy's enrollment numbers had not increased much over its years of existence.

It also was quickly apparent that Greg and Arthur had goals far grander than being attached to SPS. For years, they had wanted CUNY to create a separate and independent labor school. That was not going to happen under Matt Goldstein's leadership. Matthew felt being attached to SPS provided the opportunity to grow. Despite ongoing pressure by union leaders, a new school of labor was not going to be established on his watch.

When Matthew Goldstein retired in 2013, Greg, Arthur, and many of the Murphy staff and faculty saw an opportunity to push again for Murphy to become an independent entity. By then, the vast majority of SPS staff were also actively hoping this would happen. They had found working with Murphy to be draining and time consuming. Too often, the Murphy staff, with some exceptions, did not appreciate the assistance provided. I also had mixed feelings about Murphy's staying at SPS. I felt guilty that I had burdened my staff with the additional responsibilities of Murphy. I had also grown weary of the constant criticism from Greg and members of the Murphy faculty that somehow the SPS structure and supposed rigidity were getting in the way of Murphy's expanding its program offerings. I also resented Greg's refusal to acknowledge much less appreciate that SPS was directly subsidizing Murphy with all the services it provided. He certainly was not inclined to put aside a portion of the Murphy budget to pay for those services unless being directed by me to do so.

In February 2014, about seven months after Chancellor Goldstein left, leading members of the Murphy full-time and consortial faculty issued what they called a "White Paper on Autonomy and Governance." The document stated that "under current administrative arrangements, the full potential of JSMI as a leading national labor and urban studies teaching and research center is as yet unrealized. We believe that granting greater autonomy to JSMI, as its director and labor advisory board have requested, and giving a larger role to the faculty in JSMI governance, along the lines we suggest below, will provide the basis for programmatic expansion and greater academic excellence in the years to come."[12]

The paper recommended that Murphy have a governance plan independent of SPS governance, to include a "Murphy-wide Personnel and Budget Committee, similar to the P&B's that CUNY colleges have institutionalized." It was interesting to note that the plan indicated that the long history of the program did "concentrate too much decision-making power in the hands of the Director" and that any new structure would need "a much larger role for faculty." The plan did not specify a future structure for Murphy, only that the "issue of JSMI autonomy and its future place within CUNY needs to be addressed expeditiously." [13]

At the same time that the faculty white paper was issued, Arthur Cheliotes forwarded to Vice Chancellor Jay Hershenson a document that included 12 points on why the Murphy Institute should no longer be part of SPS. Jay asked me to respond to the points, which I did. Jay then forwarded my response to Arthur, copying Greg, Interim Chancellor Bill Kelly, and the four senior members of the chancellor's cabinet. While I disagreed with virtually all of what Arthur said, one point irked me most. It stated that "SPS is entirely enrollment driven: JSMI is partly enrollment driven and partly service driven."[14] He did not define "service-driven," but by any definition, the claim that SPS wasn't service-driven was ridiculous. By then in our degree and non-credit programs, we already were serving more than 10 times the numbers of city workers (the vast majority of whom were union members) than Murphy served. This figure grew to more than 30 times the number by 2020.

A few months later, in June 2014, J.B. Milliken was appointed as the new CUNY chancellor. Immediately, he inherited this conflict. By the early fall, the New York State AFL-CIO issued a resolution calling for the establishment of a new school for labor and urban studies at CUNY. That was followed by a letter to the chancellor on November 7, signed by all the Murphy full time and consortial faculty endorsing the resolution.

Trying to buy time and get some outside independent advice, Chancellor Milliken convened a task force on "Worker Education: Planning for the 21st Century" that was to look at workforce programs in general at CUNY but focus in particular on the role and history of the Murphy Institute. The task force was chaired by Paul Attewell, distinguished professor of sociology at the Graduate Center, Regina Peruggi, president emerita of Kingsborough Community College, and Arlene Torres, director of the Chancellor's Initiative on Latino Faculty and a member of Hunter College's Department of Africana and Puerto Rican Studies.

After months of work, the task force submitted its report. In a September 2015 cover letter prepared for the report, Chancellor Milliken accepted the recommendations of the task force. He wrote: "While calling for greater collaboration among CUNY's worker education programs, the report recommends no major organizational changes at this time either in the structure of individual programs or the Murphy Institute. It is important to acknowledge the Task Force's finding that most of the worker education enrollments at CUNY are outside the Murphy Institute." The chancellor continued: "The Task Force made it clear to us that the level and nature of CUNY support to Murphy is not widely known. As you can see, the University makes substantial annual investments in the institute, and rebates an unusually large percentage (80%) of the tuition dollars it raises directly back to the Institute. We are proud to continue our commitment to the Murphy Institute even in these challenging economic times."[15]

Despite the task force recommendation that Murphy remain attached to SPS, I was not convinced that would be the case. I was certain that

Greg, Arthur, the Murphy faculty, and other union leaders would continue to pressure the chancellor and that eventually their efforts would succeed. That happened even more quickly than I had expected.

In late March of 2016, Chancellor Milliken let me know that he was thinking about moving Murphy out of SPS. He said that at the end of a recent meeting he had with State Assembly Speaker Carl Heastie to discuss CUNY budget concerns, Heastie had mentioned that it was important for him to have a school of labor at CUNY. As Assembly Speaker, Heastie had enormous influence over the CUNY budget. In our conversation, the chancellor mentioned that he assumed that the decision to move Murphy from SPS would be welcome news for me. I responded that was largely true; however, while I understood why he needed to make this decision, it was distasteful to me to have to cave in to purely political pressure. I resented all of the Murphy badmouthing of me and SPS.

A few weeks later, then University Provost and Executive Vice Chancellor for Academic Affairs Vita Rabinowitz informed me that they would be establishing a work group to figure out where to place Murphy. It would definitely move out of SPS, and a new CUNY school of labor would be created. Vita mentioned that among the campuses under consideration to house the new school were City College, John Jay, or even a return to Queens College. When the presidents from each of these schools pushed back and declared they were not interested in housing a new school of labor, Vita asked me whether it might be possible to consider keeping the school at SPS, kind of a school within a school. Neither Murphy nor I would consider that.

Finally, after almost 10 months, the university decided to create a new school for labor and urban studies at the Graduate School and University Center. It would be given the same status as the existing University Center schools, which included SPS, the Graduate School of Journalism, the School of Public Health, and Macaulay Honors College.

A year later, at its June 26, 2017 meeting, the CUNY Board of Trustees voted to transform the Murphy Institute into the CUNY School of Labor and Urban Studies at the Graduate School and University Center. The action was intended to "provide the fields of labor studies and urban studies with greater visibility in both the academic and labor communities."[16] That was followed by the board naming Gregory Mantsios the founding dean of the CUNY School of Labor and Urban Studies, effective January 26, 2018.

On March 26, 2018, the *New York Post*, in an article by Carl Campanile and headlined "Cuomo's Budget Includes Plan to Create CUNY School Focused on Unions," stated that the governor's new budget would include a "$1.5 million line item into his election-year budget to create a School of Urban and Labor Studies at the City University of New York." The article further stated that "Union leaders have been campaigning for their own Labor School at CUNY for years" but "CUNY officials had long resisted the creation of a Labor School until the past year or so." The article continued: "It's the first time in eight years that Cuomo has put a line-item in his executive budget for CUNY's labor studies, and Albany and CUNY insiders see the move as an election-year gift to Big Labor as the two-term Democratic incumbent seeks union backing as he seeks re-election." The article also included a positive quote from the Chancellor about the move to create the new school. [17]

The School of Labor and Urban Studies (SLU) enrolled its first students in the fall semester of 2018. Although SPS lost 13% of its enrollment and three degree programs in the separation, the SPS staff was overjoyed to no longer have to deal with the stress and aggravation of trying to serve Murphy and satisfy Greg. Within a year, SPS had overcome the enrollment loss, and SPS continued to be the fastest-growing institution at CUNY.

Over its first five years, SLU has continued to advance one major facet of its mission: to increase the visibility of research in the field of labor studies. Its distinguished faculty produce important research on labor-related issues, and SLU offers an array of public programs featuring well-known speakers. It has also continued to enjoy the support of major labor leaders in New York City. And SLU had built its own administrative and governance structure. At the same time, although SLU's enrollment has grown, it remains modest, with 454 students in the fall 0f 2022.

Looking ahead, it will be interesting to see how SLU develops. What

I often observed about Murphy was the absence of a sense of urgency regarding how they approached their work. It also seemed that true program innovation was rare. Perhaps that was because they didn't need to worry about funding, since they were already receiving city, state and CUNY dollars that enabled them to maintain a sizeable faculty and staff without having to demonstrate program or enrollment growth.

Hopefully, SLU's administration and faculty will begin to serve union members more broadly and creatively. The over 30-year history leading to the creation of SLU is one of politics and power. I happened to be part of that story, and it wasn't a pleasant experience. CUNY is enriched by having a School of Labor and Urban Studies. But now that there is no longer a need to expend energy on the vision of establishing a labor college, perhaps similar energy can be directed toward creating truly visionary programming.

GRANTS GROW: ESTABLISHING THE PROFESSIONAL EDUCATION AND WORKPLACE LEARNING UNIT (PEWL)

In the dreariest of offices in our old 31st Street building, a small group of staff led by Brian Peterson and Washington Hernandez were working around the clock in 2011 to gain competence in managing a software program called Sahana. This web-based system, developed to help the country of Sri Lanka prepare for coastal storm emergencies, was slated to be used by the New York City Office of Emergency Management (OEM) to track people who needed to go to evacuation centers if a major storm hit New York. SPS had been working with OEM since 2006 to provide online training in disaster management. From 2006–2010, SPS had trained almost 14,000 city and nonprofit workers in what was called "pre-incident" management.[18]

This latest training, to learn and manage the Sahana system, was different. The staff had started to learn the system a few months prior but had not yet completed the process. We had not yet piloted it in any way. A few days earlier, however, SPS had received word from OEM that a major hurricane, called Irene, was headed toward New York. Suddenly any piloting or practicing would have to be in real time, in a real emergency. The next 48 hours would be intense, and our staff would get little sleep. To prepare, staff brought in food and let family and friends know that they would not be home until after the storm.

The storm hit the city on August 29, 2011. It was the largest hurricane to hit New York since 1972. Ready or not, the implementation of Sahana began. Evacuation centers were opened all over the city, including on CUNY campuses. Thousands of New Yorkers left their homes seeking shelter. Through Sahana, we were responsible for tracking the New Yorkers entering the centers, including accounting for their belongings and pets. Andrew Boyarsky, our project director, toured a number of the centers, including the one at York College, making sure that things were in order.

Miraculously, the system worked. In real time we were able to provide data to city officials on the location of evacuated residents. In the aftermath of the storm, senior NYC officials thanked us in a formal ceremony for the quality of our work. At SPS we also celebrated the work of our staff, proud that we had stepped up to help the city. Our work with OEM continued over the next 10 years.

From the school's opening in 2003, SPS had been committed to working directly with city and state agencies to provide training to city workers. A major goal was to assist in solving urban problems in a manner similar to that developed in my Central Office Senior University Dean unit. In addition to the Coastal Storm Project, SPS partnered with other key agencies: the Metropolitan Transit Authority, NYC Housing Authority, Human Resources Administration, and the departments of Homeless Services, Small Business Services, and Administrative Services. By 2011, funding for these programs totaled almost $4 million, with each project funded under a separate intra-city agreement between SPS and the particular city agency.

Grant-supported programs at SPS grew rapidly. Additional city and state agencies funded us to develop new programs, and we received grants from New York-based foundations, including Pinkerton, Robin Hood, Petrie, Altman, and Heckscher. By 2019, SPS was generating over $32 million in grant funds, a figure that placed SPS as the fourth—or fifth—largest grant-getting institution in CUNY.

We needed to monitor and oversee this large and growing grant portfolio, so we established a new unit at SPS that we called Professional Education and Workplace Learning, resulting in the unwieldy acronym PEWL. The PEWL unit administered more than 20 separate programs and employed more than 150 staff, all funded through grant dollars.

The largest program came about at the request of the NYC Administration for Children's Services. ACS asked SPS to partner in developing a workforce training institute that would offer professional development to child welfare and juvenile justice workers employed either by the city or community-based organizations. The program started in 2016 and was originally funded at just above $8 million. By FY19 funding had increased to over $18 million, and the program was training more than 9,000 workers annually.

We were proud of all of the grant funding we received, but we felt a special pride in a grant awarded to SPS by the Central Park Conservancy, the agency responsible for administering, preserving, and caring for Central Park. In 2017 the Conservancy's Institute for Urban Parks had issued a request for proposals (RFP) to fund an organization to develop and administer an Urban Park Leadership Program. The program would enroll park managers from throughout the United States to participate in both in-person and online "professional development experiences covering a range of topics relevant to urban park leadership and management." [19]

The funding application included a written proposal and an in-person interview with Conservancy staff and trustees. While I believed we wrote an excellent proposal and interviewed well, we still didn't expect to be awarded the grant. The other finalists in the competition happened to be Yale and Columbia. By their reputations alone, I thought our chances were slim. When we were informed that we had received the grant, we were thrilled. To be selected over two of the most elite universities in the country was outstanding recognition.

The success of the PEWL unit as a major grant-getting unit is further evidence of what can happen when the vision, scope, and role of a college are broadened. The flexibility of being able to draw on both credit/degree programs and non-credit programs was critically important to our success. By the time I left the CUNY School of Professional Studies, PEWL had become—like my Central Office unit, SUD—a place for city officials to go when they needed new thinking and innovative programs to address difficult social policy issues. Those officials knew that we would almost always say yes to new opportunities. If we lacked the requisite expertise in-house, we would find it. They also knew they could rely on us to develop and implement quality programs. At the same time, the initiative to pursue grant funding often came from us. We approached public and private funding sources whenever we came up with new ideas for programs or simply needed fiscal resources to support student success.

ESTABLISHING A FOUNDATION BOARD

I entered Midwood High School, my alma mater, trying to recognize the faces of the people milling about in the lobby. Elliott Golinkoff, my best friend from childhood and lifelong friend, and I had decided to attend our 50-year high school reunion. I was surprised that I could barely recognize anyone. Everyone looked really old. I reluctantly concluded that we must look pretty old, too.

Midwood is a large Brooklyn high school, and more than 1,000 students made up our graduating class of 1964. Mingling with classmates that day, I reconnected with several old friends. We shared stories, brought people up to date on our lives, and then moved on to talk to someone else. At one point I wound up talking to Joel Cohen, a classmate I did not know at all in high school. In our conversation, Joel told me know that while I hadn't known him, he knew me from my reputation as an athlete, and that he had attended a number of our high school basketball games. We laughed about that, and it became a story that Joel continued to tell over the years.

Joel seemed really interesting and impressive. After college he had a successful career working at JP Morgan Chase, then retired relatively early. He was currently a member of a few outside boards, including one affiliated with a small higher education institution. As we talked, I began to think that Joel would be a good fit for our relatively new SPS foundation board. The board was established in 2011 to raise scholarship money for SPS students. As were ending our conversation, I broached the idea with Joel about joining our board. We agreed to meet again soon to discuss the idea further. A few weeks later, during our second conversation, Joel agreed to join the board.

Forming a foundation board had not been a top priority when we began to build SPS. We had too much else to do. By 2011, however, with the rapid expansion of the school, it was time to establish a school foundation. All the other CUNY colleges had foundations of long standing, and some, such as Hunter, City, and Baruch, raised many millions of dollars each year from donors, many of them alums.

First, I had to find a board chair. Fortunately, one of the very first graduates of SPS was Bob Kissane. Bob, a good friend of Chancellor Goldstein, was the Chairman of CSS Fundraising, a very successful consulting firm that specialized in assisting nonprofits to raise money. Bob also served on a number of important nonprofit boards, including Human Rights Watch and the Alvin Ailey American Dance Theater. Despite his success, Bob had never completed college. With the encouragement of Matt Goldstein, he enrolled as an online student at SPS and received his degree in 2010. During his time as an SPS student, I got to know Bob well. He greatly valued his SPS degree and raved about the quality of the faculty and instruction he received. When I asked Bob to become our board chair and help develop our foundation, he readily agreed.

Over the next 10 years, we built an infrastructure for the board, established the board as an Incorporated nonprofit organization, and expanded the board membership from its initial three members to 13. Two board members, first Horace Barker and then Blake Foote, succeeded Bob as board chair. I had known Blake and Horace as members of the NYC Workforce Board and they, like Bob, enthusiastically accepted my invitation to join the SPS board. We also appointed two other SPS graduates to the board, and a number of prominent New Yorkers from finance, health care, law, and the nonprofit world. The board was hugely supportive of me and SPS, and members were generous with their time and expert advice. Most board members were generous donors. Board meetings were almost always upbeat, and I thoroughly enjoyed being around the board members, whether at formal meetings or in more relaxed settings.

By FY2018, the SPS Foundation was raising a little under $500,000 annually and was receiving gifts from almost 400 individuals and a few New York City-based foundations. The fund balance at the end of the year was over $1.2 million. In 2018 Michael Iadarola became the SPS Director of Development. Michael, who had previously worked in Development at Saint Francis and Brooklyn Colleges, was hardworking, got along with everyone, and knew when to push me and when to back off.

As much as I appreciated and enjoyed working with the board, identifying new board members and raising private money for the foundation was not one of my favorite activities. I understood that to raise money I needed to ask people who had money to give, and I like to think I wasn't bad at it. But I always found it easier to get large grants from institutions, agencies or foundations, often in the millions of dollars, than to spend time asking for private gifts one on one. Still, individual philanthropy was vitally important to SPS, especially when it came to finding support for our largely part-time student body. Since almost no public financial aid was available to part-time students, many depended on private scholarship aid to complete their degrees. Alan Fishman, a friend from college, established the school's largest scholarship program. Alan had been the board chair of the Brooklyn Academy of Music for 18 years, as well as the chair of the Brooklyn Navy Yard, the Brooklyn Chamber of Commerce, and the Brooklyn Community Foundation. While in general he gave only to Brooklyn organizations, including all the CUNY colleges located in Brooklyn, he trusted me and the SPS staff to create a much-needed, high-quality scholarship program.

Under Blake Foote's leadership, the board brought in new members, and by the time I retired, the board had become an integral part of SPS; many of its members were not only donors but also were directly involved in the activities of the school.

MANAGING SPS DURING A PANDEMIC

Early Saturday morning, March 7, 2020, I was traveling on an Amtrak train from New York to Albany. Chancellor Matos Rodriguez was hosting the annual CUNY luncheon that was part of the Somos Legislative Conference, sponsored by the NYS Puerto Rican/Hispanic Task Force. The three-day conference, attended by virtually all the major political leaders in New York State, was considered a command performance for CUNY college presidents and professional school deans.

On the train, I sat next to Ayman El-Mohandes, dean of the CUNY School of Public Health. As fellow deans of schools that were part of the University Center, Ayman and I had come to know one another well since he assumed his position in 2013. I always liked to talk with Ayman, who had lots of interests and a good sense of humor. An hour or so after we left New York's Penn Station, my mobile phone rang. It was one of my K–16 staff letting me know that she had begun to receive phone calls from anxious parents of high school students scheduled to participate the next day in the NYC Science and Engineering Fair at City College. Our CUNY K–16 office had administered the conference for the New York City Department of Education for many years. We expected several hundred of the most talented science students in the city to be exhibiting their projects.

Several parents called to urge us to delay the science fair. The first case of Covid-19 in NYC had been identified, and fears were growing that the disease could spread rapidly. I let my colleague know I would get right back to her. I turned to Ayman to get his advice on what to do. He responded that, based on the information he had at the moment, he would not cancel the fair. I called my colleague back and let her know that we would hold the fair as scheduled.

When we arrived in Albany, we immediately went to the lunch. In a very crowded room, a few hundred CUNY administrators and students mingled with many politicians. Our chancellor opened the meeting, giving short welcoming remarks. He then introduced a series of speakers, including State Assembly Speaker Carl Heastie and SUNY Chancellor

Kathy Johnson. As each speaker came to the podium, Chancellor Matos Rodriguez gave them either a fist bump or a touching of elbows, the no-handshake, no-hug Covid protocol that was being widely and quickly adopted everywhere. I asked myself if it was wise for me to attend this conference. And had I made the wrong decision about the Science Fair?

Within a week of the conference, all hell had broken out in New York City. By March 16, CUNY, SUNY, and New York's public schools were shut down for in-person learning, soon followed by virtually all of New York other than essential services. The severity of the illness was like nothing the country had experienced in my lifetime. Fear was pervasive. Many New Yorkers were dying every day. My new priority had to be to work with my SPS colleagues to plan for the changing and threatening landscape.

I immediately called our cabinet together to begin that planning. All of us recognized that despite the dire situation, SPS had a major advantage over the other 24 CUNY schools: the vast majority of our degree students were already taking online classes. Nonetheless, we still had to prepare for all faculty and staff to have the tools to be able to do their jobs at home, to arrange for the limited number of degree students who were taking in-person classes to move to online instruction, and to make sure that our technology worked. We also had to figure out how to continue to serve the tens of thousands of city workers enrolled in our non-credit programs. Perhaps most importantly, as leaders we needed to demonstrate a sense of calm, try to keep morale high, and make sure we were prepared to support members of the SPS community who were struggling with emotional issues. Finally, we needed to have mechanisms in place to support students, faculty, and staff who either got Covid or had family members who did.

Given my limited technology prowess, I worried whether I would be able to do my work at home, alone, with no one nearby to "take care of me." I was lucky that we had a great IT team headed by Bronwen Stine, whom we were fortunate to hire in 2019. Prior to coming to SPS, Bronwen had been the director of IT at Carnegie Hall for 15 years, and then at the New York Philharmonic for two years. I recall talking to her references as part of the search process and hearing one rave review after another. All of what those folks said was true, and Bronwen was perfect for these times. She was unflappable and sensitive, really knew her technology, and had excellent relationships with her IT Team and the entire SPS community. It also happened that Bronwen lived only a little more than a block away from me; she was able to stop by my house (both of us masked and keeping six feet apart) if she couldn't fix a problem by phone or join me on my computer on Team Viewer.

During the first few months of Covid, despite the horror all around us, SPS functioned at a reasonably high level. For the most part, staff and faculty were able to do their jobs, and students continued to attend their courses. Our academic directors worked closely with their faculty to make sure that we were sensitive to the specific needs of our students. That included being more flexible when it came to deadlines for assignments and scheduling to make up missed tests. Many of our students were essential workers. Throughout the early days of Covid, they were on the frontlines. Without added flexibility in their courses, far more of them would have had to drop out of school.

Those at SPS most affected by the spread of Covid were the nursing students and faculty. By 2020 nursing had become our largest program, with more than 600 students enrolled in the BSN program and more than 75 in the master's programs. Only six years old, the nursing program had grown rapidly, enabling students who were already working as registered nurses (RNs) to earn their bachelor's degree. In the pandemic, our nurses were working under the most extreme conditions, many in ICUs and emergency rooms. They were surrounded by large numbers of New Yorkers dying every day, but many of their hospitals lacked the necessary equipment—PPE, as we learned to call it—to protect the nurses. In these early months, little successful treatment for Covid was available.

The nursing faculty was similarly stressed. Many were emotionally drained, including Marge Reilly, the program's academic director. I recall one conversation when she explained that never in her long career as a practicing nurse or later as a faculty member had she ever experienced anything close to the level of patient death that our nursing students were seeing every day. Her voice quivered as she explained this to me. Marge had the aura of a tough, strong nurse, who pushed her students hard to excel and maintained high standards. At that terrible moment, however, she was drawing on every bit of discipline developed over years of professional experience. The world was beyond her control. She was working 15-hour days trying to support her students both at their jobs and in their schoolwork. Many of her students were getting Covid, along with lots of their work colleagues, including doctors. By April 4, 2020, a month after the city's first Covid case had been discovered, the city had 12,274 cases. By mid-April, hundreds of New Yorkers were dying daily. Refrigerated morgue units were backed up to hospital doors to handle the corpses.

Because of our experience with online teaching, the university turned to SPS to assist in training CUNY faculty who had been forced to move their courses from in-person to online. Prior to Covid, the majority of CUNY faculty had little interest or experience in teaching online. Only a small percentage of courses across CUNY were online or partially online. Except for a few limited start-up efforts, SPS was still the only CUNY college offering online degrees. Now all CUNY professors, most of them with no experience in online teaching and some decidedly hostile to it, would be teaching online from home and without access to onsite technical support. SPS was asked to build a professional development course that would provide these faculty members with the basic knowledge and skills needed to manage an online class. Meanwhile, teaching had to continue. There was no choice. It was the middle of the semester.

We turned to Ruru Rusmin, the Director of our Office of Faculty Development Office, to build the course and work out the details of recruiting and enrolling faculty. Ruru was assisted by Associate Dean Jennifer Sparrow, other members of her team, and a few faculty and staff from across the university. Ruru and Jennifer managed their existing full-time jobs at SPS, already complicated by Covid, while simultaneously creating a new training protocol for CUNY faculty.

The SPS team didn't complain, but rather moved ahead. Over the next 4–5 months, they trained approximately 2,000 CUNY faculty in four cohorts of 500 each. The university was pleased with our work, and even the least prepared faculty learned the rudiments of teaching online. While the approach to online teaching at SPS was asynchronous (students could sign into their work at any time), the quick training we offered to the college faculty resulted in a more synchronous approach, which was an easier adjustment. Most of the faculty offered their courses through Zoom at the same time as the original in-person class had been scheduled.

As the semester continued, SPS actually operated well, losing only a small number of students because of Covid-related issues. Fortunately, in spite of huge obstacles, most students completed their course work for the semester. While we could not hold an in-person graduation ceremony—a terrible disappointment to our students—the school did offer a dignified virtual graduation that honored the 858 students who graduated from SPS at the end of the spring/summer 2020 semester. Though worn down to the point of exhaustion by the prior five months, as a community we were deeply proud of what we had accomplished.

CHAPTER 27

My Last Year

IN EARLY APRIL 2020, JUST AFTER COVID-19 TRANSFORMED LIFE in New York City, I left the Central Office in a very understated way. The plan for a major event to celebrate my 34 years in the Central Office had to be put aside when the beginning of the pandemic got in the way. The event would wait. Instead, I said my goodbyes privately to most of my staff and others in the Central Office. As I left the building on 42nd Street for the last time, I was a little nostalgic. And sad. Still, I was certain that it was time to move on. I was ready to assume the next and last chapter of my CUNY career, as full-time dean of SPS. I could not have imagined the horror of Covid—how it would have a long and lingering impact on CUNY, New York City, and beyond.

Relinquishing my Central Office responsibility was something of a relief. I could re-focus and devote my full-time attention to SPS. I needed to provide the leadership necessary to help get us through Covid. There wasn't much of a break over the summer as we readied ourselves for the fall 2020 semester. No end of Covid was in sight. Through August our SPS registration figures showed an uptick despite the near certainty that CUNY as a whole would see a significant decrease in enrollment. When the semester began in late August, we were thrilled to see that at SPS enrollment had increased close to 15% over the previous fall. Of the 24 other CUNY schools and colleges only two, the School of Public Health and the Medical School, had an increase over 10%. Although there were undoubtedly many reasons for the disparity, one was surely the quality of the SPS online experience. Students taking online courses outside of SPS had too often found their experience makeshift and unsatisfactory. Rather than endure another online year, they decided not to re-enroll, leaving college at least for the moment. In contrast, SPS had been offering online courses for 14 years by 2020, and we offered a well-crafted and supported experience for students who came to us as adults exactly because we offered online programs.

Working from home was exhausting. True, I was saving close to two hours a day in commuting between home in Brooklyn and the school in Midtown, but that simply meant that my workday now began by 8 a.m. and didn't end until 8 p.m. or later. I was on phone calls or on my computer virtually the whole day, either in Zoom meetings, reviewing documents, or writing or responding to emails. By the end of the day, my eyes were tired, and my body stiff. I did try to fit in a walk, usually in the beautiful and historic Green-Wood Cemetery, leaving my house no later than 6:30 a.m. While I loved walking in Green-Wood, because of the devastation of Covid and with no vaccine yet available, just going outside made me anxious.

SPS staff, faculty, and students all suffered the strain of beginning a second Covid-hampered semester. I was desperate to hire additional people to relieve some of the burden on staff. Our 15% increase in enrollment meant that we had more students to serve. Every office was stretched to its limits.

Despite the need, the Central Office imposed a hiring freeze for all but what were called essential workers. I could hire only a few new staff. The university was worried that with shrinking enrollment, a flat state budget, and increased costs, many of our colleges ran the risk of incurring significant deficits. While a freeze might seem logical in those instances, implementing the freeze across the board made no sense to me. SPS had a huge budget surplus. Our enrollment had increased every semester for the past 14 years, leading to big revenue increases. In addition, our grant portfolio also had been growing, so that by 2020 we were generating over $30 million annually in grant funds, leading to a large increase in our indirect cost account revenue. We needed more staff, and we had the money to pay them. It wouldn't cost the rest of CUNY anything. I appealed to the CUNY Budget Office repeatedly for some relief, but with no success. Requests for new staff now had to be approved by the Central Office Vacancy Review Board, where requests would languish for many weeks, finally either being denied outright or returned for more evidence as to need.

I wasn't the only president irate about the Vacancy Review Board or the freeze. Some raised the issue quietly; others, me included, brought it up occasionally at the chancellor's Council of Presidents meetings, which had moved online. Neither approach worked. None of us had any luck in changing the policy, even after new Federal Cares Act relief funds brought hundreds of million dollars to CUNY. To the CUNY presidents, the freeze demonstrated that the Central Office lacked confidence in their ability to manage their budgets. Why not give the presidents that authority and then hold them accountable for the results? The policy was having a terrible effect on staff morale. It compromised our ability to serve our students. Having to explain to staff our inability to hire without blaming the chancellor was not easy to do. The situation infuriated me.

At the end of January 2021, I called Executive Vice Chancellor Jose Luis Cruz to complain one last time about the harm the Vacancy Review Board was doing, particularly to CUNY schools that were growing. I explained how the delay in hiring decisions was affecting SPS staff; many of them were overworked and angry. The executive vice chancellor listened politely but insisted there was nothing he could do. He sounded almost apologetic. He didn't dispute the logic of my argument but indicated that he lacked the power to change the policy at the time.

MIDDLE STATES

Despite the frustrations, the fall 2020 semester went well, highlighted by our Middle States site visit. The Middle States Commission on Higher Education (MSCHE) is the regional body that accredits colleges and universities in the Middle Atlantic States plus Puerto Rico and the Virgin Islands. The MSCHE accreditation process, repeated at eight-year (formerly 10-year) intervals, is demanding and stressful. A critical evaluation can damage a school's reputation and in rare cases put an institution in jeopardy of losing its accreditation and threaten its future. To prepare for the assessment, the institution being evaluated submits a self-study prepared according to strict guidelines. MSCHE forms an external evaluation team selected from peer institutions. Then this team of evaluators assesses the self-study and conducts a site visit.

In several important ways, our assessment would be far from typical. In the first place, our Middle States site visit had originally been scheduled for the previous spring but was postponed because of Covid. It was now rescheduled for the fall, but it would be a virtual review instead of an in-person visit by the evaluating team. Secondly, SPS would be assessed not on its own but rather as a component of the CUNY Graduate School and University Center, which would be evaluated as one institution. Therefore, in preparation for the visit, representatives from all five University Center schools and the Graduate School worked collaboratively for months to develop a joint self-study mandated by the assessment process. Our SPS representatives were led by Abi Morrison, who became one of the leaders of the entire process.

Having to integrate the stories of five distinct schools into one unified, coherent document was not easy, but actually may have worked to our advantage. That is not to say that we hadn't submitted a thorough and thoughtful self-study or represented ourselves well in front of the evaluation team. We had, and all of us were confident that we deserved to be reaccredited. It is only to say that considering the stresses of Covid, a virtual visit, and the uniqueness of the structure of the Graduate School and University Center, it would have been difficult for Middle States to arrive at an outcome that was any less than satisfactory. At the standard exit interview conducted by the visiting team, their comments were largely positive, and near the end of 2021 we received word that the Graduate School and University Center had been reaccredited. It was cause for celebration. One of the reasons that I had delayed my retirement was to make sure that when I left, our accreditation was in place. We had accomplished that goal.

WINDING DOWN

Despite the many difficulties of the pandemic and remote work, the SPS staff adjusted to administering a school that was now almost fully remote. Our enrollment continued to increase, with the spring 2021 enrollment again up by double figures. As happened everywhere, a number of faculty, staff, and students got Covid, and many members of our community had family members get sick. We did our best to offer support and be flexible when it came to managing work and personal responsibilities.

in early January 2021, I let Chancellor Matos Rodriguez know that I would be leaving CUNY in the summer. We discussed when I would inform the SPS community. He was gracious as to the time frame. Although I was still a Research Foundation employee, the university was very fair to me; I received the same severance benefits as former presidents with similar years of service. My last day of service at CUNY would be August 7, 2021, when I would begin what is called Travia Leave. (Named after a speaker of the State Assembly, this is a retirement benefit, giving employees a retirement leave of absence consisting of half of their accumulated days sick leave, at full pay.) I would officially retire on January 7, 2022.

Meanwhile, I continued to respond to requests, and SPS continued to rack up milestones. In the fall of my last year, Susan Herman, a senior advisor to the mayor and director of the Mayor's Office of Community Mental Health, called. Susan was thinking about establishing a new mental health academy and wondered whether SPS would be interested in partnering with the city to run it. Susan explained that many nonprofits and city agencies worked with clients who had mental health issues, but these agencies often lacked trained mental health professionals on staff. The Mental Health Academy would provide training to social service providers and opportunities for their employees to enroll in an array of professional development activities where they could gain the skills needed to address clients' behavioral health issues.

Six months later, in June 2021, the Academy for Community Behavioral Health launched. SPS would administer the program in partnership with the Mayor's Office for Economic Opportunity and the Mayor's Office of Community Mental Health. We signed a three-year, multi-million-dollar agreement with the city to serve more than 5,000 workers over that period of time. Opening less than two months before I would leave CUNY, the academy would be the last large CUNY project developed under my leadership. The project was consistent with how SPS—just as our SUD unit had been—was a partner of choice for government to help build and implement new and important projects.

Change is difficult. It is a constant in life, but that doesn't make it easier to accept. Throughout my career, I had considered myself an agent of change. I often had to persuade, cajole, entice, or confront those resisting change. At times, I myself had had to adapt to new situations and new personnel. I left New York City Tech and came to the Central Office. Chancellors and vice chancellors came and went. So did members of my own teams. I understood that was to be expected. People moved on. I moved on. As my career was winding down, however, I was forced to reflect more closely on my own response to change. Covid-19, of course, forced a major re-examination of the workplace everywhere. But other political and social trends also brought significant changes.

The political climate in the country certainly affected my last year at CUNY. On May 25, 2020, George Floyd was brutally murdered in Minneapolis. The reaction to that murder was immediate and intense at CUNY, a university that prided itself on its long history of serving the underserved, and its commitment to social justice and racial equality. The chancellor responded quickly, writing many times directly to the entire university community to deplore the killing and recommit the university to the fight against police brutality and racial injustice. The presidents also issued statements and held open forums to provide opportunities for members of the community to express their anger and anguish. At SPS we held campus meetings and encouraged staff to share their thoughts and feelings.

Discussing issues of racial justice, diversity, and inclusion was not new to SPS. We had formed a very active diversity, equity, and inclusion committee to examine our own campus climate. The goal was to assess our commitment to diversifying our workforce, hire more persons of color to senior level administrative positions, and provide promotion opportunities to existing young staff of color. These were difficult conversations, requiring everyone to re-examine their assumptions and behavior.

I also struggled to navigate issues of gender and bias. Accusations were made regularly by some staff members regarding unconscious bias on the part of their supervisors or colleagues. Some of these accusations of bias were exceedingly troubling to me, while others seemed far less consequential. All of them, however, had to be investigated, taking enormous time and energy from our HR staff. Often the results of the investigation were inconclusive and satisfied no one.

As was happening all over, other changes occurred. Some staff members were no longer defining themselves as male or female. Pronouns were changing, including a preference for "they" rather than 'he" or "she." That was absolutely fine with the vast majority of our staff and with me. But even with attention and effort, I would sometimes absent-mindedly get a pronoun wrong. I regretted that.

We worked hard to address issues of inclusion and diversity; however, conversations could easily end in conflict. At one of our town hall meetings, I was asked whether it was permissible for SPS staff members to march at a Black Lives Matter demonstration under the banner of SPS. I wasn't really sure whether the university had a policy related to demonstrations. I turned to our school's legal counsel to answer the question. She was an experienced attorney who had been at CUNY for a long time, both in the Central Office and at campuses, and who had liberal politics. She also was white. She said that while as a staff person you could participate in any demonstration, she believed that it would violate CUNY policy to march under the SPS banner. That answer did not satisfy many of the participants in the meeting and led to further, more hostile questions. The Counsel responded with lengthy answers that included attempts to let the audience know how committed she had been in her life to fighting for civil rights and social justice. I tried to intervene and lessen the tension but was not successful.

Later that day, I received a number of emails criticizing the response of the counsel, including one that asked me to fire her. The counsel and I met the next day to discuss the incident. Firing her or even punishing her would not have been appropriate. She was deeply saddened, agreeing that she had not handled the answer with sensitivity. I called the university's general counsel to make sure that our counsel had stated CUNY policy accurately. He said that her description was accurate, but he wanted to think about whether it made sense. The counsel, Derrick Davis, was relatively new to CUNY. He got back to me a day or so later to say that he planned to change the existing policy. I let the SPS community know about my conversation, and the issue died down.

Issues related to race and gender did not have a direct impact on my decision to retire, but they made me increasingly aware of a generation gap between me and many of my younger staff. Furthermore, because of Covid and working at home, I had not met or interacted with the many new staff members whom we had hired beginning in the winter of 2020. I had always made a point of getting to know new hires, either by walking around our facility or inviting them to my office for introductory meetings. Now although I tried to introduce myself to new staff through Zoom or regular phone calls, the interaction tended to be more formal and less relaxed—the opposite of what I was seeking. Informal day-to-day interaction was something that I really missed, and the lack of face-to-face contact necessitated by Covid may have contributed to a loosening of the cohesiveness of our staff.

In the early spring I announced to the entire SPS community staff that I would be retiring in August. For most of the members of the SPS community, other than my key staff, it came as a surprise. I think that was largely because, like the boy who cried wolf, I had been hinting at retirement for years. Most staff had come to doubt it would ever happen.

Meanwhile, the pandemic continued to control much of our activity. Recognizing the toll that Covid had taken on so many of our students, we resolved to offer whatever support was needed to students expected to graduate at the end of the spring semester. We expanded our emergency assistance program with the support of the Robin Hood and Petrie Foundations. We supported a food insecurity program with micro grants through a new Food Access Initiative that was supplemented by over $50,000 from our Student Association. Faculty remained flexible and supportive, doing everything possible to see that their students were able to complete their courses in time to qualify for graduation.

For the second time during Covid, the 2021 SPS graduation was virtual. Our students deeply missed having an in-person celebration, but the planning team, led by Heather Zeman, organized a beautiful tribute to honor the 1,100 plus students who were awarded degrees and certificates. This was the largest SPS graduation to date, and despite being virtual, it still honored and celebrated our students. I briefly mentioned that this would be "the last commencement ceremony where I will preside as dean of SPS, having recently announced that I will be retiring after serving as the School's founding dean since 2003." I added, "I have conferred degrees on over 7,700 students who have trusted CUNY SPS to move them forward on their educational journey, and I can't begin to tell you how happy I am about all of your successes."

Sitting at home on my computer for the virtual graduation was emotional. And a bit lonely. Bonne was at my side for support, but I missed being with our students, faculty, and staff. I believed deeply, however, that the school we had built was uniquely designed and that most of the graduating students were earning their degrees directly as a result of our work in creating SPS.

Two beautiful virtual tributes were organized over the summer of 2021 to honor me and celebrate my career. The chancellor hosted the first event, on July 21. Attendees included members of the Chancellery and the Board of Trustees, college presidents, provosts, former CUNY-wide colleagues, and members of my staff. Many colleagues offered eloquent remarks, recognizing our accomplishments and stressing the innovative nature of the programs we developed.

The second event, on August 24, was organized by my SPS staff. It couldn't have been nicer. The event featured a 14-minute video produced by Shannon Taggart, a filmmaker who originally worked at CUNY Prep, and later was hired to be our unit's videographer. The video blended brief comments from staff and colleagues, clips of me at events, creative sub-titles, good music, lots of humor, and a snappy pace. This was the second video Shannon had produced celebrating my career. The first, the previous year, was of similar length and had been the highlight—for me, at least—of an event organized by my SUD staff to celebrate my time at the Central Office.

I treasure these two videos. Over and over again many people have let me know that the retirement videos were the best such tribute they had ever seen, capturing the breadth of my career and its impact on CUNY and the city. After these two events, whenever I felt even a bit sad, I watched the videos again. My mood immediately brightened.

By the beginning of August, I was done. I spent a little time back in the office cleaning up files, but with the university still largely working remotely, the nearly empty building lacked its usual pre-Covid energy. I was ready to move on, but it still felt odd and lonely to walk out of the building one last time, saying good-bye to the few staff who were around. I wasn't sure what retirement would bring. I had no concrete plans. Once home, I came to realize that I was no longer the dean. It sunk in. CUNY-related emails and phone calls pretty much stopped. An interim SPS dean, Jorge Puras Silva, appointed by the chancellor, began immediately. The pace of my life slowed down. I knew that would happen. I expected it. That was the plan. But I had a lot of adjusting to do.

AFTERWORD

Reflections

"John, there is a specific issue I have been meaning to talk with you about, because I heard you address this in a podcast about your career. It had to do with making changes/breaking rules in institutions like CUNY. I don't have to tell you that institutions are stubborn things, and they are not easily transformed by anyone or anything. I know you are a transformative leader, but I don't know if you feel that you transformed CUNY (via your OAA unit or SPS) or were able to do great ground- and rule-breaking things within an institution that did not otherwise change, grow, and so on."

Email to me from Vita Rabinowitz,
former CUNY Interim Chancellor and Executive
Vice Chancellor for Academic Affairs and
University Provost, October 21, 2021.

AS I HAVE THOUGHT ABOUT MY CAREER AND TRIED TO ASSESS ITS impact on CUNY and New York City, I have given considerable thought to the point raised by Vita Rabinowitz two months into my retirement. I have no doubt that the institutions we created and the many programs we developed did indeed permanently change CUNY. We provided new educational and career opportunities for students and New Yorkers, worked to solve urban problems, and redefined what was an appropriate and necessary role of an urban public university. So, in some ways, Vita was right: we did transform CUNY.

Having said that, I don't believe that we changed the overall culture of CUNY. The University Faculty Senate and college governance still too often resist meaningful change and rebuff challenges to the status quo. Campus leaders, whether administrative or faculty, too often do not welcome new projects and ideas. On most CUNY campuses a risk-averse mentality limits innovation. Large, bureaucratic institutions breed inertia. At CUNY, new degree programs take years to create, and the process itself is exhausting. It is an unusual president who considers it worthwhile to enter into battle with senior and entrenched faculty and staff in order to implement change. The ever-present fear is that pushing too hard will only lead to conflict and criticism. Campus leaders have a convenient scapegoat in the Central Office, which they are eager to blame for getting in the way of initiating change. But it is also true that the Central Office sometimes adopts unreasonable edicts that are promulgated without consultation and that diminish the authority and autonomy of college presidents.

An adversarial relationship between the union and management also works against change. From 1986 when I first started working at the Central Office until my retirement, especially during the Goldstein years, the relationship between the Central Office and the Professional Staff Congress was frequently contentious. While understanding the necessity for strong unions, I have struggled with the formality and rigidity of the relationship between labor and management and the inherent tension that arose whenever the two parties got together.

The actual contractual negotiations between the PSC and the Central Office, already complex, were complicated further by the roles of the state and city in the process and the need for their signoff before a new contract could be approved. On the university side, negotiations were led by the vice chancellor for labor relations. I can't imagine a more thankless job. For many years, as a member of the chancellor's cabinet, I heard regular briefings on the progress (or more often lack of progress) of contract negotiations. The slow, painful process of reaching an agreement took years. At times, even when a matter needed immediate attention and could be settled quickly, there was no movement from either side.

A good example was the lengthy negotiation related to the status of teachers and staff working in the CUNY Language Immersion program and CUNY Start. When the programs began, teachers and staff were hourly employees with few benefits. As the programs grew and became permanent, we program administrators agreed with the union that the faculty and staff should have permanent status and enhanced benefits. Although costly, it was the right thing to do. Beyond that, these programs were fiscally sound because under New York State Education Department guidelines non-credit remedial programs generated significant state aid. As the program grew, the dollars provided by the state, based on a formula tied to student attendance—"contact hours" —also grew.

At the same time, both sides understood that until an overall contractual agreement for the university was reached, nothing would be done. The negotiation process prevented a quick solution. Neither side would give up what might become a potential bargaining point as the process dragged on. Ultimately, CLIP and CUNY Start staff did not receive permanent status and benefits until a university contract was signed. It took seven years.

Unions must secure decent contracts and fight hard for their members' rights. That is their role, and one I fully embrace. But it is hard to explain the consistently adversarial and hostile response of the PSC to programmatic initiatives that would not violate any contract provisions or affect working conditions but would bring change to CUNY. Joining with the Faculty Senate, the PSC voiced intense opposition to each of my largest, most important projects: ASAP, SPS, CLIP, CUNY Start, and Guttman Community College. These programs created new jobs and generated revenue, and more importantly, directly helped students. Now demonstrably successful, they have been fully accepted and embraced by the PSC. No one appears to remember that they ever opposed them.

The other dynamic of being able to transform the university permanently relates to changes in leadership. Chancellors come and go, as do other senior leaders. Negative aspects of a bureaucracy can outlast even a visionary leader. I worked for eight chancellors. While all of them expressed the desire to bring change to CUNY, it was really only Matthew Goldstein who accomplished that in a meaningful way. I have often marveled at how and why. Matthew combined vision, courage, and specific ideas. He didn't give in to either political pressure or criticism, and always backed up his staff when they were attacked. My unit and I were beneficiaries of Matthew's vision. In turn, we were his go-to shop, both for ideas and to lead and administer new projects.

I was fortunate to work on Matt Goldstein's senior team during his 14 years as chancellor. It wasn't that our unit didn't do good and important work under other chancellors. We did. The difference was that Matthew truly wanted to change CUNY and was relentless in pursuing that change. He also had the advantage of having a very supportive board chair in Benno Schmidt. When Matthew left, the university entered a period that, while not static, lost much of the energy and desire to take on entrenched interests and create new programs. Over the next eight to nine years, CUNY had two interim chancellors (Bill Kelly and Vita Rabinowitz) and one short-term chancellor (J.B. Milliken) before the appointment of the current chancellor, Felix Matos Rodriquez, who almost immediately had to confront Covid-19. Felo also has been limited by an intrusive board, and for his first two years, a hostile governor in Andrew Cuomo. During this time, several college presidents brought change to their institutions, but the energy coming from the system office was often not there.

Felo and his first executive vice chancellor, Jose Luis Cruz, privately and publicly voiced support for the work of our Senior University Dean unit. Even so, it was apparent from the outset of their administration that they were going to weaken or even eliminate the unit upon my departure. And that is exactly what happened. Initially, in the months before I retired, EVC Cruz, an incredibly smart and talented administrator, appointed several of my senior staff to his cabinet, which expanded to close to 16 people. He asked me to join the cabinet as well, but as I was already a member of the chancellor's cabinet, I declined. The SUD members still reported to me, but I rarely interacted with the vice chancellor. And only rarely did Jose Luis or Felo reach out to me. When I left Central, my position was not filled. The programs and staff were assigned to other areas in the Office of Academic Affairs. Having worked for so many chancellors, I expected that a new administration would bring in its own senior leadership. Some degree of restructuring of the chancellor's office was inevitable. I did, however, strongly disagree with the chancellor's decision to eliminate the SUD office.

About seven months after retiring, I had the opportunity to share my feelings about that decision with Chancellor Matos Rodriguez over lunch. I told him that I felt it was a mistake to eliminate the SUD unit, pointing out that as a result of that decision, he no longer had an innovative arm at Central that worked together to share ideas and to be able to react quickly to city and state requests for assistance in solving problems. The chancellor responded by describing the relationship between the Central Office and the colleges as a pendulum, with power swinging back and forth between the two entities. SUD had been very effective, he said, but now it was time to return greater authority to the presidents and colleges. The message was hard to miss. In its heyday, our unit had too much independence, authority, and responsibility.

Ensuring that campuses and their presidents have the authority to do their work does make some sense. But it needn't be done by diminishing the power and authority of the chancellor and the Central Office or the benefits of an integrated university. Over my long CUNY career, the greatest innovation and productive change at CUNY happened when the chancellor had a clear vision for CUNY's future and an implementation strategy that led to essential changes.

STILL SO MUCH TO BE PROUD OF

So, the first part of my answer to Vita's question about transforming CUNY is a sober but realistic assessment: the permanent structure is still largely in place and many aspects of the culture have not changed. It also is true, however, that in the face of that entrenched culture and structure, the accomplishments of our unit over 35 years were extraordinary and unprecedented. Who would have thought that a small continuing ed unit originally responsible for overseeing the university's non-credit programs—and led by an anxious leader—could become the driving force for change at CUNY for decades? And at the same time that this modest unit would also redefine the university's relationship with the city where it resides?

Guttman Community College and the School of Professional Studies exist because of our work. Guttman was not only the first new CUNY community college in 40 years, but it implemented a new and successful model of community college education. SPS, designed to serve an exclusively adult population, brought online degree programs to CUNY. ASAP demonstrated that it was possible to dramatically increase graduation rates at CUNY's associate degree programs, growing from an original pilot of 1,100 students to 25,000 students; CUNY Start introduced a new way of addressing the needs of our most unprepared degree students; and the CUNY Language Immersion program changed the way we approached ESL instruction. Both CLIP and CUNY Start helped set the direction for the end of remediation.

We built huge units in K–16 and Early Childhood Education, each supported by grant funds that approached $30 million annually and staffs of over 100 people. The K–16 unit, working in partnership with the NYC Department of Education, built 20 Early College High Schools and three new specialized high schools, while College Now, one of the largest dual enrollment programs in the United States, enrolled over 20,000 high school students annually in college credit classes. The Early Childhood Professional Development Institute provided professional development opportunities to tens of thousands of early childhood workers, while also developing a process to assess the quality of early childhood programs throughout New York State.

We worked with virtually every city and state agency to train workers and offer new opportunities for professional development. We set up special units at the NYC Human Resources Administration and a Workforce Training Institute at the City's Administration for Children's

Services, and we worked closely with the NYPD, the Office of Immigrant Affairs, and the Departments of Correction, Homeless Services, Emergency Services, Small Business Services, and Transportation, to name just a few of our partners. We also partnered with the Mayor's Office of Adult Education to create the Emmy Award-winning television series "We Are New York," establishing our own television production company.

Our work with the city and state assisted government in solving problems and addressing issues of poverty, mental health, inequality, and public safety. When government sought a response that was both rapid and high quality, they turned to our unit. Over the years we became one of the major training arms of city and state government.

We also developed CUNY-based programs that included the CUNY Service and Cultural Corps, The Dream.US, CUNY Prep, and the CUNY Adult Literacy program, as well as a series of programs for public assistance recipients that enabled tens of thousands of low-income New Yorkers to earn a college degree, increase their basic skills and English language proficiency, and find employment and career opportunities. Through our John F. Kennedy Jr. Institute for Worker Education, we founded a series of programs to better service New Yorkers with developmental disabilities, and we became advocates for improving the working conditions of direct care workers. Virtually all of these programs were funded outside of the regular operating budget of CUNY, enabling our unit to become the largest grant-getting entity in the history of CUNY.

Our work was framed by a deep belief that to be great, a public urban university must look beyond providing degree programs. It must use its intellectual resources to assist government and the private sector in solving the most difficult urban problems. We believed that CUNY wasn't as good as it needed to be and that far too many students did not get to the finish line. Through our programs, we extended and, in some measure, redefined CUNY's role and mission.

Our success was built by a gifted staff, made up of talented, passionate people who brought energy and enthusiasm to work every day. Our leadership understood that it was crucial to pay attention to detail and to be customer friendly. We also welcomed criticism and serious debate. We liked our work, being around each other, creating community, and solving problems. We also understood that at times we had to make compromises to achieve success. We realized however, that we needed to respond aggressively to criticism and attacks. We advanced new ideas to consider, took risks, knew how to design and implement programs and measure our results. Not everything we tried worked, and we did have disappointments. But the vast majority of our programs succeeded, some far beyond what we had imagined. We were committed to working with the New Yorkers who were the most disadvantaged, both educationally and economically. We fought for social justice and racial equity. Most importantly, our focus was always toward our students and what we could do to help them succeed.

We also created future leaders. Many of our staff assumed senior level positions at CUNY and beyond. We were really good at hiring exceptional staff and understood that nothing is more important than the hiring process. Some staff members had impressive formal credentials, but many did not. Credentials were not that important to us. Because we were successful in our work, our reputation grew, and that attracted talent. We wanted people who would say yes to opportunity, and we had no patience for naysayers.

We tried hard to treat our campus partners with respect. As is clear throughout the book, we had our critics, but we also worked closely with hundreds of faculty and administrators who welcomed the opportunity to tackle new projects. If some folks thought we were arrogant and know-it-alls and others believed that we were too powerful, I do feel that overall, we were well regarded and appreciated.

As for me, I have had an amazing career in education. I look back at those 49 years with enormous pride and often disbelief at the long list of accomplishments. I was neither an intellectual nor a scholar, but I did have a sense of how to get things done. I believe I became a good leader who was trusted by staff to do the right thing. I cared about our staff and took an interest in their professional and personal lives. I also was good at selecting staff and surrounding myself with can-do people. Most importantly, I cared deeply about the students we served and did everything possible to build new opportunities that would reverse past setbacks.

As I look back, I often think about the wonderful graduations that SPS held at Lincoln Center, filled with joy. I can't quite believe I was at the podium addressing thousands of people, still a bit worried that I might have a panic attack, but exuberant as I looked at the students in their caps and gowns. I never could get over saying the following words at the conclusion of the graduation: "Now, by virtue of the authority vested by law in the Board of Trustees of The City University of New York, I confer upon each of you the degrees and certificates for which you have been recommended, with all the rights, privileges, responsibilities and obligations appertaining thereunto, and I offer my sincere congratulations."

It was hard for me to say the words "appertaining thereunto" without bursting into laughter at the formality and stuffiness of the phrase. Me conferring degrees? Not possible. But I said the words with enthusiasm and excitement, honoring the students who had worked so hard to get to this place. These were grand moments to be cherished. I shared the excitement with everyone who helped make my career possible.

EPILOGUE

What's Next for Higher Education?

AMERICAN HIGHER EDUCATION IS UNDER THREAT. CONFRONTING an erosion of public funding and support, as well as shrinking enrollment, higher education faces questions about its value and its costs. People are concerned about what is taught and how instruction is delivered and by whom. Challenges are being made to how higher ed's institutions are governed and decisions are made. Until now, these concerns have been met with powerful and often unrelenting resistance to change from colleges and universities asserting that they represent timeless values and thoughtful processes. Nevertheless, despite internal resistance, institutions of higher education are in fact being changed profoundly and permanently from the outside.

Without deep self-examination and active redefinition, many institutions will find themselves greatly diminished and even irrelevant. Some will close down. When the Editorial Board of the *New York Times* publishes an editorial entitled "See Workers as Workers, Not as a College Credential," it is time for higher ed to take notice. The editorial argues that for a large percentage of both the public and private sectors, the bachelor's degree requirement to qualify for a job is a barrier to employment for far too many qualified people—especially Black and Hispanic job seekers who area "less likely to have bachelor's degrees than non-Hispanic whites and Asian Americans." The editorial congratulates those states, including Maryland, Utah, and Pennsylvania, that have eliminated the requirement for a bachelor's degree for many jobs in state government.[1] Certainly, more states will follow this example.

State governments are not unique in moving away from requiring a college degree for certain jobs. The private sector is also embracing this concept, particularly in the tech area where companies seek job prospects who can demonstrate defined skill levels that may or may not come with a diploma. In New York City, agencies like Per Scholas and Year-Up offer short term training and internship opportunities that lead directly to well-paying jobs.

While I have spent almost 50 years in higher education, I have no argument with the decision to eliminate the college degree requirement for certain jobs. As the *Times* editorial says, for too long, a degree requirement has prevented many qualified job prospects from being hired for jobs that they could do well. I would argue, however, that as this trend continues, higher ed can have a direct and important role during this transition; higher ed can help ensure that those foregoing college will actually have the skills that employers need. And further, higher ed can make sure that low-income families do not receive the message that a college degree is worthless or not for them. That message, intended or not, diminishes even more the number of minority students who enroll in college and complete their degrees. With a degree or not, employers are not going to hire individuals who don't have the educational background and skills to do the job. Colleges and universities are still among the best places we know to instill skills and competencies across the gamut of life paths. The research is clear. College educated people live longer, healthier, more prosperous lives.

It is not surprising that higher education is vulnerable to threat. For way too long, much of higher education has accepted low graduation rates. We have paid only lip service to partnering with the business and nonprofit sectors. We've refused to be flexible in offering credit for prior learning or accepted credit earned from other colleges in the transfer process. And we've declined to work closely with K–12 systems. We've watched costs continue to rise, and it is no exaggeration to describe the college loan situation as a crisis. These failures, among others, have created many of the elements that have led to the mistaken mindset that a degree is not worth the time and money it takes to earn one, and that the number of years it takes to earn a degree would be better spent as a full-time wage earner.

Throughout this book, I have tried to demonstrate that change and innovation are possible in higher ed. It's been proven through developing programs like ASAP, building new colleges and schools like Guttman Community College and SPS, and creating alternatives to traditional remediation like CUNY Start and the CUNY Language Immersion Program. Those initiatives have shown that innovation can be brought to scale and lead to dramatic increases in graduation rates for all groups of students, particularly those at community colleges.

We have demonstrated that public higher education institutions like CUNY can successfully partner with government and the private sector to address the serious problems facing cities. This can often be done through their adult and continuing education units, where new programs can be designed and implemented quickly.

So how should higher education respond to this uncertain future? And to the growing view that earning a college degree education is not essential? Or that it might actually be an obstacle to addressing issues of inequality? How can higher ed respond to so many students with serious debt and no degree?

Foremost is to make sure that higher ed is at the table with government and the private sector when these issues are discussed and to fight like hell for the value of a college degree. But at the same time, higher ed must be flexible enough to broaden the scope of who it serves to include the tens of millions of people who either have no college or have left college with credits but no degree. Whether that includes creating new workforce development programs, bringing curricula up to date, expanding apprenticeship and internship opportunities, developing new credit or non-credit certificate programs, or expanding online programs, it is imperative that the programs be of quality and that the results are carefully measured. Future funding should be based on achieving positive outcomes and, like ASAP, the most successful programs should be brought to scale.

Real change will take more than just talk. It demands true and quick action to change business as usual. As I have said throughout the book, bringing change to universities is not easy, but can and must be done. It will take bold leadership, new ideas, and a willingness to listen, compromise, and challenge entrenched interests and obsolete ways of doing things. Finally, it will take the recognition, indeed the insistence, that the number one priority of higher education is to serve its students.

ACKNOWLEDGMENTS

Many people encouraged me to write a book about my CUNY career. But the first person to propose the idea was Gerald Markowitz, distinguished professor of history at the CUNY Graduate School and John Jay College. I couldn't be more grateful to Jerry for the time he spent with me on my oral history. His insightful questions pushed me to discuss not only successes, but also the struggles and disappointments my team and I had. He was a wonderful partner.

Over a long career, I was fortunate to work with committed and talented people. Much of my effectiveness was a result of what I learned from them. To have Fannie Eisenstein be the first CUNY person I met was, if not a miracle, a matter of the greatest luck and good fortune. Fannie, my role model and mentor, introduced me the world of higher education and the potential of adult and continuing education to change people's lives.

During my 13 years at New York City Community College, now New York City College of Technology, I worked with many talented educators. I learned from all of them, and several became lifelong friends. Those included Judy McGaughey, my direct supervisor for a number of those years, along with Mae Dick, Sandy Weinbaum, Will Saunders, Linda Brown, John Garvey, and Barbara Ritchin. I also want to thank Jacque Cook; at the dark moment when I didn't get the dean's job at City Tech, she invited me to join her staff at the Literacy Assistance Center.

Regina Peruggi introduced me to the CUNY Central Office. It was an honor to be part of her team and to watch how she approached her job. She taught me how to deal with the politics of "80th Street." No one worked harder or was more respected.

None of the success of our Central Office unit could have been possible without the support of a series of chancellors and vice chancellors. For 14 years, I had the privilege to be a member of Matthew Goldstein's team. He was a true visionary who turned to me and our unit to implement the change he believed necessary to enhance the status of CUNY and better serve its students and New York City.

I also thank the other chancellors that I worked for during my years in the Central Office: Joe Murphy, Ann Reynolds, Christoph Kimmich, Bill Kelly, J.B. Milliken, Vita Rabinowitz, and Felix Matos Rodriquez.

To Richard Freeland, Louise Mirrer, Selma Botman, Lexa Logue, and Vita Rabinowitz, the leaders of the Office of Academic Affairs during most of my time in the Central Office, thank you for always being there for advice and encouragement, to help me solve problems, and to refine new ideas. Your support never wavered, and you often rescued me from individual mistakes and bad decisions.

Thanks also to Rick Schaffer, Jay Hershenson, Iris Weinshal, Matt Sapienza, Pam Silverblatt, Richard Rothbardt, John Kotowski, and the late Ernesto Malave, all senior CUNY officials during the Goldstein administration. They were always approachable and made sure that the CUNY structure and bureaucracy didn't stand in the way of implementing new programs.

I reserve my deepest gratitude to my many colleagues at the School of Professional Studies and those in my unit at CUNY Central. It is because of their hard work, creativity, can-do attitude, passion, intelligence, and commitment to student success that we were so successful in our work. They put up with unreasonable deadlines, long hours, and my endless nudging to build programs that provided opportunities for our students and helped change lives.

It is not possible to name all of the staff, but I do want to acknowledge and give a special thank-you to those colleagues who were part of my senior staff. They were gifted leaders who led the many projects we developed. At the Central Office, I thank Leslee Oppenheim, John Garvey, Bill Ebenstein, Deborah Douglass, Margaret Panciera, Suri Duitch, Tracy Meade, Donna Linderman, Cass Conrad, the late Derrick Griffith, Angie Kamath, Mia Simon, Gary Dine, and Sherry Cleary.

At the School of Professional Studies, thanks to the members of my leadership team: Brian Peterson, George Otte, Rachel Levine, Washington Hernandez, Jennifer Grace Lee, Michael Iadarola, Jennifer Sparrow, and Tracy Meade. I am grateful to the members of the SPS Foundation Board, with a special thanks to Bob Kissane, Horace Barker, and Blake Foote, who chaired the board during my time leading SPS.

To academic directors of SPS, thank you for assuming the academic leadership of the school. You led the development of our degree programs, hired and supported our faculty, and always kept the students' best interests in mind. To the hundreds of faculty members who so capably taught our students, I am forever grateful. Any college or school is only as good as its faculty, and you were exceptional.

Throughout my time as dean of SPS, I interacted with many CUNY college presidents and deans of professional schools. Many became friends. During difficult and good times, they were always available for constructive advice, support, and encouragement.

Members of my direct support staff looked after me, making sure that there were few surprises. Thanks to Lia Kudless, my chief of staff, and Josephine Cherry and Dianne Vargas, my administrative assistants. They were at my side for many years, putting up with my quirks and calming me down when I got too excited.

The students served by our programs were of all ages and backgrounds. For over 49 years our programs were focused on providing education and career opportunities for them. They came first in all we did. We helped thousands become, first, college students and then, college graduates. Interacting with our students was the best part of my job. Watching them grow and succeed was inspirational. I learned so much from our students; being around them always put a smile on my face.

I am grateful to Peter Sloane, president of the Heckscher Foundation for Children. I was honored to be named a Heckscher Leadership Fellow. That has enabled me to learn about the foundation world from the inside, while at the same time, being supported in writing this book.

Special thanks to my ad hoc production team, who brought their professional expertise to help this novice author get his words into print. Good listeners all! Tim Harper provided generous, no-nonsense editorial advice. Joe Lops designed an attractive, readable book. Kelly Cunningham gave it a beautiful cover. And Justin Miracle Jones shepherded it—and me—through the production process. Thanks to Lawrence Kim for an elegant website.

Finally, I want to thank my family. To my wife Bonne, a gifted educator herself, who has been a partner for almost the entire 49-year CUNY journey, words can't express my gratitude for supporting me through the ups and downs of many years, for putting up with my worries, regrets and anxiety, and for all of the reading and editing she did as I wrote this book. She has been the love of my life. Bill and Marian Mogulescu are always there to share ideas and offer support. To my daughters, Amy and Laura, their spouses Patrick and Zach, and my grandchildren, Miranda, Phoebe, Nathan, Max, and Julian, you bring me joy and love. You have all lived the CUNY story, which has certainly been a part of your lives as well as mine.

NOTES

CHAPTER 3

1 Arthur Laurents, *Original Story By: A Memoir of Broadway and Hollywood* (New York: Applause Books, 2000), 247–8.
2 Fannie Eisenstein, Keynote, CEA/NY Region Annual Meeting, Baruch College, May 18, 1995.
3 Anonymous detainee, Graduation Speech, Prevocational Education Program, Brooklyn House of Detention, April 3, 1975.

CHAPTER 6

1 Mary Catherine Bateson, *Composing a Life*, (Boston: Atlantic Monthly Press, 1989).
2 Ann Reynolds, Letter to John Mogulescu, October 29, 1997.

CHAPTER 8

1 Final Report 1996–97, CUNY Language Immersion Program, CUNY Office of Academic Affairs, February 2, 1998.

CHAPTER 9

1 "The City University of New York: An Institution Adrift," Report of the Mayor's Task Force on the City University of New York, June 7, 1999, 107.
2 "The City University of New York: An Institution Adrift," Report of the Mayor's Task Force on the City University of New York, June 7, 1999.
3 "An Institution Adrift,"13.
4 "An Institution Adrift," 8–9.

CHAPTER 10

1 Greg Donaldson, *The Ville: Cops & Kids in Urban America* (New York, Ticknor & Fields, 1993; updated edition, New York: Fordham University Press, 2015).
2 "Streetwise: Language, Culture, and Police Work in New York City: Training for New Officers of The New York City Police Department in the African/Caribbean-American, Chinese, Haitian, Hispanic, Lesbian/Gay, Bisexual/Transgender, Russian and South Asian Communities," A Project of the New York State Regional Community Policing Institute and the New York City Police Department developed by the City University of New York, 2000.
3 John Marzulli, "Rookies Get Crash Course in Cultures," *New York Daily News*, 1999.
4 NYPD Board of Visitors, "Preliminary Report," June 2000, 4.

CHAPTER 12

1 "The New Life Café" *We Are New York: Television that Makes a Difference*, pilot episode, WNYE TV, June 27 2009.

CHAPTER 13

1 Scott Kennedy, Keynote, 1st Annual Service Corps Conference: Celebrating Our Inaugural Year, May 9 2014, Lehman College.

CHAPTER 14

1 *A Partnership for Student Achievement*, CUNY Office of Academic Affairs, 2004, 3.
2 Karen W. Arenson, "Gates to Create 70 Schools for Disadvantaged," *New York Times,* March 19, 2002.
3 Matthew Goldstein, Memo to college presidents, June 21, 2006.
4 Working Group on Collaborative Programs, *Final Report*, November 2006.

CHAPTER 15

1 Carl Campanile, "New CUNY School Aiming to Drag in Dropouts," *New York Post,* September 15, 2003.
2 nypost.com/2003/09/15/new-cuny-aiming-to-drag-in-dropouts/.

CHAPTER 16

1 *Crescendo! The Power of Music*, https://www.imdb.com/title/tt3909442/?ref_=tt_rvi_tt_i_1.

CHAPTER 17

1 *Center for Economic Opportunity: Evidence and Impact*, January 2010, vii.
2 David Hansell and M. Patricia Smith, Letter to Governor's Economic Security Cabinet, February 13, 2009.
3 Hansell, David, Letter to Governor's Economic Security Cabinet, March 3, 2009.
4 *Jobs for New York's Future*, City University of New York Jobs Task Force, 2012, 5.
5 *Career Pathways: One City Working Together,* Jobs for New Yorkers Task Force, n.d., 5.
6 In just one example of the impact of workforce issues, *The New York Times* reported that more than 104,000 public school students were homeless at some point during 2021–22 school year. The parents of many of these children were working but did not earn enough to provide housing for their families. "More than 104,000 NYC Students Were Homeless Last Year," October 28, 2022.
7 *Real-Time Labor Market Information and Environmental Scan of Vendors and Workforce Development Users*, Summary Report, CUNY Labor Market Information Service, October 2014, https://www.gc.cuny.edu/center-urban-research/new-york-city-labor-market-information-service/other-projects-and-publications.

CHAPTER 18

1 Bill Ebenstein, Memo to John Mogulescu, September 26, 2002.

CHAPTER 19

1 Natasha Lifton, Memo to Josh Starr, December 12, 2003.
2 Natasha Lifton, Memo to Josh Starr, December17, 2003.
3 Natasha Lifton, Letter to John Mogulescu, January 22, 2004.
4 *Learning About the Workforce: A Profile of Early Childhood Educators in New York City's Community- and School-Based Center*s. Study conducted by the NYC Early Childhood Professional Development Institute & the Cornell University Early Childhood Program, 2007, 3.

CHAPTER 20

1 Henry Levin and Emma Garcia. *Benefit-Cost Analysis of Accelerated Study in Associate Programs (ASAP) of the City University of New York* (Center for Benefit-Cost Studies in Education, Teachers College, Columbia University, April 2013).
2 Susan Scrivener et al, *Doubling Graduation Rates: Three-Year Effects of CUNY's Accelerated Study in Associate Programs (ASAP) for Developmental Education Students* (MDRC, February 2015). https://www.mdrc.org/project/evaluation-accelerated

-study-associate-programs-asap-developmental-education-students#overview. MDRC has continued to follow ASAP, including replication efforts in Ohio.

3 Ann Hulbert, "How to Escape the Community College Trap." *The Atlantic*, January/February, 2014. https://www.theatlantic.com/magazine/archive/2014/01/how-to-escape-the-community-college-trap/355745/.

4 "Community Colleges Pay Student Expenses Beyond Tuition Hoping to Boost Graduation Rates." PBS News Hour, May 9 2023. https://www.pbs.org/newshour/show/community-colleges-pay-student-expenses-beyond-tuition-hoping-to-boost-graduation-rates.

5 Sarah Weissman. "Scaling the Secret Sauce for Completion Rates." *Inside Higher Ed*, July 6, 2023. https://www.insidehighered.com/news/students/academics/2023/07/06/efforts-replicate-asap-program-spread.

6 Sharon Otterman, "Could $2,000 a Year Keep Students in College?" *New York Times*, September 12, 2023.

7 Ari Paul, "Protecting a vital resource for students: Members urge the city to fund ASAP, ACE." *The Clarion*, July 2023, 4.

CHAPTER 21

1 Selma Botman, Email to CUNY presidents, February 14, 2008.

2 Alexandra Weinbaum, Camille Rodriguez, and Nan Bauer-Maglin. *Rethinking Community College for the 21st Century*, (The New Community College at CUNY, 2013).

3 *A New Community College Concept Paper*, CUNY Office of Academic Affairs, August 15, 2008.

4 Barbara Bowen, Email to Matthew Goldstein, February 26, 2009.

5 Matthew Goldstein, Letter to Barbara Bowen, March 3, 2009.

6 Barbara Bowen, Letter to Professional Staff Congress members, October 22, 2009.

7 John Mogulescu, "For the Record: The Facts on CUNY's Proposal for a New Community College." CUNY eNews, November 2, 2009.

8 Gail Mellow, Letter to John Mogulescu, September 9, 2008.

9 David Moltz, "Shaking Up the Community College Concept." *Inside Higher Ed*, February 6, 2009. See also Moltz, "The Great Community College Experiment" *Inside Higher Ed*, December 2, 2009.

10 Elyse Ashburn, "City U. of New York Plans a Grand Experiment: A New College," *Chronicle of Higher Education*, April 18, 2010, https://www.chronicle.com/article/city-u-of-new-york-plans-a-grand-experiment-a-new-college/.

11 *Rethinking Community College for the 21st Century*, 15.

12 Matthew Goldstein, "CUNY's Newest First, Reshaping Community College." *New York Post*, August 24, 2012.

13 The overall amount of the gift was $25 million, of which $15 million was allocated directly to the new college.

14 https://guttman.cuny.edu/.

CHAPTER 22

1 *CUNY Start: Analysis of Student Outcome,* CUNY Office of Academic Affairs, 2013, i–iii.
2 Susan Scrivener, et al, *Becoming College-Ready: Early Findings from a CUNY Start Evaluation* (MDRC, 2019), https://www.mdrc.org/publication/becoming-college-ready. Since its preliminary study, MDRC has continued to follow CUNY Start and analyze its outcome data.

CHAPTER 23

1 https://www.thedream.us./.

CHAPTER 24

1 David Kirp, *The College Dropout Scandal* (New York: Oxford University Press, 2019), 135.
2 J.B. Milliken, Email to John Mogulescu, October 2014.
3 David W Chen, "U.S. Investigating Finances of City College's President," *New York Times*, July 15, 2016.
4 David W Chen, "Lapses by CUNY Officials Made System Ripe for Abuse, Report Says." *New York Times*, November 15, 2016.
5 Jane Sovern, Email to campus presidents, April 20, 2017.

CHAPTER 25

1 Frederick Schaffer and Louise Mirrer, Letter to Robin Dasher-Alston, June 9, 2003.
2 CUNY Board of Trustees, Resolution, June 23, 2003.
3 Matthew Goldstein, Letter to Susan O'Malley, June 9, 2003.
4 Brian McLaughlin, Letter to Matthew Goldstein, July 1, 2003.
5 CUNY School of Professional Studies, Three Year Report, April 2007, 36.
6 Theodore Kheel (1914–2010) was a well-known attorney who negotiated many labor disputes, both in New York City and nationally. Kheel was active in many causes including civil rights, the environment, employee health and welfare, and others.
7 CUNY SPS Three Year Report, April 2007, 19.
8 Jacob Gershman, "CUNY Plans Online Push to Entice Students to Return," *New York Sun*, October 6, 2005, https://www.nysun.com/article/new-york-cuny-plans-online-push-to-entice-students.
9 Susan O'Malley, Letter to Joseph Frey, March 15, 2006.

10 Joseph Frey, Letter to Susan O'Malley, April 3, 2006.
11 CUNY SPS Three Year Report, April 2007, 20–21.

CHAPTER 26

1 Vita Rabinowitz, email to CUNY history professors and college provosts offering MA programs in History.
2 CUNY SPS, Proposal to Establish a Master of Arts Degree in American History, 19.
3 History Discipline Council, Letter to Vita Rabinowitz, May 18, 2017.
4 Barbara Bowen, Letter to Vita Rabinowitz, May 24, 24 2017.
5 Andrew Robertson, Letter to James Basker, May 15, 2017.
6 John Mogulescu, Email to Vita Rabinowitz, May 25, 2017.
7 Vita Rabinowitz, Email to attendees of May 25 meeting, June 2, 2017.
8 The similarly named Center for Worker Education at City College, founded in 1981, has a different history.
9 Gregory Mantsios, Email to Jay Hershenson, August 25, 2004.
10 Michael Zavelle, "White Paper on the Worker Education Program at Queens College," December 6, 2004, 14.
11 Arthur Cheliotes, Letter to Matthew Goldstein, May 5, 2005.
12 "JSMI Faculty White Paper on Autonomy and Governance," February 13, 2014, 1.
13 "JSMI Faculty White Paper," 3–4.
14 Jay Hershenson, Email to Arthur Cheliotes, February 19, 2014.
15 J.B. Milliken, Cover letter for "Task Force on Worker Education" Report, September 3, 2014.
16 CUNY Board of Trustees, Resolution, June 26, 2017.
17 Carl Campanile, "Cuomo's Budget Includes Plan to Create CUNY School Focused on Unions," *New York Post*, March 26, 2018.
18 External Assessment, CUNY SPS, 2008, 3.
19 https://sps.cuny.edu/academics/non-degree-programs/urban-park-leadership-program.

EPILOGUE: WHAT'S NEXT FOR AMERICAN HIGHER EDUCATION?

1 "See Workers as Workers, Not as a College Credential," Editorial, *New York Times*, January 28, 2023, https://www.nytimes.com/2023/01/28/opinion/jobs-college-degree-requirement.html.

INDEX

Made in the USA
Middletown, DE
29 January 2024

48752593R00201